The Essential Earthman

THE
ESSENTIAL
EARTHMAN
Henry Mitchell

HOUGHTON MIFFLIN COMPANY

Boston   New York

for my wife, Ginny

For information about permission to reproduce selections
from this book, write to Permissions, Houghton Mifflin Company,
215 Park Avenue South, New York, New York 10003.

Library of Congress Cataloging-in-Publication Data
Mitchell, Henry, date.
The essential earthman
p.   cm.
Originally published: Bloomington : Indiana University Press, © 1981.
Includes index.
ISBN 0-395-68632-6
1. Gardening.   2. Gardening—Washington Region.   I. Title.
[SB455.3.M57   1994]
635.9′09753—dc20   93-44884
CIP

Printed in the United States of America
BP   10   9   8   7   6   5   4   3   2   1

Printed on recycled paper

Contents

Henry Mitchell
1923–1993

Henry Mitchell, for almost twenty-five years a columnist for the *Washington Post*, died on November 12, 1993. The day before, he had seen the proposed cover for this new edition by Susan Davis, whose cartoons had illustrated his *Post* column. He died, with dirt on his hands, helping a neighbor plant daffodils.

In one of his last columns, he wrote: "You wonder after many years if any of it was worth the bother. The answer is, I think, more or less yes. . . . Entire sections [of the garden] have to be rethought and old friends given up. All seems to be nothing but change and irregular advances and collapse, as if paying little attention to the gardener, who is seen to be far less consequential than we had supposed."

Here is an appreciation of Henry Mitchell which appeared in the *Washington Post*. It is followed by the last "Earthman" column he wrote for the paper.

The Glorious Bloom
of the Gardener
by Sarah Booth Conroy

As Henry Mitchell wrote of the tall mullein, a member of the figwort plant family: "O for a lute of fire to sing their merits."

I feel the same way about Henry, who, no matter what he said, had a lute of language, which he played well nigh unto a quarter of a century in the *Washington Post*.

His own words are the best song of his merits. Certainly he deserves the ones he typed about Joseph Wood Krutch: "As for his very long friendship with the English language, that turbulent shrew, it appears that with him she did not kick and bite so much as usual, and was almost tameable."

Of Henry, who died yesterday, it could be said that the muse of words stayed him with flagons, comforted him with apples (unsprayed with pesticides, one hopes). Ah, apples. He was ambivalent about them, warning gardeners of small plots that an apple tree would never fit. He did, however, like to expound on "where apples come from." In one of his more celebrated dissertations (from his book *One Man's Garden*, a collection of his "Earthman" columns), he wrote, "I shall speak today of sex in apples and other plants, which operates very much as sex in humans does."

"Henry is a Victorian writer," Shelby Coffey, now the editor of the *Los Angeles Times*, is said to have warned one of his editors when he ran the Style section.

True, the old words, the poetic phrases, the King James Version, rolled not only from Henry's computer but from a deep and resounding voice that would not have disgraced an organ. He also liked to spice up his conversation among friends with prissy sayings from the front porches of his youth: "Jane Wilson as was" for the maiden name of a married woman, for instance. He coined the phrase "zub zub zub" for "and so forth" and is generally credited with its widespread use.

He always had time to tell a story or to listen to one. He was an accomplished actor, managing gestures, speech patterns of place, age and education adeptly and inoffensively, until the characters in his stories appeared before your eyes and echoed in your ears.

I remember his story about the family who lived in genteel shabbiness and had to entertain the family of their daughter's fiancé. They carried it off with great elegance by lighting the whole house with candles. And the Thanksgiving dinner when a mouse gnawed its way through the ceiling. "Nobody noticed it, naturally. In the South at dinner, you are not supposed to notice anything short of a three-alarm fire," he wrote.

Henry believed, as Southerners do, that "despair is surmounted through the act of verbalizing."

When Eudora Welty, the Mississippi novelist, short story writer and friend to Henry, was awarded the Presidential Medal of Freedom, Henry called her "as pleased as a dog with two tails." And he added, "The nobility her readers mark . . . is built in, not stuccoed on." When Maria Callas was met with roses and dignitaries at the airport here, Henry reported that it was like the "arrival of a phoenix in a chickenyard." Both could describe Henry Mitchell.

Henry's illness was long and painful. But it had one good thing to recommend it, so to speak. His friends, journeying from his homeplace of

Memphis, from Bethesda and Brazil, from London and Williamsburg, came in such hordes to say goodbye and bon voyage that he hardly had time to worry about where and when he was going.

Not that any of us doubts where, though it's true he railed to considerable extent against the modernization of the Book of Common Prayer and his inability to keep it from being read at his funeral. But surely the Good Lord shares his taste.

Henry was a man who respected all of God's creatures. He built a perch for dragonflies in his lily pond, after seeing one drown for lack of a landing place. He also liked wasps and hornets and bumblebees: "All these creatures commonly fall into fish pools. . . . Often a stick or a tuft from some plant can be extended to them to fish them out. It is astonishing how many bees which seem dead in the water will revive if fished out and set on the ground to dry."

He was respectful and agreeable to the homeless on the street, to the old fellow who took up residence in his servants' house in Memphis—and lived there fifteen years on the Mitchell charity.

As for children, he remembered well the time as a child he discovered that "grasses" bloomed in his neighbor's yard and brought home a hundred crocuses. Many years later, he wrote: "The quickest possible route to hell, it has been said, is to growl at a child for picking crocuses. . . . Now of course if the child gets into *lilium langkongense* or the irises, well, that is something else again and a tub of boiling oil is recommended."

Still, Henry was opinionated. He did not suffer fools at all, much less gladly. He was also bullheaded. Because of his talent for vituperation, his victim would yellow along the edges and wither away.

He had no kindly feeling nor soft words for those whom, as he would say, he "took against": warmongers, violators of others' civil rights, garden shop clerks who sold innocents unworthy plants, editors who changed a word or a comma of his sacred text, maple trees, presumption or cold weather. ("Sleet, incidentally, is the worst five-letter four-letter word I know.")

He was a man of ups and downs. He was variously described as a Southern gentleman, a curmudgeon, a true friend, contrary, pigheaded, kind, thoughtful, sensitive to others' feelings. He was all those things and some for which only he knew the name.

He could be untiringly helpful, spending afternoons planning the gardens of friends, going over a back yard to point out the poison ivy clumps, searching for an hour at a hardware store to find a shovel to be plied without bending over. He answered his mail—much of it impassioned. He gave endless advice to people who called him, not only at the office but often at home. His phone number was always listed.

Henry was clothed in much authority. He, unlike most writers, could spell. His reputation was such that he spelled *lavender* as *lavendar* for ten years before anyone challenged him. Even the glinty-eyed super-speller *Post* readers never wrote to the editor or to Henry about it.

Henry's memos—to the publisher, the executive editor, the editor of the section, his own editor—were legend. One that has survived deserves to be published, if only in an expurgated version. He turned down an assignment to cover the auditions of small girls for *Annie* at the Kennedy Center, writing, "The kind of story that will really work is a street guy with a mangy dog who needs an operation the man cannot pay for."

Henry knew all about dogs, mangy and otherwise, and he had the veterinary bills to prove it. Thus he meant it kindly when he said of Elvis that "he had the same open manner, the same artless eyes and the same natural dignity that you find in hounds of good quality."

The other day, we were all talking about Henry, and why those of us who have neither dogs nor gardens read every word he published. And the general view was that Henry used gardens and dogs and bumblebees as metaphors for life.

He was a pessimistic man: "It is not nice to garden anywhere. Everywhere there are violent winds, startling once-per-five-centuries floods, unprecedented droughts, record-setting freezes, abusive and blasting heats never known before. There is no place, no garden where these terrible things do not drive gardeners mad."

Henry was a gardener who knew what the Garden of Eden looked like, and that paradise was forevermore unattainable. He was a writer who knew Milton, and feared he could not equal him. He was a human so far superior to the average walker on the earth that he must have despaired of making us mortals understand the vision he saw and described.

But Henry had a place of solace, which all could envy. He would sometimes tell about the year he took two weeks off from his job in Memphis during the peak of the iris season. Every morning after he drank the first of his twelve cups of coffee, he'd go outside and watch the two thousand stalks, with about seven flowers on each. Curiously, he said, not many have ever seen an iris actually blooming. But he saw these open, shudder "like an animal" and lay back their petals to a full bloom of glory.

Ever after, in times when darkness lay on the face of the deep, he would call up the memory of the irises, and they would bloom again, in his mind. And his heart would rejoice.

∴ x ∴

The Dawn Lies in Wait
by Henry Mitchell

The weather gods can deliver some sharp slaps in November to present masses of seemingly dead leaves, and the subtropical canna called *C. iridiflora* is a fine example.

Early in the month a clump is a sight to melt the heart, as its seven-foot-high flower stalks nod over to display coral rose flowers, not too large, not at all gross.

Behind it I see a few gentian-blue flowers of the blue dawn flower, *Ipomoea acuminata.*

But now the dawn flower is withering on its ten-foot stems. It must be protected for the winter, either by bringing the plant indoors or by mulching it with six to eight inches of litter where it grows.

Neither of these plants has yet produced the effect I know it to be capable of. I want a sheet, a tapestry wall of blue for the canna to stand against, and I would like a dozen or so flowering stems of the coral flowers. In a garden some two such plants will settle in promptly to produce the beautiful sight one intends, but sometimes it is a matter of several years. At the moment all looks brown and dead, but the gardener should pay no attention to the surface, knowing that abundant life is still in the crown and roots, ready to shoot up stronger than ever in the spring.

A delightful plant this time of the year is the wild Italian arum, *A. italicum pictum*, with arrowhead leaves of rich green marked with gray-white veins.

While most other plants are dying down, this one is sprouting anew.

I like to brush back fallen leaves to admire the young arums gathering strength. They are fresh all winter, no matter how dismal the sleet may be, and they reach their greatest beauty in March and April, when they may serve as a lush, seemingly tropical background to many anemones, crocuses, scillas, chionodoxas and the like.

Once the garden has a few good shrubs and perennials in it, great pleasure comes from examining them through the seasons. Some leaf buds, now dormant and waiting for spring, are varnished and gleaming. Others are fuzzy. Some stems erupt in little explosions of scarlet berries, and these may be globular or almond-shaped. Sometimes crimson leaves attend the fruit (as in *Viburnum wrightii*) while others bear pointed, hanging leaves like knives (as in *Viburnum setigera*, a shrub worth its space in even a small garden).

The little star flower from South America, *Ipheion uniflorum*, though the name floats about among four or five genera, has an alarming habit of sending up new leaves in November, in good time to face the worst weather of the year. The little leaves are narrowly strap-shaped, perhaps eight inches long and curving over so that you get fine fat tufts of gray-blue from the leaves, long before the flat, salver-shaped sky-blue flowers appear in March.

What a beautiful beast it is, slithering along with dark ivy and displaying its tender growth against heavy cold slate, while to its back there is the rich green of boxwood in several varieties. The gardener must acquire plants, but amassing treasures is not the aim or the goal. The aim is to peer intensely at all of them, to enjoy the way in which they sprout up and in due season die down.

Flowers have turned to black berries on the common ivy, and deep tints have spread over the commonest epimediums—two plants that are not doing anything spectacular but are full of interest and a quiet beauty.

Sometimes daffodils surprise us by sending up new leaves for spring before winter has arrived. Sometimes those leaves are killed or torn to pieces by ice, but again they may endure unscathed and accompany the April flowers in firm clean shape.

Always there are little irregularities, and always a hastening back (you might say) to old ways as if it were dangerous to stray very far from ancient tracks.

One of the joys never called attention to is the state of any clematis in late fall. Often the seed head, like some gray Medusa who has gone off half-cocked, remains to shed a few more gray seeds. Always it is interesting to look down to the dormant leaf buds that will not open and reach out for several months, but are silky or fuzzy now, affording interest along some stems that one would swear were dead.

I have only a few crocuses and none in bloom now, though gardeners who have troubled to make small collections can have these brilliant chalices for many weeks. I like to see the common fat yellow kind huffing and puffing against brick edging—the flowers threaten to smash the bricks.

On the Defiance of Gardeners

One. ☐ As I write this, on June 29, it's about time for another summer storm to smash the garden to pieces, though it may hold off until the phlox, tomatoes, daylilies, and zinnias are in full sway.

I detect an unwholesome strain in gardeners here, who keep forgetting how very favorable our climate is, and who seem almost on the verge of ingratitude. Disaster, they must learn, is the normal state of any garden, but every time there is wholesale ruin we start sounding off—gardeners here—as if it were terribly unjust. Go to any of those paradise-type gardens elsewhere, however, and see what they put up with in the way of weather, and you will stop whimpering. What is needed around here is more grit in gardeners.

Now I guess there is no garden in the world more dreamworthy than the one at Tresco Abbey in the Scilly Isles. It rarely approaches freezing there, off the mild coast of England, and wonders abound. Palms grow luxuriantly against soft old stonework, medieval in origin, and there is hardly an exotic rarity of New Zealand or South Africa or Madeira that does not flourish. And yet they can have their daffodils, too, for it never gets hot in those islands, either; and if you view such a garden in the long slanting light of a summer's late afternoon, you will think you have got to heaven in spite of yourself. Indeed, almost any garden, if you see it at just the right moment, can be confused with paradise. But even the greatest gardens, if you live with them day after decade, will throw you into despair. At Tresco, that sheltered wonderland, they wake up some mornings to discover 500 trees are down—the very shelter belts much damaged. The cost of cleanup is too grim to dwell on, but even worse is the loss not of mere lousy Norway maples, but of rare cherished specimens that were a wonder to see in flower.

Or there may be—take the great gardens of Gloucestershire—a drought, and the law forbids you to run the hose. Not just a little dry spell, either, but one going on month after month. There you sit in your garden, watching even the native oaks dry up, and as for the rarities imported at such cost, and with such dreams, from the moist Himalayas, the less said of their silent screams the better.

Or take another sort of garden, in which the land to begin with is a collection of rusting bedsprings and immortal boots. Old shoes simply do not rot, in my opinion, but just stay there forever. The chief growth the gardener finds (I am speaking now of the great garden of Sissinghurst in Kent) is brambles and bracken and dock, maybe broken up by patches of stinging nettles. Amenities include the remains of an old pig sty. You convert it, let's say, into one of the sweetest gardens of the world, with roundels of clipped yew and a little alley of lindens, rising over a wide walk, almost a terrace, of concrete cast in big blocks (not one in a thousand knew it was concrete) with spaces for a riot of primroses and spring bulbs, bursting out everywhere in lemon and scarlet and gentian and ivory. The lindens all die. The pavement has to be replaced. The primroses start dying out—they develop a sickness, they wear out the soil, and no mulches of manure, no coddling of any sort will preserve them. So you grub out the dying and start anew with something else.

Wherever humans garden magnificently, there are magnificent heartbreaks. It may be forty heifers break through the hedge after a spring shower and (undiscovered for many hours) trample the labor of many years into uniform mire. It may be the gardener has nursed along his camellias for twenty-five years, and in one night of February they are dead. How can that be? Well, it can be. You have one of the greatest gardens of the Riviera, and one night the dam of the reservoir breaks. The floor of the house is covered with a foot of mud once the water subsides. The reservoir was built at endless labor and cost, since the garden would die without water from it. And now it is gone, and in the flood everything has gone with it. Be sure that is not the day to visit that great garden.

I never see a great garden (even in my mind's eye, which is

the best place to see great gardens around here) but I think of the calamities that have visited it, unsuspected by the delighted visitor who supposes it must be nice to garden there.

It is not nice to garden anywhere. Everywhere there are violent winds, startling once-per-five-centuries floods, unprecedented droughts, record-setting freezes, abusive and blasting heats never known before. There is no place, no garden, where these terrible things do not drive gardeners mad.

I smile when I hear the ignorant speak of lawns that take three hundred years to get the velvet look (for so the ignorant think). It is far otherwise. A garden is very old (though not yet mature) at forty years, and already, by that time, many things have had to be replaced, many treasures have died, many great schemes abandoned, many temporary triumphs have come to nothing and worse than nothing. If I see a garden that is very beautiful, I know it is a new garden. It may have an occasional surviving wonder—a triumphant old cedar—from the past, but I know the intensive care is of the present.

So there is no point dreading the next summer storm that, as I predict, will flatten everything. Nor is there any point dreading the winter, so soon to come, in which the temperature will drop to ten below zero and the ground freezes forty inches deep and we all say there never was such a winter since the beginning of the world. There have been such winters; there will be more.

Now the gardener is the one who has seen everything ruined so many times that (even as his pain increases with each loss) he comprehends—truly knows—that where there was a garden once, it can be again, or where there never was, there yet can be a garden so that all who see it say, "Well, you have favorable conditions here. Everything grows for you." Everything grows for everybody. Everything dies for everybody, too.

There are no green thumbs or black thumbs. There are only gardeners and non-gardeners. Gardeners are the ones who ruin after ruin get on with the high defiance of nature herself, creating, in the very face of her chaos and tornado, the bower of roses and the pride of irises. It sounds very well to garden a "natural way." You may see the natural way in any desert, any swamp, any leech-filled laurel hell. Defiance, on the other hand, is what makes gardeners.

Earthman vs. the Seasons—Winter

Two. □ The days are now at their shortest and the gardener should keep it in mind that his ill-humor and (as it may be) gloominess is directly linked to this nadir of the year. All that is necessary is to hold on until spring or a few sunny days which will surely come, in January, February, March, April, or May at the latest. Meanwhile, several activities will help the gardener keep cheerful.

• Whenever it snows, go out with a broom and swat all conifers likely to be broken down by snow.

• Whenever there are ice storms, pull the window shades down.

• If you have planted roses, camellias, or other plants smack dab against a house wall, water them.

• When Christmas gift plants, if any, stop blooming, either give them conditions they require or else throw them out. There is no point making yourself miserable by watching a poinsettia, cyclamen, or greenhouse azalea die over a period of three months.

• Resolve not to try delphiniums, tuberous begonias, or carnations again.

• Force yourself, for once, to order the varieties of annuals you want from a seedsman in January, so you will not find yourself in a snit in March when you can't find what you want at the drugstore.

• Start saving money to buy next fall's bulbs.

• Borrow money to chop down those maple trees.

• Decide those old gardeners are correct, who have been saying for the past few hundred years that nothing is lovelier or more cheerful in winter than common ivy, common holly, and common yew. And, you might add, junipers.

• Do something now to keep dogs off daffodils, tulips, and other plants that soon will emerge from the ground, since you know perfectly well they will step, sit, sleep, or otherwise intrude on them unless you devise some means to keep them off.

• Feed the birds. You won't get anything much but grackles, starlings, and English sparrows. What did you expect, flamingoes?

• Do not throw rocks at cats. It merely frightens the poor creatures and you never hit them.

• Feed squirrels. This is the same as "feeding birds." Squirrels eat a lot of bulbs—they are in heaven when they find the cyclamen and crocuses—but they keep the garden interesting for the family dog and besides, the squirrels are more attractive than the cyclamen probably would have been.

• Put a couple of logs in lily pools to absorb or deflect some of the pressure of the ice. Do not chop holes in ice. Fish in the pool do not need air holes.

• If it ever gets warmish again, admire the swelling buds of elm, ash, azalea, flowering quince. Make up your mind once and for all whether you will give space to a pussy willow bush. Whichever you decide, decide, and stop being of two minds about it.

• Thank God you do not have to stay in the garden all winter like a blasted snowdrop (which should, incidentally, be showing some signs of activity within the year's first month). Gardeners, on the other hand, will stir about April 8.

The Wrongs of Winter, the Rites of Spring

A gardener must not feel sorry for himself, even in winter, and no matter how great the cause.

When I was a lad there was a man who had the most splendid garden around: the main axis was half a mile long and instead of an old tub with a rosemary leaning out of it (as ordinary gardeners have) he had seventeenth-century marble urns. If there was some plant you had mentally been saving up for to buy next year, you could be sure he had at least a dozen mature specimens of it in his woodland. But if you openly envied him his garden, it was clear he felt a bit abused because his fountains were not as good as those of the Villa d'Este and he could not grow rhododendrons like the ones at Ghiga and his camellias were nothing much to those at Middleton.

Which was perfectly true. But I thought at the time, I must never let anybody know I suffer because my ornamental water (a horse trough with a water lily in it) is less than I would like. Even the great gardens lack many things, and that should comfort us if our bird bath is not so blue or palm-fronded as the lake at Como. In a nutshell, I was sorry because I had no lorapetalum, and then I met a man who had no snowdrop.

As you may perceive, I am trying to rev us all up to that gratitude gardeners ought to feel for our many blessings, much as parents sometimes point to the turnips and say "but Tim, they are delicious and besides they're good for you—many a child in China would be happy etc., etc." And that is true, too, as so many parental sayings are. Or were.

We do not, in our gardens, need rarities, nor more land, nor a better climate (though one can conceive of improvements here). We merely need more labor and less grumbling, more brains and fewer store-bought gewgaws, and most of all more awareness of what is in front of us in the garden. What good would a whole orchard full of daffodils be, if our minds were preoccupied with palm trees?

Which brings me to today's major news: I have two clumps of the crocus 'Violet Queen' in bloom, and three flowers out on the crocus 'Goldilocks,' and one snowdrop. Furthermore, I can already tell there will be some flowers (the buds are getting pinkish) on the double plum *Prunus* × *blirieana* (possibly the name "blirieana" suggests something bleary or weary or disheartened, though this small tree is among the most festive occupants of the vegetable kingdom and blooms early with the forsythias).

It is true the daffodils 'Tête-à-Tête,' which are very early, are not up as they should be. The doubtfully hardy ceanothus (a broadleaf evergreen with panicles of sky-blue flowers like vitex or small lilacs in spring) is resolving the doubts in a way I do not like. It may not make it through the winter.

Also, the hyacinths apparently suffered even more than I thought when last year the old hound discovered they made a grand place to nap. The hound has never been born that does not know how to demolish a few little wooden stakes that are supposed to "protect" the plant, even if they are driven eighteen inches into the ground. They can be snapped off, bent sideways, etc. Anyhow, I thought, well, the hyacinths will be all right next year. As I say, they are not.

The daffodil 'Grand Soleil d'Or' has virus. I have read the entire stock of this variety does, but thought mine would not.

The squirrels have stopped eating the crocus bulbs since we took to feeding them massively on peanuts and sunflower seeds, but they still pull them up and leave them on top of the ground uneaten. Only a few are pulled up, but it is annoying. It is too soon yet for them to start chewing off the flower buds of the rhododendron and the Knap Hill azaleas (which they do, and if you cover them with little sacks made of nylon stockings, they leave the twigs with the stockings on the ground—they never succeed in getting through the nylon to the bud, but they do gnaw the twig off, so not much is accomplished if your idea was to have flowers).

Iris danfordiae is not doing right. Neither, for that matter, is 'Harmony,' a brilliant deep blue hybrid of *Iris reticulata* and *Iris histrioides*. They are not doing right because they are not up, and they should be.

The grapes are deficient in vigor. The mock orange 'Belle Etoile' has not grown as it should. The fig has been seriously damaged by the winter, because I did not get around to correcting a drip from the roof on it. Dear Lord, you can't do everything.

There are winter days I look around out there and quite lose faith. Nothing looks like anything. The stachys has caught a fungus—it will revive in the spring probably—and the myosotis has got that black bacterial blight that it gets in winter in damp places. It is always threatening to die in the winter, then romps all out of bounds all summer. *Viburnum* × *juddii*, with sweet-scented pink ping-pong balls of blossom in early spring, is only going to have two flowers—I had counted on twenty. The winter jasmine, which is a positive weed, is taking unconscionably long to get going, and the Carolina jasmine still has four leaves and four only, as it did last spring. Does it not know it is to clothe an arbor, the great bare posts of which are still sitting there waiting?

In brief, I am no stranger to the anxieties or disappointments of a garden. A fine gardener once said his garden had a certain origin: "This garden is the result of doing unnecessary things which we could not afford at the wrong time of the year," he used to say, and the garden was quite beautiful. Of my own garden I might add, in addition to all that, "and furthermore nothing is doing all that well and it looks utterly hopeless."

And then one bleak winter day as you blast out the front door in a sprint for the bus there, by the grace of God, is *Crocus sieberi* 'Violet Queen' in full bloom two weeks earlier than scheduled. And there (as you slow down, though of course you must get to the office) is 'Goldilocks' and there (will wonders never cease) is one snowdrop and (what wondrous life is this I lead), incredible as it seems, the cyclamineus hybrids are pushing through the much-too-deep mulch after all, and the wild cyclamen have revived despite being stepped on—it is not to be believed how otherwise civilized people will step on wild cyclamen even as you very tactfully suggest avoiding them—and I do not go so far as to say God's in his heaven or anything of the sort that I know nothing about. But I do say it takes very little to convince a gardener he will make it right into spring.

Earthman vs. the Seasons—Spring

Three. ☐ When we complain of weather we are always on firm ground. It is not imagination or idle dreaming; there is excellent reason for complaint. This time of year, a day may bring temperatures of 90 or 25. You never know.

The gardener knows those early April days when the air is soft, the sun not too bright, and the thermometer at 63. There have been soft rains, there is little wind. The gardener thinks such weather is his right, this time of year. If a wind of seventy-two miles an hour follows a cold snap and the temperature shoots to 83, followed by hail, he is fit for the madhouse and really should be safely stashed away there for a few days. And yet such weather is not only normal but inevitable—if not this year, then next. Nothing in the natural world is "always reliable."

One thinks, "Well, at least the lilacs are always on time and always good," but there are years they all freeze. There are years the irises do not bloom at all. There are years the roses are blown right off their stems, and years the chrysanthemums are frozen dead just as they come into bloom. If you think of it, most of us garden on land where things have been planted pretty steadily for a couple of centuries, and it would be a paradise by now except for disasters along the way.

The first time a storm rips all the peonies to pieces—the gardener has waited two years and done a good bit of scratching about with wood ashes and has chopped out tree roots and has set up stakes—the pain is severe. Within a few years, however, the gardener begins to realize there has never yet been a single year in which everything did well. And (usually after forty years or so) he notices that no year is without some special splendor. Most of us can remember years when the irises were unearthly in their perfection, day after day after day of flawless flowers. I have seen two such years myself in the past forty-three.

I remember one year the daffodils reached such glory that almost any one in the garden would win a blue ribbon. One year. Once the trout lilies outdid themselves. Several times the azaleas had no blemish anywhere. The gardener, naturally, remembers those years and is in a snit for decades afterward if the insolent wind presumes to blow. He remembers the year it didn't.

It is amazing to me that nurseries without any exception I can recall send dormant blueberry plants at the end of two weeks of perfect planting weather. The plants arrive (nurseries are especially clever at timing deliveries when one is out of town) just before the temperature soars to 80, with plenty of wind. Or, sometimes, just before the sleet storm.

The truth is, of course, that there is no day of the early spring that is safe. Usually, after the gardener has carried on a good bit and made life miserable for a number of people, the weather settles back and the gardener stops hollering everything is going to die. But already I dread those terrible days in May when torrents will fall and it will get cold and raw. How gross and clumsy Nature is. How ill-planned and slipshod. On the other hand, who could stand a really revolting climate, like Southern California or the South Sea islands? Lucky is the gardener who has learned first-hand and early that Nature is outrageous everywhere and, as the schoolteacher said in one of Eudora Welty's novels, when the tornado headed for the schoolhouse and she had to think of something quick, "We're in the best place right here."

Rumor, as we know, is almost the only home of truth.

Daffodil Time

Since the daffodil season lasts six weeks, if both early and late varieties are included in the garden, it is not surprising that every year, without exception, there is gnashing of teeth. From mid-March to May we are bound to have some of the most unsettled weather of the year. There are certain to be days of cold wind and a touch of frost on still-bleak nights. We can count on several hot

days as well, and any daffodils opening then will promptly wilt
and flag. Every year some will have poor texture, or short stems,
or the scarlet will come orange, not red, or the petals (supposed to
be like white kid or refined beeswax) will be full of slight ribs or
have a puckered finish like crepe. A certain number of stems will
be snapped, or some flowers will be flattened and then mud-spotted.

So every year, without fail, the dirge goes up. It has never
dawned on gardeners, and still less on daffodil fanatics, that chancy
weather means chancy flowers. And you have only to read a couple of decades of yearbooks on the daffodil (in which you may find
the most concentrated of ill-humored weather complaints in the
world) to realize things are no better and no worse in England or
Ireland than here.

I will spare you, therefore, a litany of disappointments in this
year's daffodils and say simply that on April 23 I had a handful
of the most beautiful flowers imaginable.

There is a pink-crowned white flower, 'Passionale,' which is,
not to split hairs about it, supremely beautiful. Beside it, the well-
known 'Accent' looks coarse and unworthy of cultivation, even
though it has a splendid firm perianth. Another flower of ultimate
beauty is the white trumpet 'Rashee,' which with me has always
been distinctly small and not likely, therefore, ever to win any
major prizes at a show. It is more beautiful, however, than 'Vigil'
or 'Empress of Ireland.'

Something got into 'Easter Moon' this year, causing its stems
to be much too tall for the size of the flower. One bloom, however,
was flawless. This was an excellent year also for 'Easter Morn,' a
variety more than fifty years old now; it's a white with short
white cup and great refinement. Certainly nobody would plant it
nowadays (for one thing, it is not in commerce), but it is pleasant
when a very old daffodil quite surpasses itself. All daffodil nuts
know the refinement brought to white daffodils (the short-cupped
whites) by 'Silver Coin.' One of that type, 'Silver Salver,' always
did well in my former garden, and sometimes I took wicked pleasure in showing a bloom to someone whose newer and better
whites were not all equal to it.

The lemon daffodil with a white cup, almost a trumpet, called
'Daydream' has been without blemish this year for me. Mine are
always on the small side, but this year perfect. The hound sat on

two, giving me an excuse to cut them. A rather large white with a shallow rose-madder crown called 'Coral Light' has outdone itself this year. I have never seen that particular color in a flower. It is soft but assertive and the cup has a deeper red rim, quite astonishing. It would have won something in a show if the show had been ten days later.

Always there are years in which some flower like 'Coral Light' blooms finer than you have ever seen it. I like those years, and in them I can recapture the excitement of the fellow who bred the flower and who could not believe his eyes when it first bloomed for him in great perfection. 'Double Event' is a ball-shaped flower of white with light yellow segments scattered among the white petals. Almost every year it comes perfect, on firm fine stems. The double canary yellow with scarlet segments called 'Tahiti' always is astonishing, and flawless. It has everything except an ultimate beauty, which escapes it.

Both 'Falstaff' and 'Ceylon' are yellow with medium-large red cups, and both are sunproof—the red does not fade or bleach. Of the two I prefer 'Ceylon,' though there is not much to choose. With me it is a trifle smoother, the pose of the flower a trifle better, and to my eye it is just a bit more beautiful. And yet, I remember well the years I longed for 'Falstaff' and could not afford it. One bulb produced fourteen flowers in its third spring.

Two small-flowered daffodils, 'Pipit' and 'Mockingbird,' are alike in having white cups against yellow perianth. 'Pipit' is paler, more delicate, while 'Mockingbird' is a strong lemon and showier. I always wondered what happened to 'Arbar,' a white flower with a red cup, which I once saw in complete magnificence about twenty years ago in a friend's garden. With me it was always wonderful but never quite perfect. In my new garden I assumed 'Arbar' was lost in the shuffle, and never noticed it in the spring. But this year a little patch of it turned up in what was supposed to be 'Sun Chariot' (a yellow and red flower that was not up to snuff for me this season), and I cannot think how it got there.

One year I had a 'Silver Chimes' better than any I had seen elsewhere. It grew and grew (this one stem) almost to the stature of the old tazettas you find in southern gardens with unreliable names but none the less beautiful for that. It can be an astounding thing. There must have been more than fifteen flowers on the stem, each rather large and beautifully spaced (of course, you have to push them about a little with your fingers) and of unparalleled smooth texture. Up here, however, I have never had a decent bloom, and this year I see all the bulbs have disappeared. It blooms late and is fine for cutting.

The old white trumpet 'Cantatrice' came on very long stems this year with coarse texture and uneven perianth. It needs digging and dividing, but I had never before seen it really lacking in beauty.

Most of my daffodils have severe defects, by show standards, but then they make a brave show all the same. I have several that are to my eye distinctly ugly, but I like them too. One is a bicolor trumpet, white perianth with a really gross megaphone sticking out in intense neon-lemon, frilled to beat the band, like a whore on Easter. I never saw anything quite like it.

I also have some glorious yellows with red cups, a little like the old 'Red Goblet' but better—except that the cup burns to ashengray after two days of sun. Then I have a good-sized patch of 'Spellbinder,' which is greenish lemon with white trumpet, eventually, and nothing gives me more pleasure than seeing it at the beginning of the season though it lacks refinement.

Many gardeners could with profit buy some of those Dutch mixed daffodils that come in net bags. There is great variety there, and they make a loud show. But I hope any gardener will try at least a few of the most beautiful sorts, like 'Passionale.' Even one bulb.

Perennials

This time of year nurserymen sell perennials in cans and pots or flats, and it is perfectly sensible to buy them that way rather than not get them at all.

Field-grown clumps, planted in the fall, are best, but since most gardeners refuse to get around to tending to such matters then, it can all be tended to now. All perennials that I can think of require a while to settle down and show what they can do.

Phlox, for example, or baby's breath or baptisia or hostas or daylilies or peonies—you name it—need to be in the garden two or three years before anything approaching their full beauty is to be seen.

Virtually all perennials require sun. Some, like soldiers and sailors (*Pulmonaria*) or the big forget-me-nots (*Cynoglossum*) plus ferns, of course, and hostas and bugle weeds (*Ajuga*) accept woodland shade, since woodlands are quite sunny in the early spring. For those dark places where the sun never shines, the best that can be hoped for is a good-looking paving with ivy, pachysandra, ferns, and hostas, and even these will benefit from coddling in the way of careful watering and good soil.

Foxgloves (*Digitalis*) are too often overlooked for positions in dappled light. Most foxgloves are short-lived perennials, dying out after two or three years, but in congenial places they seed themselves. So do many poppies, though they require the nearest thing to full sun the gardener can offer. The soundly perennial Oriental poppies (in white, orange, crimson, scarlet, rose) like the same sort of position that corn does—plenty of sun, and good, deep rich soil. There is no point expecting them to look like much for a couple of years.

I have enjoyed my white and yellow primroses this spring. They are very easily grown, but are not plants that can be stuck in and then forgotten. Every year, or every other year at maximum, they must be dug out, separated, and replanted in good rich soil. This is done in May. Mine grow at the east end of a raised pool, and are shaded most of the day. If left alone, they get thick and then start to die out. If replanted every year (it is good to have them out of the ground no longer than it takes to pull them apart and reset them) they go on forever, increasing at a great rate. They will not take being dry in the summer, by the way.

For some reason columbines never seem to seed themselves with me, probably because the earth is disturbed by scratching around before they have time to sprout. Columbines sometimes settle down for five years or so, but often they die after two or three years. Like everything else, they take a good bit of space (like a bushel basket) but their foliage is handsome even when the plants are not in bloom, and they flower from late April right through May.

The coral bells (*Heuchera*) are among the most rewarding perennials for gardeners with small places, since they bloom for two months or more, knee-high slender stalks hung with delicate bells of red, rose, white, or green. They have handsome leaves the size of a small hand, usually with a reddish tint, and these are much appreciated in November, say, when most perennials are sad. They flower from late April into July. They are admirable in clumps along a walk, forming neat hummocks. The only problem with them is that they easily heave in the winter, and need to be pushed down when it thaws. They make little offsets, and should be kept coming along from these, since old plants get increasingly woody and do not do so well. But I would not want to say anything that might discourage the planting of these splendid flowers which contrast so well with almost everything else in the garden.

Everybody, I suppose, likes hollyhocks. I often come to grief with them because I jam other things up against them, and hollyhocks like plenty of space and air and full sun. The alleys of Washington are sometimes showy with them, for they are not fussy as long as they have room and sun.

Shasta daisies are far more agreeable and lovely than one thinks they are going to be. The average collection of daylilies, incidentally, would be much brightened by a few clumps of these white daisies to bloom with them in late June. These daisies are among those plants that should be dug up, separated and replanted every year or so, in April or else in September. It does not do at all to separate them in November, because they die over winter. I do not see why anything so hardy should not settle in promptly, even in November, but experience convinces me to separate these daisies either in April or around Labor Day.

Peonies do quite well planted from cans in the spring. I myself would always buy the bare roots in October and plant them then, because they are cheaper and usually better. But I have seen fine peonies from spring plants, which can look splendid after three years.

This is a great time, by the way, to prepare daffodil beds for planting next fall. In the garden where space is short, daffodils can be planted eight inches apart and left for two or three years before being dug up, separated and dried (in June or early July) and replanted in September. So a good many will fit in a small space. If the earth is deeply dug, with peat mixed in and a bit of rotted manure (an inch or two, dug in and mixed with the soil) you can grow vegetables there this summer, clearing them away and digging again lightly in late September and planting daffodil bulbs in

October. As any gardener knows who has tried various methods, daffodils do far better in a bed prepared the spring before, instead of being stuck in any which way in the fall.

There are certain terrible grasses that form massive clumps, so that when they are dug up with a spade a whole bushel of dirt comes up also. These grasses dearly love to sprout among daylilies, shrub roses, or anywhere else they can get a foothold. They must be got up now, or they will form truly enormous clumps this summer, and nothing—literally nothing—can grow through them. Again in early fall they should be dug up, if any have managed to get started during the summer. I have been getting some out of old clumps of daylilies, and it meant digging the entire daylily clump up, working all the grass out, and replanting. There is no point thinking the daylilies will shade these clump-forming grasses out. They will not. Fortunately the grass comes up clean (along with half the dirt of the garden) so once the clump is up, you don't have to worry about oddments sprouting all over the place.

Interlude

In the Merry Month of Mayhem

Four. ☐ There is nothing like the first hot days of spring when the gardener stops wondering if it's too soon to plant the dahlias and starts wondering if it's too late. Even the most beautiful weather will not allay the gardener's notion (well-founded, actually) that he is somehow too late, too soon, or that he has too much stuff going on or not enough. For the garden is the stage on which the gardener exults and agonizes out every crest and chasm of the heart.

Now of course May will bring us the most awful days of the entire year, in which the sky suddenly turns gray and the temperature drops to the point one needs a coat, and this lasts three to five days and then all is well again until the first sky-wrecking torrential rain of June.

It was the poet Hopkins, who was not ever a gardener but who nevertheless learned a thing or two just by thinking about things, who noticed that the great pleasures of life come rather incidentally, and not at all as the result of much craft and planning. We all know by now that as the irises and roses and peonies reach a great climax we are likely to have a storm so severe it batters flower stalks and blooms to nothing. So we are braced for it. And then there will come a day in which things we do not expect all bloom together and the light is of some curious quality and all things take on a glow and richness that transfigures them.

This year I was alarmed at the failure of the great ditch grass (*Arundo donax*, which is said to have played some sort of role in the draining of malarial swamps in Italy) to appear as soon as it should have. But now I see its conical spikes pushing up. In Washington it rarely sprouts out from its old stalks but starts up new every year. My neighbors always inquire, when this grass first overtops the fence in June, if I am growing corn, since that's what it looks like if you don't see much when you look.

A plant that is supposed to do nicely in ill-drained heavy earth without full sun is *Peltiphyllum peltatum*, which in April sends up little stalks only a foot high, decked with clear rose-colored saucers half an inch wide, in clusters at the top. It is nothing much to see, but there it is. Before the flower passes, the leaves begin rising from the ground, and they are circular, pleated, all squinched up like a moth's wings fresh from the cocoon. These leaves in a few weeks grow to a foot or so in width, borne on a stem (one leaf to the stem) of ample strength to withstand any weather. They are like water-lily leaves rising out of dry land. It's a new plant with me, but I have greatly admired its effect by the waterside in certain gardens.

In Williamsburg recently a kind gardener gave me some cowslips, the pale-yellow unimproved sort you don't see much now. I used to grow them in a town with longer and hotter summers than here, and they protested every July by going dormant, but revived a bit in the fall and bloomed heavily every spring.

Dahlias and gladioli, if not already planted out, can go in now and you can keep planting them for the next month or so. Within reason, the later you plant a gladiolus the quicker it blooms. If you plant it in mid-March it may take it a hundred days or more to flower, while the same corm planted out in mid-May may bloom in seventy days. I allow ninety days for gladioli (some varieties bloom in sixty-odd days, others in one hundred days) but if planted late in July you have to allow for the effect of cooler nights in early fall. I have never planted them as late as August, but suspect they would do well enough, provided the gardener didn't go into fits if an early freeze got them.

Coral bells (*Heuchera*) bridge the gap between late daffodils and tulips, and the heavy flowering of peonies. Here the spring is so jammed up and comes on so quickly that we do not have to wait many days between the first flowers of spring and the last. Even so, there are a few days when columbines and honesty and coral bells and woodruff seem to be the main things going. In a garden across the river in Virginia there is a solid bed of coral bells that I envy. It is rather large and it goes on blooming into July.

The wild Japanese *Iris tectorum*, in its white form, was the first iris to open this year with me. It is as beautiful as any flower but only a foot tall, so it makes no great show, even if you have a whole bed of it. It is one of those plants you should keep coming along from seed, since it is not long-lived, and besides it quickly exhausts the soil.

The tremendous Japanese iris of gardens (for the little white one is not a major garden plant) grow for me in a whiskey barrel. When I think of it, which is not often enough, I give them a flooding with the garden hose. Fortunately we do not often have to complain of a shortage of water in our springtimes, but the Japanese iris—with flat flowers of crumpled crepe in complicated colors—can never have too much water from March to June. It also likes heavy mulches of manure in the winter. It likes full sun, but I have seen a very beautiful clump of it greatly shaded (though open to the south sun in early spring) by a hemlock tree. As with many other plants, it sometimes obliges us by growing in conditions it would not have chosen for itself.

The Fluffy Majesty of the Peony

The fattest and most scrumptious of all flowers, a rare fusion of fluff and majesty, the peony is now coming into bloom to mark the highest of high spring. Most of my scruples against ponderous shapes in flowers are swept away in the general confusion of the peony season. I say confusion only because I have never been able to settle down with a handful of varieties I consider the best. It's gradually becoming clear to me that if I had space for two hundred, there would still be a few hundred more to be desired and, worst of all, I have never had the chance to grow a few hundred so that at the last (that is, in a small city garden) I could settle for a handful to serve as well as a thousand.

When I was a boy there was an old man who sold peonies and opened his garden once a year for the town to admire. There you placed orders and in due time, late in September or October, he showed up to deliver the roots. His favorite was 'Le Cygne,' a swan of a flower indeed, though not as hearty a grower as one might wish. As far as I know he had no other plants but peonies, and when they were over, he aestivated.

When he was in his 90s, he dropped by unexpectedly—since I had not ordered anything in the spring—and said he wanted me to have three roots, 'Festiva Maxima,' 'M. Jules Elie' and, I think (for I did not grow it), 'Edulis Superba.' He died a few days after that, and I suspect he thought the time had come to go around and make sure plenty of people were growing peonies, and that he had better start them off right with a few that would grow and bloom well for anybody. I never see those varieties but I think of him. 'Festiva Maxima' is the fat double early white with occasional crimson flecks that you see everywhere. It was bred and put on the market in 1851. The second, which is one of those rare flowers of which gardeners manage to get the entire name right, 'M. Jules Elie,' is a huge medium pink, the petals curving up somewhat like a chrysanthemum, and the color slightly veiled by silver-gray. But do not imagine it is a dull color—it is flawless and as luscious as strawberries in cream. The third, which came out in the 1820s, as I remember it, is a sort of rose pink, a trifle too blue to suit many gardeners, and round and not too large. But like the other two it blooms early in the peony season and is, of the three, the most perfumed. It used to be a great cut-flower variety, and once or twice I have seen it at flower stalls in Washington.

To bring some sort of order to the peony tribe, for gardeners who may not be familiar with them, let me mention the general types. First, there are the full doubles, very like dahlias that have gone to heaven and been transformed. These are the tremendous sorts that girls used to carry in bouquets for graduation day from high school in the North. Many of them are big as a cantaloupe. When the petals fill with rain, most of them bend down on their stems and never quite stand up straight again. Needless to say, it is prudent to provide wire rings or stakes for them.

Second, there are the semi-doubles, with fewer petals. The anemone-flowered kinds have a row or two of flat outer petals— not always flat, come to think of it—and thinner petalodes, like shredded petals, in the middle. Sometimes they have yellow stamens showing, sometimes not.

The Japanese peonies are somewhat similar, only with the stamens transformed into floral parts. That is, there is a great flat saucer of petals and a grand sunburst of stamens looking like yellow confetti in the middle. Sometimes the Japanese sorts have the middle the same color as the petals, which is very handsome, and sometimes there is a contrast. These great single flowers, once quite expensive, are now as cheap as any other sort of peony. Some are red with yellow centers; some white with tawny gold; some pink with red centers; some rose with whitish centers; some vaguely lavender, and in some the pink petals are edged with lighter color. Having only the single row of petals, they do not get waterlogged so badly as the massive doubles, and they stand up better in rain. It is not true, however, that you need not stake them. Last year my 'Largo,' a deep rose with yellow centers, flopped about in the rain and covered a circle five feet in diameter. It is merely one of many spectacular varieties, and I also grow 'Christine,' a white; 'Westerner,' a rich wonderful pink; 'Plainsman,' blush; 'Sitka,' another white; and 'Chocolate Soldier,' a glossy red with occasional yellow dots on the petals, one of the earliest kinds. 'Gay Paree' is pink with red centers; 'Doreen' has several tints of pink in it; 'Sword Dance' is a late-flowering red and yellow; 'Isani Gidui' and 'Toro-no-maki' are whites with yellow centers. And there are dozens of others, all of which I would grow if I could.

This may be the place to say that lists of the "best" varieties are inherently absurd, since if you dislike deep red with yellow centers, you clearly should not grow reds with yellow centers, no matter what list they appear on. Likewise, if you think the whites with yellow are too elegant, and want something flashier, like pink and yellow, then clearly you should grow the pinks. Most lists provide a wide assortment of types and colors, and I dearly love lists of the best this and the best that, but I never follow them very closely in my own selection. I do not think a gardener can go wrong with peonies, except in two ways: he can wind up with so many of the massive doubles that the effect is heavier, when they are in flower, than he intended, or he may not be prepared for the staking that the heavy kinds require. Apart from that, I don't see how anyone can go wrong. Some of the very double kinds, especially the late-season ones, will fail to open properly in hot weather. They are a gamble, and to begin with the gardener should perhaps concentrate on earlier-season sorts.

I have not mentioned the singles. These have a row of petals, like the Japanese, but lack the big central tuft. Such varieties as 'Dawn Pink,' 'Sea Shell,' 'Krinkled White,' 'Pico,' and 'Le Jour' are among the esteemed sorts.

Also I have not mentioned the hybrids—peonies in which more than one wild species is in the ancestry. As a group, these bloom earliest of all, and their colors are especially brilliant. Or fierce, if you prefer. They bring the fire of the Oriental poppy to the garden before those poppies bloom, and since they are strong in orange-reds, intense cherry, etc., some restraint (if possible) probably should be exercised. Well-known kinds, besides 'Chocolate Soldier,' which has the Japanese form of a central boss, include such single reds as 'Bright Knight,' 'John Harvard,' and such full doubles as 'Red Charm,' which virtually everybody likes since it is fully and clearly red without setting off the smoke alarms, and such whites as 'Requiem,' a flat lightly built bloom. There are also many curious pinks, and many creamy cerises—colors otherwise lacking in garden peonies. Among the doubles, since they are entirely too gorgeous to gloss over, are 'Florence Ellis,' 'Mrs. Franklin D. Roosevelt,' 'Nick Shaylor,' 'Myrtle Gentry,' all considered pretty reliable pinks. Whites include 'Kelway's Glorious,' 'Mary E. Nicholls,' 'Elsa Sass,' among many; and good reds 'Kansas,' 'Philippe Rivoire,' 'Karl Rosenfeld,' and 'Richard Carvel.' Again, let me insist that one should not assume varieties not listed are somehow maybe not as good as those that are.

'Big Ben,' for example, is not found on lists of the "best" reds, I think, but it is tall, early, reliable, and one of the very best for the South since it does not fail to open properly.

Peonies should be planted in October, the growth points or eyes (those fleshy red swellings on the roots from which stems emerge in the spring) just barely covered. No more than an inch of dirt over them. They should be given full sun, if convenient, or at least as sunny as one has. They will not grow under trees, like azaleas, and they like good soil such as tomatoes require.

The sensible thing (although I am quite aware I am dealing with gardeners) is to decide how much space can be given to peonies and just where. All gardeners like to say, "Well, now, let's just go through a few catalogues," and they make tremendous lists and fidget over them for a while, then (as July arrives) cut them drastically, and finally (as October approaches) madly order a few peonies almost at random, having forgotten which ones they were so keen about in May. There is a public display garden of labeled peonies in the National Arboretum, well worth a few visits.

Once the gardener decides he can manage half a dozen, or three, or twenty-six, or whatever it is, he should have a precise idea which spots in the garden they will occupy, and this will prevent color clashes, assuming the gardener can remember that the fiery climbing rose 'Dortmund' does not look so hot with the pink Japanese 'Sky Pilot.' Likewise, certain tender-colored pink peonies do not blend (except in a whirling sort of way) with certain fiery orange poppies that may bloom at the same time.

If planting stations are prepared now, digging in plenty of humus and some manure (but no manure at planting time, or around the stems in future years, since it is supposed to invite fungi and rank growth both), then a stake can mark the spot, and the whole thing may be allowed to settle without attention until October. Then pull up any little weeds that may have been missed, and plant the peonies about October 10. Most of them bloom the first spring, in my experience, but it will be the third spring before they look fully contented and prosperous. Most peonies have excellent foliage. Even when out of bloom, the plants have a solid air, as if the gardener knew what he were doing, and this of course has endeared them to gardeners for centuries. Many of the hybrids, however, die down in late July, and this is alarming the first time it happens. One cannot imagine the plants will be healthy and vigorous the next spring, but they are. Do not plant the hybrids (such as 'Red Charm'), therefore, in a place where you require fine foliage in the fall.

Try not to go hog wild. A peony will occupy a circle thirty to forty inches in diameter, as a rule, and nothing else will grow in that space. Also peonies abhor tree roots and grass. They greatly dislike being moved, once they settle in. Like irises, they like the best spots in the garden. So do roses. Try to be careful, remembering peonies only bloom a few weeks—an individual plant only a few days. But don't be too restrained.

Advice for the May-Struck Gardener

I always warn myself (with very little result) against the beauty of the late May–early June garden, which can overpower and unbalance the entire rest of the year—to say nothing of the gardener. It is the time for peonies, the last of the tulips, the first of the roses, and columbines and lupines and violas and pansies and Oriental poppies and irises. Usually the gardener commences with admirable restraint, remembering well that there must be space for early bulbs and daffodils, space for summer perennials and annuals, space for fall flowers like Japanese anemones and chrysanthemums and perhaps cleomes and cosmos.

Besides all that, there must be plenty of space for those plants that are not much in flower, but which have foliage of great interest and importance: plants that give texture and tone and substance to all the rest, such as rue and wormwood and angelica and hostas and mulleins.

It all sounds very reasonable, when you see it in print, and the alert gardener usually makes a note to add some clumps of Italian arums and hellebores and wild cyclamen and the like for winter interest. The trouble arises (as it usually does in all fields of endeavor) only when you stop reading and start doing. The first year or two commonly goes well. A peony here, an iris there, a soft pink poppy over yonder. Disaster (as far as balance is concerned) usually strikes either the second summer or the third spring of the gardener's career, when it dawns on him, like the sun of Rangoon, that there is no reason at all he could not really get himself some color if he put in a few more peonies, and why settle for one clump of poppies, and Lord, what can be done with irises. In no time at all reason is out the window and extravagance and gaud take over. Oh shame, shame, I always say.

By the fifth year—for satiety is said to follow orgies usually—the gardener generally decides it would be nice to have something to look at, once the three weeks of May are done. Chrysanthemums, which are often the first thing to be pitched out, in the interest of spring splendor, are grudgingly fetched back in extreme moderation. Daylilies are allowed to expand a little, even at the expense of peonies and irises and poppies, since they are so reliable for July when the irises are a dismal mess.

It must be admitted, however, that once the taste for splendor or opulence or gaudiness (it is nice to be able to choose your own word, perhaps) is acquired, then the garden is restless ever after, or at least the gardener is. Only an uneasy truce prevails. The gardener perhaps makes room for September or July flowers, but his heart generally is back in spring, and he is usually on the verge of throwing something out that doesn't flower in May. It is a marvel that chrysanthemums bloom at all in those gardens where the gardener is forever glaring at them, holding them up to poles and trimming things off and muttering that they certainly take a great space.

Fortunately, by the thirtieth or fortieth or fiftieth year or thereabouts, the gardener strikes that balance by which he has the best of all seasons. By the time one is eighty, it is said, there is no longer a tug of war in the garden with the May flowers hauling like mad against the claims of the other months. All is at last in balance and all is serene. The gardener is usually dead, of course. If he should live to 100, however, then needless to say it takes somewhat longer to achieve balance in the garden.

If I may venture one suggestion to the May-struck gardener it is this: do not allow the total space occupied by irises, peonies, roses, poppies, forget-me-nots, violas, clematis, and the other glories of late May to occupy more than 63 percent of the space. Unless, at an absolute maximum, they are allowed to occupy 76 percent. It is unthinkable that they should in any case hog so much as 94 percent of the arable area. Usually.

Earthman vs. the Seasons—Summer

A [Brief] Season to Enjoy

Five. □ There is a brief time in July when the gardener has nothing to do but enjoy his flowers. Oh, there may be a few things, like tying in the dahlias, discreetly staking the chrysanthemums, picking off the dead water lilies, keeping an eye on the roses for blackspot, soaking the azaleas and camellias, cutting the grass, tying in the huge new canes of climbing roses, and like that.

But by and large it is a time of leisure, different from the panic of the great fall planting season and free from that sense of frantic tidying up that afflicts the spring.

If you have planned ahead, in fact, this respite can last even into August and September. A garden planned for late August (and for January as well) will give the greatest pleasure, because spring and early summer tend to take care of themselves. Even a little thought for these too-neglected months will go far in keeping the gardener from muttering and snapping. But the average gardener pays too little attention to August and September, and it may be safely said that the average garden goes to pot on July 16 as regular as clockwork.

Daylily Days

July is full of daylilies, which have progressed from their former state of being useful to their present state of substantial beauty. As there are now about 20,000 named varieties, however, the sensible gardener is much at sea if he wants only a dozen. The best way to choose is to spend twenty-five years looking at various sorts in many gardens and shows, but this is not always practical. Another is to pick current favorites from the latest "recommended" lists put out by the local or national daylily societies. Most such lists attempt complete coverage of the colors now found in daylilies, along with a complete range of sizes, from flowers two inches wide to those seven or eight inches across, and include some early (June 13 or before) and some late (August 7 and after) varieties. But no collection of a dozen or even twenty-five plants will cover the full range of daylily beauty. The daylily collection at the National Arboretum, by the way, is well worth visiting. They have a fine assortment there, labeled, that will give you a good notion of what daylilies are like today.

In small city gardens the gardener must decide whether to attempt a long season of bloom, using early and late flowering varieties, or to concentrate on the main midseason varieties only, which bloom from about July 2 to July 20, and whether to devote all the space to one's favorite two colors (say, lemon and cantaloupe, or scarlet and buff, or lavender and near-white), or have the full spectrum, and whether to concentrate on the smaller sorts or the mediums or the largest ones.

Whichever sort one chooses, daylilies are so nearly a perfect garden flower that it seems silly to note their few defects, and I will instead describe how I think they are most readily used in small gardens. The usual town garden in the capital is rather like a cat run. My own is 40 by about 100 feet or so, and its main feature is a walk from the kitchen door to the alley gate. It is not blessed, in other words, with any God-given feature except the sun itself. It would have suited me better if I had old pink brick walls, with Ely Cathedral at the back boundary and a lake to the west. On the other hand, I might easily have wound up with something the size of a rug, overhung with maples and hemlocks—disgusting creatures.

Now daylilies have increasingly insinuated themselves into this garden, such as it is; I now have maybe a hundred varieties, and I can see how this happened. First of all, they are healthy animals, reminding me a good deal of bassets I have known, to whom, once whelped and given their shots, nothing much happens vet-wise until they at last die. Daylilies, similarly, once planted sit there like Rocks of Gibraltar, shading out weeds, resisting droughts and hurricanes and plagues, for years on end, never requiring spraying or pampering or even fertilizing. Besides the long blooming season and freedom from pests, daylilies bloom at the most settled season of the year. There is no danger of cold snaps, incredible weather, or other terrors. The days are long, and one can sit out enjoying the flowers until night falls. The shape of the flower is good, the texture is good, and the slender stalks holding the large blooms are reasonably dramatic.

To give occasional height and bulk I use roses that make shrubby growth, and I have a few tallish yews and junipers and a few rounded blobs (Russian sage, lad's love, arborvitae, false cypress) and then I have my favorite plants whose mission is not so much to bloom as to have good-looking leaves (a few sorts of yuccas, hostas, *Rudbeckia maxima*, tamarisk, Japanese butterbur, variegated miscanthus, yellow ivy, giant reed, purple smoke bush, coral bells). I use them freely enough that even if nothing much is in bloom, I get a certain pleasure from the contrasting leaf shapes and colors. I also go quite berserk for grapes. These major plants have the places of honor, where I think they show up best, and in back of them are the daffodils, irises, peonies, roses, and daylilies.

Daylilies, as I say, have become increasingly important because they look after themselves so well and are such admirably behaved plants. They do not run about, coming up here, there, and everywhere, and they do not die out in the middle, either. They stay where you put them, getting better as the years pass.

Results are best if daylilies are given a good deeply dug bed in full sun, with plenty of leaf mold or composted cow manure or peat moss dug in. Allow each plant space the size of a bushel basket. They need water from late May onwards if the season is dry. With plenty of water they usually exceed the size and height that catalogues say they will reach.

In choosing daylilies you should, of course, select the ones you think are most beautiful. They are all beautiful, but personal preferences differ. This all seems obvious, but often gardeners choose varieties that are highly regarded and are then annoyed. I myself, years ago, acquired 'Rare China' because it grows well, blooms madly, makes a brave show, and so forth. But it is medium yellow flushed at the edges with tawny rose, a combination I do not like, so I was quite put out when it bloomed in its typical fashion. Also,

increasingly, I have learned not to choose varieties that merely complete the spectrum and add variety. It is pointless, really, to acquire the best dayglow oranges or black-reds if you dislike those colors. The colors of daylilies are far richer and subtler than words can describe. A visit to a good collection, as at the Arboretum, will not only help you to avoid colors you may not like at all, but may startle you with the discovery that there are many colors you were not aware of that you like enormously. Then get a specialist's catalogue or price list and order all the cheapest kinds in your favorite colors. You will find this an entirely satisfactory method of acquiring daylilies. Or if price is no object, order from some list of "the best." But do not attach too great importance to "the best," or assume that a flower much talked about is bound to be superior to one that is on nobody's list.

The Zinnia's Revenge

August is the month I have always thought of as the time of the Zinnia's Revenge, because this is when zinnias—and also marigolds, petunias, bedding begonias, black-eyed susans, and all those other dull flowers—come into their own, somehow finding their way into even the most elegant gardens, and one might conclude at this time of year that it is because there is nothing else.

God forbid! First, phlox is hanging on well (given good drainage, full sun, rich soil, and a great deal of water), and there are dahlias, which come in such wonderful colors, shapes, and sizes that one forgives their lush weediness. They are at their very best in September, but a comfort in August as well. Cannas are not as despised as they used to be, and August is the month for cannas. Nothing else makes quite such wonderful sheaves of foliage, and flower colors tend to be pure and sparkling.

August flowers need not be screaming shades of orange, red, or yellow. There is also blue. A great favorite of everybody who grows it is the Russian sage or *Perovskia*, with almost white aromatic leaves and stems and very narrow spikes of mid-blue flowers. It is semi-woody but very light in effect. I suppose many people grow aconites or monkshoods, which are gloriously blue as summer turns to fall. In light shade they are very valuable. I have said nothing of the perennial *Aster frikartii*, with soft lavender-blue petals surrounding a small gold boss, and neat though not elegant pointed leaves, blooming from late July sometimes even into November.

If the chicory of our roadsides is divided in the spring, it blooms in August rather than early July, and its sky-blue daisy flowers are to my mind quite beautiful. Some other admirable weedy things that bloom now are the liatris (in purple, purple-magenta, or white), the lythrum, with vivid pink spikes like clusters of skyscrapers, and the physostegia or obedient plant, rather like a starved snapdragon, in lavender or white. The cleome, or spider flower, has grand magenta, white, or rose-pink blooms, and interesting foliage and an unusual flower shape that redeem it from coarseness. The old-fashioned tall cosmos have ferny leaves and bright, silky flowers. There are four-o'clocks too, fine weeds from South America with little trumpets of red, magenta, yellow, white, and striped flowers. I do so admire four-o'clocks. All these weedy things are best grown in clumps here and there and not allowed to dominate the scene.

Toward the end of August the first flowers appear on *Anemone japonica*, the Japanese anemone, and its five-petalled, two-inch saucers in pink or white will brighten the garden into October. They are not showy, but I never ran into anybody who did not admire them. Their broad palmate or hand-shaped leaves are basal; from them arise several wiry stems, each with several dozen blooms opening off and on as the spirit and the waning sun move them. For small gardens, which require of a plant not only handsomeness of flower but good-looking foliage and orderly habits as well, the Japanese anemone is a perfect choice. Moreover, its wonderful combination of vigor and refinement is especially welcome in late summer when most things look a bit blowsy. It is soundly perennial, and spreads a bit but could hardly be called invasive. Nothing is handsomer against old box bushes or walls clad with ivy or winter jasmine. I also like it by garden pools, since it blooms just as the hardy water lilies are slowing down for the season.

The late-blooming bugbanes (*Cimicifuga*) are also worth a space, and if there is a bit more sun the sternbergia (like a large gold crocus) and the fall crocuses (especially *Crocus speciosus*, in various tints of blue-lavender) are wonderful. Where they settle in, the wild cyclamens (especially *C. neapolitanum*) are flawless plants for small gardens, since they stand up to the most critical inspection, not only of their little flowers on four-inch stems, but also their leaves which stay green all winter.

All along alleys and tumbling down banks and over fences we now have the white, honey-scented bloom of the Japanese clematis (*C. paniculata*). If I could only have one clematis, it would certainly be this. Unfortunately, it does not flourish in England, the nation that dominates clematis lore, so it is not made much of in books. Furthermore, snobs dislike it because it is not rare, and although it is easily controlled with a yank if it gets carried away with itself, it grows like a weed. It is a plant, however, that—like the dogwood—has no faults and every virtue. If you stop to think of it, few vines have total grace. But this clematis does and, again, it is glorious just when everything else looks tired, dusty, and vaguely discolored.

People who are away part of the summer and who return in late August should keep these flowers in mind (along with morning glories if there is enough sun, and those hostas that only bloom in late August). It can be depressing to come home to a garden full of run-out petunias, marigolds, and zinnias.

Earthman vs. the Seasons—Autumn

Plant Now . . . Loll Later

Six. ☐ Virtually all hardy shrubs may be planted from October till Thanksgiving, but a nurseryman told me most people like to wait until the spring sunshine inspires them to run about like rabbits through clover. This is understandable, but fall—not spring—is the great planting season for woody things. If, in other words, you had thought of lolling in the warm weekends admiring the chrysanthemums and the dogwoods turning red, congratulating yourself perhaps that the weeds are losing heart, let me cheerfully remind you that you should be exhausted (not lolling) since this is the busiest of all garden seasons. When you are not planting bulbs, digging up bindweed roots, rooting out pokeweed, soaking bamboo, there are still other tasks. Thousands of them. You are terribly behind. The very idea of just sitting about in the sun!

A surprising number of people ask about water lilies and pools, and many gardeners report nothing in the garden is so rewarding. The fall is a fine time—the best time—to build a pool. It is not a project to be undertaken lightly, without thought. Mine holds 12,000 pounds of water, as I recall it, so something pretty substantial is called for. Cast cement is best, as far as I am concerned, with walls six inches thick. Directions on just how to go about construction will be found in G. L. Thomas's book, *Goldfish Pools, Water Lilies and Tropical Fishes*. Needless to say, the more sun the better, but with three to four hours of sun on the water, you can get water lilies to bloom well—varieties doing well with this much sun include: 'James Brydon' (rose red), 'Chromatella' (primrose-sulfur yellow) and 'Yellow Pigmy' (ivory yellow). All these are still blooming at the end of September as they have bloomed since the first of June. They are perfectly hardy and just sit in their tubs in the water all winter, though ice freezes all around them.

This is a good time to make rose cuttings. Climbers especially root well from cuttings, but many bush varieties do too. For climbers, cuttings a foot long are sliced off with a knife or clippers, leaves are removed from the bottom eight inches and the cuttings are set right in the ground with four to six inches sticking up above ground. Sometimes I put a jar on mine, sometimes not. The ones that root will leaf out nicely in the spring and can be moved to permanent quarters a year from now—late October or November is a good time.

You will recall some pages back we dealt with peonies, and needless to say you followed directions. You prepared a place for them and ordered roots to be planted in October. Now that the time is here, you are rightly pleased with yourself. I think it wise to mulch the new planted peonies a couple of inches deep after Thanksgiving, removing the mulch in March. I do not mulch peonies except their first winter.

In the unlikely event you have done nothing at all that you were supposed to do, you can plant peonies all through October. Simply dig a hole the size of a bushel basket, making sure the earth is nice and friable, and plant the roots, taking great care that the growth buds (the reddish knobs on the roots) are not more than an inch below ground. It does not harm them to be at ground level, but certainly not deeper than an inch.

In a final word, let me suggest pokeweed be grubbed out in the fall, unless you are growing it as an ornamental (it is very ornamental). It comes up late in the spring, and you won't find it in late March when you try to dig up its vast root. So if you don't want it, dig it out in late October. Its splendid berries stain shirts in a royal and permanent way, but by late October the mockingbirds have usually finished them off.

Tidy Time in the Yard: Fall Priorities

Now we have reached Tidy Time in the garden. The secret of success in tidying up the garden is, simply, not to start new projects. Some tidiness is worthwhile, some is not. It is well, probably, to say a word about leaves to start with. These fallen leaves are great diversions for people, since "cleaning up the leaves" gives them a grand sense of activity, as if they were participating in the world of nature. There are even deeper causes, I think, than that. There appears to be a large element of tree worship in us Americans, and anything remotely connected with a tree is approached with a numinous awe. People who are slothful by nature and who never get around to cutting down the peony and lily stalks in November (though this is well worth the labor) and who never divide the irises on time, or plant the daffodil bulbs before Thanksgiving, or prune the climbing roses—such persons nevertheless leap into action when leaves fall, as if the fate of the garden depended on raking them immediately. I do not intend to comment on that situation, on the grounds that fiddling with leaves is no more harmful than cocktail parties, marijuana, stock car racing, and other little bees people get in their bonnets.

Assuming, however, you have duly wasted some weeks on collecting leaves, perhaps there will be time to do something useful as well.

Peony stalks should be cut to the ground, preferably a bit below the ground, so you cannot see any trace of them. This is said to prevent disease spores over-wintering in the dead stalks, and I am inclined to think it is worth doing. You will find that next spring's growth buds, somewhat like pink pointed peanuts, are quite close to, if not actually touching, the old stalks. When cutting the old stalks, do not injure those pink growth buds. The way you avoid damaging them is to gently—the word is worth repeating—scratch away the soil so you can see them. With sharp shears (not that the average gardener has anything that will really cut anything clean) cut out the old dead stalks as well as you can. Anybody can do the job perfectly, provided he pays attention and does not let his mind wander, or (another common hazard) does not try to do a row of peonies in twelve minutes before he positively has to take a bath for dinner.

Removing the old stalks of daylilies is much quicker. You simply cut them off at the ground. The only possible pitfall here is a series of hasty yanks. Though the stems look quite weak and withered and sere they are still firmly attached to the roots. A determined yank will often pull out part of the root or even a fan of leaves or two. So cut, don't pull. Of course, if you don't remove the old stalks until next March, they will yield readily to a light tug. I am assuming, however, you are cutting the stalks down now, when you should. It is also a good idea to get rid of a lot of matted dead foliage that accumulates around these plants.

Often it is said, in books, that the dead foliage protects the plants during winter. Since, however, I have not noticed that they need any protection, I like to clean up the clumps before winter—especially since I already have more than six million slugs and sowbugs (which adore daylily stuff to dwell in) and do not need any more.

True lilies should also have the stalks cut off just below the ground, to prevent water and perhaps varmints from going down the hollow tubes to the center of the bulb. Sometimes it is recommended that you give a mighty yank on the stalk, with a slight twist. The stalk will come up, the books say, and so it will. Without going into it, I may say I prefer cutting. I have cut stalks, pulled stalks, and left stalks alone, and I prefer to cut them.

Roses should be pruned now to the extent of shortening any whippy growths that over-balance the bush and bode ill in ice storms. I have a young plant of 'Mrs. Whitman Cross' which needs discreet trimming back, not because I intend to prune it, really, but simply because it should not enter the winter with long sappy growth. Trim it back to where the wind will not whip it about is all I propose to do.

Hybrid tea rose bushes can often make six or seven feet of growth in six months. A plant of 'Medallion,' a rather nice, vaguely apricot-buff rose, is one I should tend to and I will gently whack it back to five feet.

Many of the modern "climbing" roses, like 'Joseph's Coat,' are as much shrubs as climbers. They often like to send up a nearly bare stalk, then branch at five feet above the ground. This is fine if they are tied with rope to a support, but if not supported (that is, if left to become the fine shrubs they will become if not trained) then of course this top-heavy growth will bend the stem to the ground or break it with the first good slushy soggy snow; so such stems should either be staked, or tied, or pruned sufficiently to correct the top-heavy branching.

In our merry efforts we must resist the urge to divide more perennials. Shasta daisies and phlox, for example, to say nothing of chrysanthemums (which can be very touchy indeed), will often come through the winter fine if left alone, but will perish if divided now and left to face the winter unestablished.

We must also resist the urge to prune clematis and grape vines now, even if we have some to prune. We prune grapes in February and clematis in March.

Tulips should be planted now, though they involve the risk of the gardener's getting fascinated and deciding "You know, it was dumb of me not to plant more daffodils in September; why don't I just run over to X and get a few more. . . ." This does nothing for the budget. Also, it usually means that, like impulse buying, the bulbs are not carefully thought out and the gardener winds up getting 'General Patton,' a daffodil he does not care a hoot for, instead of 'Ceylon,' which cannot be found in the stores. The correct way is to plan ahead and once your daffodil budget (in space or cash) is reached, then *stop*. I will not take your time explaining how I know all about this.

Tulips, to get back to them, should be watered after they are planted. Watered? When it's cold? Yes. Watered. Once. Thorough soaking. Then leave them strictly alone.

I will spare you the news that this is a fine time to replace fence posts (if they need replacing) and I will not remind you that any painted exterior wood (as sometimes in an arbor, say) requires a minimum of three coats of paint, and that painting should be done only when the temperature is above fifty degrees. Also, all wood that touches the earth should be treated with a preservative, or else charred in a fire and then dipped in tar (a procedure likely to result in burning down the neighborhood). Posts subject to strain (things pulling on them, like tight wires for grapes) should be braced or set twenty-four inches deep or in concrete, or all three.

Leaves should be kept out of lily pools. When they begin to decompose in "warm" spring weather, they emit noxious gases, at least fish think so. Of course, if you have a lake, don't worry about leaves. After a weekend of tidying up, it will be convenient to jump into.

Reflections on the Cycle of Life

By the end of December we will be looking for signs of spring, because the days will be getting longer and here and there the buds of many plants will start to swell. But the low point of the year, with the days still getting shorter, is the period from Thanks-giving to Christmas, in which the light of the sun is still retreating and the life of plants seems to be still draining away, not building up at all.

Gardeners, however, do not think November is a terrible time. Many like it better than the full summer.

Why? If gardening consists of amassed colors, then this is a terrible period, and if the pleasure of gardening consists of shaping, fertilizing, spraying, exhibiting, picking, and boasting, then this is a bad time indeed.

I have heard people say—people who are not garden nuts—that the trouble with the peony or the iris or some other plant is that it only blooms two or three weeks during the year and then you have nothing. That is true, to some degree, and that is why most gardeners learn to resist giving all their space to flowers that have a brief glory and then die. But even in a garden devoted entirely to daffodils or irises or lilies (the individual flowers may last no more than two days or as long as two weeks, but hardly longer) there is plenty to occupy the gardener. The first shoots of spring emerging from the ground, the developing leaves changing shapes and colors over a period of months, the buds, the stages of decay itself, are all different from the week before, so there is no monotony for the gardener even in those occasional gardens where one sort of flower is doted on to the exclusion of almost all else.

It soon becomes clear to the gardener, who has probably started out to achieve a certain bloom, that the cycle of life in the plant is a good bit more enjoyable than the bloom itself. I cannot imagine a gardener consenting to have his daffodils plopped into his borders in full bloom and then taken away as they begin to fade. He may say he grows them because of their bloom, but you will notice he wants them there for their whole cycle. Even if he could, he would not want them introduced by magic only at the instant of their peak. There are people who want flowers magically appearing for the time of their bloom and then whisked away, to reappear next year only when they are at a climax. But such people are not gardeners in my sense of the word, and they do not enjoy the deep vibrations at all.

Most of the maples by now have shed their leaves that were so flamboyant a few weeks ago. But some of the Japanese maples that we lost patience with in October because they sat there in their dull and somewhat tired summer green have turned to plum and mahogany and dark olive and orange and pink, sometimes in marvelous mixtures. Sometimes flashy, sometimes somber.

Some dogwoods hold their color longer than others. Young and well-fed trees have larger leaves, hold them longer and color them later.

Judd's viburnum, which is never thought of as much of a foliage plant (being grown for its masses of sweet waxy flowers in early spring with the daffodils), sometimes turns in late November to rich wine, and Wright's viburnum, celebrated for its dark wine-red leaves and berries like garnets, often brightens its hues a good bit after its initial fall coloration of purple-red. Maries' viburnum, which may or may not color well, turns yellow-green flushed with orange. Sometimes it fruits, sometimes not.

The andromedas (leucothoes and pierises as we should now call them) vary in this month in their colors, according to the sun they get. The more sun the more colorful, but they are equally beautiful in deep woods where they remain rich black-green.

Some of the grape hyacinths have their new leaves for next spring well above the ground now, almost full length, and these leaves will endure all the winter weather and still be there when the flowers appear in April. The same is true of the blue starflowers (*Brodiaea uniflora*) and certain alliums.

Hypericums often surprise us by the gorgeousness of fall leaves in reds, oranges, and yellows, often in color for weeks. Neither these nor crape myrtles nor pear trees even seem to make the list of plants that color splendidly in the fall, yet often they are among the most sumptuous.

Gardeners who have planted yews and hollies and crabs and thorns in their gardens along with the flowers do not need to be told how rich they look in late November. Some days you will see cardinals in the dark green yews eating berries, or sometimes white pigeons seriously at work on the hawthorn's clouds of fruit.

Various junipers now turn to violet and rose—extraordinary colors in a conifer—and many azaleas settle in for the winter with highly polished black-purple-red leaves, though the rest of the year they are ordinary green.

Feathery seed heads of many clematis still hang on, catching sparkles of ice which are beautiful in morning sunshine, or soft buff and gray at other times. The stinking hellebore (a plant of exceptional beauty possibly handicapped by its totally undeserved name) is preparing to flower, and it will not be too long before the dandelions rev up. The winter buds of sedums and sempervivums, superb rosettes, are ready for anything the winter brings.

Yuccas and cryptomerias, roses and hollyhocks, spurges and willows, cupressocyparis and witch hazel are all at some special stage of beauty now, to those who can see.

One of the things I learned to do as a young gardener was look at plants bit by bit, to see if there was anything that delighted me. Never mind what the plant is famous or infamous for. Look, and see for yourself. If a book did not tell me the smooth bark of crape myrtles is one of the great sights of this world, I found it out anyway, just by looking. I learned it made no great difference if lumbermen said the silver maple or the white willow or the paper mulberry were weed trees, because I began to notice they had exceptional beauty of bark or outline. I learned that sometimes thorns may be the most ornamental aspect of a rose (as in *Rosa pteracantha*) and that the fruit of the tea crab (though rarely mentioned since the praise usually concentrates on the flowers and their scent) is one of its major glories.

People do not tell young gardeners, necessarily, that the common polypody fern will creep about in fissures of tree bark or festoon the branches of old hackberries in a startling way nor, for that matter, that hackberry leaves can turn an incredible chartreuse color in October.

If it were not for these things, which have nothing much to do with tulips or irises in full bloom, I would certainly not waste my time on gardening. Even when I had all the irises I wanted, about five hundred carefully selected varieties, and even when they were in full bloom, I was perfectly aware I would not bother with them at all if there were not oaks and photinias as well.

It is the spectrum, not the color, that makes color worth having, and it is the cycle, not the instant, that makes the day worth living. Sometimes the big thing in the gardener's day is irises and roses and peonies all together in a gorgeousness suitable for keeling over at. Other days it is a squirrel loading a dry oak leaf in his mouth—God only knows why he picks one and not another, but he shops around—and you would think from his nervousness with the leaf that he was carrying a bushel of lightbulbs across the Beltway.

Flowers are of course a sexual display unmatched in the living world and anybody who does not respond a little probably has no blood in him. But they aren't everything, or even the most important thing, at least not for the gardener.

Life, as they say, is even bigger than sex and has occasional moments of interest apart from sex, and that is as true of plants as of primates. In the garden there is always life, right through the year, and gardeners are merely those people who, while admiring the sex of plants as much as or more than anybody else, go on even beyond, and admire as well the bones and skin and guts and all the rest of it, and who admire more than anything the totality of it in all seasons. Compared to gardeners, I think it is generally agreed that others understand very little about anything of consequence.

The Vine List

Honeysuckles

Seven. ☐ Honeysuckle, if I remember right, is a word that entered our language with Alfred the Great and has remained the same through all those centuries, though it used to mean the clover and not the honeysuckle, but by the reign of Elizabeth I it was applied to the honeysuckle as we know it.

I can't think of many things that so improve a new house as a honeysuckle over the door. Often the front door fairly cries out for a set of little posts and a canopy—to keep you dry while fumbling for the key—and on those posts few plants are a happier choice than a honeysuckle. Maybe with a big hefty sweet rose (the old alba 'Celeste' is a flawless choice) to one side.

Now sometimes I think garden nuts, including all garden writers, dream up obscure plants to recommend, but on the matter of honeysuckles I can recommend one that is a severe pest of hedgerows in the Middle Atlantic States, the white and gold Hall's variety of the Japanese honeysuckle. It is one of the very few true aristocrats of gardens that can be acquired simply by pulling some up off the side of the road or a back alley. It can be a fierce pest in the garden, as in the pasture, but when it is kept in bounds it is a very beautiful thing—of far greater quality than most plants you see in Washington gardens.

But of course there are other honeysuckles, and I am more than slightly pleased to notice the great general-gardening catalogue of Wayside Gardens is now listing a native honeysuckle, *Lonicera flava*. As almost any gardening authority will tell you, it is very rare and very beautiful. It has leaves smooth on top and glaucous beneath, with whorls of soft bright yellow trumpets at the tips of its growth. The length of the tube is sometimes given as one inch, sometimes as two inches, and you think, "Well, that does not sound very showy or very pretty." It is, however, a vine to treasure, and you will not find it offered for sale very many times in a lifetime, so if I can collect myself to send the outrageous sum demanded—about $9—I shall myself have a vine I have always wanted. (You must not think I have any special affection for this nursery. Over forty years I have frequently been angry with them for one reason or another, but increasingly they list outstanding woody plants hard to find elsewhere.)

One of the finest honeysuckles is *L. heckrottii*, of hybrid origin, and to speak the truth I think nobody knows what its parentage is. They also sell that one. When I got this new garden six years ago, one of my concerns was to find *L. heckrottii*, which I finally got from Spring Hill Nursery in Ohio, which puts out an inelegant catalogue with some good things in it. The honeysuckle is rose madder or vaguely pinkish wine in the trumpet, and inside it is soft yellow. It blooms in clusters throughout the warm weather. It has a good smell, but only at night. So often, what we really need to know is whether a plant is first-rate, not what its dimensions are, and I can conceive of no garden too fine for *L. heckrottii*.

The yellow Chinese *L. tragophylla* has long yellow trumpets, not scented, and I know of no source for it, but if you see it listed, you may acquire it with every assurance you will like it. Two hybrids, *L. tellemaniana* and *L. brownii*, are presumably worth growing. Telleman's is much like heckrottii, and Brown's is much like the wild native scarlet honeysuckle, *L. sempervirens*. The wild one, sempervirens, is as beautiful (I sometimes think) as any plant in cultivation. The hybrids, in their best forms, merely capture its loveliness. Why the wild plant is so rarely sold I cannot say—it is hardy, easy to grow, and altogether desirable. *L. brownii* may be equally good, though I have learned to be suspicious of hybrids that are "just as beautiful" as their wild parents.

Boston Ivy

It sometimes happens that a startlingly beautiful and useful plant is used in one way that is wrong. There is a perversity in gardeners, that much I am sure of, and of course it takes some ingenuity to think to yourself, "Now surely there is some way I can use this plant so it will be a nuisance, a chore, and thoroughly unattractive." And then to discover that very way.

The Boston ivy (*Ampelopsis tricuspidata*) is one of the greatest Asian treasures, a vine of innumerable merits. Yet it is often used where all its merits become liabilities—as if a monumental statue were chosen to be a lamp base. If a vine is used with flagrant disregard for what it can do, then of course we will complain of results. This great creeper holds itself firmly to any flat surface, such as brick, stone, or wood walls, or tree trunks, or window screens, or anything else. It has little tendrils bearing tiny pads, like the cross-section of a grain of rice, and these stick like a natural epoxy to a wall. The foliage of this vine is wonderful, somewhat like poison ivy, but glossier, and in the fall it turns crimson and bright. Then it drops its leaves and is neat until the spring, when it sprouts anew. Few vines cover anything so densely, so uniformly, with foliage so free of bugs or diseases.

The way to use this vine, obviously, is on a fairly ugly solid fence where nothing more is desired than a wall of neat, tight, brilliant green foliage. It is a vine that grows quickly and is ironclad hardy. It endures any fluctuation of temperature our climate offers: there is no such thing as a bad year for the ampelopsis.

With all these merits, it is perversely used as a vine on house walls. There, its vigorous growth is an embarrassment and a defect, not a virtue. It grows right over windows. It inquires into gutters. It works its way among roof shingles. Only constant clipping makes it possible to see out of the house or, indeed, to get in the front door. You also often see it on walls of beautiful masonry, where its growth totally obscures the fine work. The garden of Blair House, where the brickwork is handsome, is converted into a jungle wall of green—a sad mistake. It is even a worse mistake to let it grow on carved stone, which it will promptly obscure. The old National Geographic building is covered, on a back wall, with this vine that has reached perhaps 75 feet in height. The wall is sufficiently ugly that the vine can only be called an improvement, so it does no harm. But it is a reminder that the vine is chock full of vitamins and has never yet lost a beachhead.

But think of another, happier, use for this vine: think of a huge old silver maple that does nothing much but scatter leaves over the adjoining fifty acres and fill up its sector of the city with roots. What an ornament this vine is, if grown up such a tree. It need not be tied, or pruned—it goes right along and finds its own way. It does not fall off in storms; it does not have to be led out on a branch. It makes a most beautiful clothing of shimmering green. In the fall it turns glorious—with the western sun shining through it, it is indeed something to see. It hangs in swags (when it can grow no farther).

Another splendid place to use this vine is at the top of a massive stone retaining wall. The wall that keeps the Seine out of the basement of Notre Dame in Paris is hung in great festoons of greenery. Imagine my surprise, some years ago, to discover this was a common ampelopsis.

Since it is extremely hard to find a foolproof vine that will support itself for heights of an eight-story building, and that has excellent dense foliage, with fall color and no quirks about exposure, it seems a pity not to use the vine where all these merits can have full scope to show. You would not plant such a vine on a young or delicate tree, or on anything like a magnolia, but on an old locust or silver maple or the like, the result can be exciting.

Clematis

Clematis may be planted in March in a sunny place (but well shaded at their roots by a shrub or stone) and there are only two problems:

- Which, among dozens of sorts, to choose.
- How to make the dratted things grow.

The first problem, which kinds are most beautiful, may be glossed over, since they are all pretty glorious, but the second question—how best to grow them—will require several minutes of effort on the gardener's part. It should be said, though without any intention of adding to the world's already adequate store of guilt, that the average gardener is surprisingly lazy and, not to split hairs about it, pigheaded. Every book in Christendom says the ground should be "well-prepared" or "well-dug" or "in good heart" or "well-drained" and "reasonably full of humus." The gardener, therefore, having thought about these things all winter, leaps forth in March, about the time the very first daffodils are blooming, to

chop a hole the size of a coffee can in some godforsaken spot encumbered with couch grass (since it is easier to dig where coarse
grasses abound) and plops in his clematis or rose or whatnot, and
sits back to await the promised splendor.

The usual cause of failure with clematis, or anything else in
the garden, is slovenly planting. In my own case (perhaps more
tactful than considering yours) I have rarely lost a plant that I
really wanted sufficiently to prepare a reasonable spot for it to
grow in. A place the size of a bushel basket, dug twenty inches
deep and filled with good garden soil, will do. Good garden soil is
as follows: it is whatever soil you have, to which two heaping
shovels full of peat moss, one shovel full of sand, and one or two
shovels full of leaf mold have been added. By "added," I mean
that in this spot for the small clematis plant, you dig in the things
I have mentioned until the mixture is quite uniform for a depth
of 18 inches or so. This is watered, allowed to settle and when it is
dry, it is firmed down with the feet. Then, after a few weeks, you
plant the clematis there.

"It's too wet to dig all that in," the gardener says.

Which is why you are constantly advised to do it in October.

"I wasn't thinking of clematis in October."

Well, why not?

In March, therefore, you do as well as you can, and set the
young clematis (which comes in a small pot or plastic bag) into
the hole with the crown two inches below the soil surface. The
crown is the point at which the roots spring out from the main
stem. Thus two inches of the main stem are underground. I find
it helps to put a couple of bricks on top of the ground over the
roots. The edge of the flat brick touches the stem. This helps a
little in keeping the soil over the roots moist and even in temperature, and also reminds the gardener not to dig another little hole
there and stick in a hollyhock. Many clematis are lost through
failure of the gardener to remember exactly where he planted
them. Slugs and cutworms and, I suppose, other monsters like to
chew off the tender shoots of the clematis as it sprouts in April.
Do not let them do this. Once the plant is a couple of years old and
soundly woody, there will be no great danger, but the first year
put a device (such as a coffee can with both ends out) around the
clematis to discourage dragons from coming in. At the time of

planting, set in a slender stick or other device for the young vine to climb on. The clematis twines. It does not like to flop on the ground. If the aim is for the clematis to cover a post, then give the post some wires. Do not expect the clematis to wrap itself around the post without assistance. A strip of wire fencing (painted to match the post—all this done last fall, of course) can be nailed flat to the wood post and the clematis will romp right up it.

I say romp. But often the clematis straggles up for three feet and then sits. The gardener is annoyed, his head being full of visions of total luxuriance. And it is just here that many clematis are lost. Do not be in any way discouraged. Keep weeds away from the young vine, even if it makes only a few inches of growth the first year. "It will be a century at this rate," the gardener commonly says, when his new clematis ceases growth in May and just sits there week after week.

It is unbelievable that a clematis that grew hardly at all the first year can grow eight or ten feet the second. Covered with flowers.

Now there is the matter of the clematis wilt. This is a disease that can carry off a clematis plant in the matter of a few days and it is, needless to say, the strongest argument against divine providence that I can think of. Some put their faith in benomyl sprays and drenches. But it would be sheer perversity to worry so much about wilt (from which the clematis often recovers if you do absolutely nothing) as to forego the pleasure of growing these happy vines.

Let me say there are only three kinds of clematis as far as I am concerned: the ones that bloom early, with wisteria and tulips; the ones that bloom with irises and roses and into the summer (and many of them tend to rebloom a bit in late summer or early fall); and the ones that bloom around Labor Day.

Of the first batch, the early ones, we have *C. montana* in various kinds. The pink montana is the easiest to find, but there are garden forms and hybrids too, such as 'Elizabeth' and 'Tetra Rose.' There are allied early pink clematis—*C. spooneri, C. vedrariensis, C. chrysocoma*. There is not as much difference among them as you might think from reading the passionate comments of clematis nuts. *C. vedrariensis* is the most beautiful, without splitting hairs, and I do not know where it can be bought. Once I saw a good col-

lection of these early pinks at Kew, in London, and asked myself
if *C. montana rubens* was so overshadowed in beauty that I would
not want it: the answer was no. It is not quite so lovely as *C.
vedrariensis*, but there is not really much to choose.

Then of the warm-weather clematis, the ones with flowers like
saucers, there are several dozen kinds in commerce, in white
(like 'Henryi'), purple ('Jackmanii Superba'), or pinkish-rose-lilac
('Comtesse de Bouchaud'), and winey mahogany red ('Ernest
Markham'), or whitish with rosy-wine stripe ('Nelly Moser'), and
so on. Some of them, like 'Lady Betty Balfour,' bloom in late June
and early July, when its rich blue-purple contrasts handsomely
with daylilies. Some hot-weather sorts like *C. tangutica* (yellow)
are small and urn-shaped.

The end-of-summer sorts are summed up with *C. paniculata*
which grows all over the place and seeds itself about, producing
almond-scented, inch-wide white stars in tremendous quantities,
falling like a white veil over fences, garages, old stumps, etc.

Christopher Lloyd's book, *Clematis*, is the best I have run into
on the subject.

At the Chelsea show in London in May you can see a rare
plenty of clematis in bloom, including many uncommon kinds not
generally to be had here, but there is no need to be heartsick since
the garden effect of such old kinds as 'Jackmanii' is fine enough.
The crying need, in my view, is for *C. vedrariensis* to be raised by
our nurseries. There is a garden in Ireland where the common
blue wisteria, the yellow Banksian rose, and this pink clematis all
flower together in great masses against a monumental background
of gray stone. Glorious.

Ivy

The common English ivy (*Hedera helix*) and its dozens of varieties are commonly ignored by gardeners who itch for rarities.
Assuming, however, that the gentle reader has eyes and can see
for himself that the ivy is the most beautiful and practical of all
evergreens grown in Washington, we might pause for a minute to
salute its merits and suggest a wider use for it.

Christmas is, of course, a great season for ivy. As everybody
knows, or used to, the traditional Christmas greens are ivy, holly,
yew, juniper, rosemary, bay (*Laurus nobilis*), and mistletoe. Or

so we always thought when I was a boy in Tennessee. Nobody grew the bay, which is not hardy there (or here) and rosemary everywhere is so scraggly and always on the verge of giving up the ghost that we used the others without them, substituting leaves of the magnolia or bull bay. Magnolia leaves, needless to say, were never heard of in Europe before the 1500s (the first one was imported to the botanical garden at Padua) and have no business among traditional Christmas greens. Still, there they were.

Getting back to ivy, there is no reason whatever for calling it "English" ivy, except that's the common name. It grows wild in England, but its range extends across much of Europe to Central Asia and down into North Africa here and there. Any plant that grows from England, where the sun never shines, to sunny Africa may be expected to vary a good bit, and the ivy does.

Gardeners will find it agreeable to grow a dozen or so varieties of the ivy, though some of them are not hardy. The variegated Madeira ivy (with creamy variegation flushed rose madder) is quite pretty and often deceives the gardener by growing along for two or three years in the garden, then dying. It grows very nicely in California. You can grow it in a pot indoors, of course; and this is true of all ivies.

Many delicate little ivies acquired as pot plants can surprise the gardener outdoors. I once transplanted one with tiny leaves an inch long from a pot to the base of an elm near a pool, thinking the delicate foliage would look good. So it did, and so it does now, some years later, when it has romped perhaps thirty feet up the trunk. There it sends out woody branches with smooth (not incised or cut) leaves and flowers in September, following this with clusters of agreeable but inconspicuous black berries.

As far as I know, all ivy flowers in late summer, once it has produced its woody branches. This is called the arborescent (or woody, or mature) phase of the ivy, in which the leaves become smooth, sometimes much darker and the juvenile distinctions of leaf (for which the variety was selected, often) are lost. If the gardener does not like the mature phase of the ivy he has only to keep pruning it and it will stay juvenile forever, I think. But in my view the ivy is never so beautiful as when it is old or has reached the top of the tree or wall or other support; and has begun to grow heavy woody branches and to flower and to fruit. Those who ride the L buses will notice some fine examples smothering trees in a vacant lot on the north side of Connecticut a few blocks east of Chevy Chase Circle. And, of course, examples are all over the city. The wall of the Bishop's Garden at the Washington Cathedral is a particularly good example since the wall is low and the woody aspect of the ivy can be examined closely.

English sparrows, which will nest everywhere except the exhaust of a jet, are especially fond of ivy. Theoretically, you can knock the nests down, but I have yet to meet a gardener who could do it, in spite of much rough threatening. Besides, the sparrows will simply move over to the drainpipe, chimney, etc., so nothing much is accomplished that I can see by chasing them out of the ivy.

In Washington, ivy grows on walls facing any direction. It is most useful on a wall facing north, where fewer things will grow. It attaches itself by means of aerial rootlets. It is very nice on brick, or stone. On wooden siding it is clever at getting under the boards and prying them loose. Ivy should not be allowed to grow on young trees since it will smother them; it is ruinous on dogwoods, for instance. But on old trees it does no harm and is beautiful.

Ivy can be planted from pots acquired at nurseries, garden centers, or dime stores and set outdoors in the spring. A light rich soil will get it off to a good start, though it takes it two to three years to start climbing lustily.

It is often used as a green ground cover. Rats are very fond of banks covered with a thick mat of ivy and they should be dealt with, since as I understand it they may attract cats.

Ivy is also used a good bit by the French (and in the gardens at Dumbarton Oaks in Washington) to form designs in flat parterres. This is a rather simple-minded way to use plants, possibly, but the result is charming enough provided you don't mind the endless clipping and provided you don't keep thinking how asinine a thing it is. Ivy clipped against a wire fence makes a good screen and soon covers the ugliness of a chain link barrier. Of course, if one likes to look at the plain wire (some otherwise sane people do) he should keep ivy off, since it readily grows to the top.

Ivy, to conclude on an uplifting note, circled the mast of the ship that first brought Dionysus to Greece. It has always surprised

me that I never learned anything useful or interesting like that when I went to school, but then I never got very far in any classical language. Do not imagine, in other words, that I am drawing on my Greek, an irksome habit that some people have. For all that, Sophocles says of Attica that it is the country "of lovely horses" and

> In the green leaves sings the nightingale,
> As she sits in the ivy among the branches:
> Here is the forest home of Dionysus....

I always try to keep that in mind when the sparrows start fighting in the ivy outside my bedroom window.

Bad Trees and Good Trees

Woodman, Don't Spare That Tree!

Eight. ☐ Recently, a speaker at a men's garden club observed that he had acquired a nice house and lot that once belonged to a fellow who went wild over trees and shrubs and had 97 genera or species on an acre lot (210 by 210 feet). The speaker was from Arizona and was amazed at the amount of leaf-raking to be done. His wife had been shown the joys of this task, he indicated. But far more serious than the slightly male-chauvinist notion that women are suitable for raking leaves (most of them are not, and can be quite dangerous with sprouting clematis and other delicate plants) is the current balderdash that Trees Are Good Things.

It's only a step—and this nation has taken it—to saying that trees are sacrosanct things. The result is that the entire eastern part of the continent is becoming overrun with trees, at least in gardens, and the work our forefathers accomplished with so great pain and sweat is now set at naught. The first thing they did on arriving in America was start cutting down trees, and the gardens of this seaboard would be vastly improved if this good work had been kept in mind.

The proper place for trees may be summarized easily. They belong in parks, which we need more of; along streets, where they relieve the monotony of bad architecture; in the country, where cows may doze beneath them; and in gardens *in extremely limited numbers.*

For some reason—carelessness of observation, for starters— many persons believe trees grow slowly. They also believe that a little switch of a tree should be planted ten feet from another little switch of a tree; and they believe this in spite of the evidence of one-hundred-foot yellow poplars, oaks, and so forth all over the city. The average city lot of fifty feet might easily accommodate a dogwood, an ironwood, a persimmon, a crape myrtle, or something of that kind. One is enough of a tree to satisfy anybody but a Druid, I should think. Instead, the choice runs to oaks, elms, maples, hemlocks, liriodendrons, ashes, and so on; all of them glorious trees (except hemlocks, for which there is no earthly excuse that I have ever heard except that they unfortunately exist). No sooner do these trees get going nicely, heaving up paving, getting honey fungus, clogging drains, soliciting clouds of starlings, and generally behaving like trees, than the gardener begins to inquire why his roses won't grow. "What, please, is the matter with my roses? I have had the soil tested and corrected; I spray faithfully. And yet I get scarcely any roses. Modern varieties have no stamina. . . ." What is not said is that the roses are shaded most of the day by a beech the size of the Capitol dome, and the rose bed is solidly infiltrated with the roots of three elms, two maples, and a hemlock.

If space permits, nothing is a nobler ornament than a tree. I yield to no man in the fervor of my tree worship. I can point to a seventy-foot oak I planted recently from an acorn (it was not all that long ago, when I got out of the Army) and to a yellow poplar I planted with four leaves on it; an evergreen magnolia I planted when it had but eleven leaves; a metasequoia planted when six inches high and now a forest-type specimen, and on and on.

But I expect all my other sins to be forgiven in reward for one proud virtue: I have never in my life planted a tree in the smack dab middle of the garden where it would prevent the growth of virtually all desirable flowers; nor ever planted one on a boundary line where it would ruin my neighbor's garden.

Do yourself a favor, and do society a favor: use your influence on behalf of parks, arboretums, open countryside, tree-planted highways, and shrub-planted neutral strips. And cut down a few trees around the house.

Longing for Tall Trees

Some have accused me of being anti-tree merely because I have well-founded and correct hatred of Norway maples, hemlocks, wild cherries, and silver maples. I have suffered much from all of them. Hemlocks are worst.

But if I had room, my real passion would be trees. Once I helped someone choose magnolias for a great planting of these glorious creatures; and while they did not take my advice to have plenty of *MM. salicifolia, sargentiana robusta, veitchii*, etc., still it was exhilarating even to contemplate several acres devoted to the Asian magnolias.

Usually I am grateful for the little dabs of stuff I grow, and when in my right mind I thank God for my sixth of an acre. But there are other times—shameful, of course—when I feel much abused. Lately I have been mourning, for the thousandth time, my lack of black locusts. What is more beautiful than the locust with its light shade, its flowers like little white wisterias in May, its furrowed bark and picturesque old age? It never occurred to me as a young man that I would not have plenty of locusts, but now I suspect I never will. There is a bright yellow-leaved one called 'Frisia' I also covet.

The honey locusts, quite a different sort of cat, are also tempting beyond words. The ones with the vicious thorns are especially beautiful, and so is the yellowish one called 'Sunburst.'

If it were not for the fact that I have four forest trees on this forty-foot lot, I could at least have some things I like better than the present trees. Can anybody resist the sourwood? The persimmon? The shad? The most beautiful of all trees is the ginkgo. Unless it is the white oak. Or—wait a minute—the bald cypress. Or the sophora. Those are the trees of such beauty that it makes me sick to think of the damned maples planted all over this capital, many of which do not color in the fall or have any other merit except (if you have a taste for it) the production of gloomy darkness and gunk that drips.

But banish them from your mind; there is enough misery in the world without thinking of Norway maples. Think rather (even if like me you have no room for them) of the great beauties like the ones I have mentioned. Or the beech. Both the American and European beeches are beautifully rich in texture, and almost unparalleled in the delicacy of their bursting leaf buds in the spring. They are every bit as bad as the Norway maples in their roots, and nothing but pachysandra can be grown beneath their shade, but at least they are beautiful beyond belief at several seasons of the year.

There are ugly hollies, but you have to search long and carefully to find an ugly variety among the several hundred in commerce. I am glad to see our American holly is admired more than formerly, for it is a glorious plant. The English hollies, the Chinese hollies in many varieties, the yaupons and cassines and inkberries are all elegant small trees too.

Flowering trees are usually a snare and a delusion, like those people you meet at cocktail parties who seem so glamorous and exciting and whom, after the third time, you hope never to see again. The dogwood is the standing reproach, however, to snobs and purists who distrust flashy flowering trees. Our wild dogwood is the most generally valuable garden plant of the continent. It is utterly without fault and has so many startling virtues that I assume it was the last tree created, once Providence really got the knack of things. And there are other examples worth mentioning. The shadblow in flower is as beautiful as any flowering tree in the world. It seems to me the flowers last less than a week. But then that is the snare of flowering trees in general, the flowers never last more than a couple of weeks. That is why shads and dogwoods are fine, they have so many attractions apart from flowers. The Asian witch hazels do too. Some of them turn the most wonderful tomato and orange and rose colors in October.

I do like Blirey's plum, which not only has copper-purple leaves but is covered with pink aspirin pills in the spring. The flowers are double and I would not expect a man of my taste to like it, but I do, very much.

If a gardener wants a flamboyant show in a flowering tree, why not grow the cerise-crimson double-flowering peaches and be done with it? No crab is as showy as the flowering peach, after all.

Resistant as I am to dozens of flowering crabs, I confess the flowering peach is irresistible. It carries extravagance beyond all bounds and thereby achieves a sort of triumph. It is somewhat like dogs—if you are going to have great ears and paws, you might as well go all the way like a basset or a bloodhound and not settle for being merely a beagle. Indeed, the trouble with many flowering trees is that they have all the drawbacks of blatant display without really achieving drop-dead flashiness.

Laburnums and hornbeams and mountain ashes; sour gums and Arizona cypresses—Lord, what a feast. And me with nothing. *Nothing.*

Narrowing the Choices

Certain garden varieties of tree grow upright and narrow in outline, resembling an exclamation mark or a rather plump telephone pole, and such trees are pretty magnetic to gardeners. For my own part, I have always resisted them, however, partly because I know how striking (and therefore domineering) they are, and partly because I never can decide which one of them to get. Also, of course, there is the problem of never being quite organized enough to order them in time for spring planting.

First there is the upright narrow Hicks Yew, one of the really fine conifers for small gardens where something twelve feet high and two and a half feet thick is desired. Like all yews, it confers a remarkable air of solidity, cheerfulness, sobriety, and a sense of great age to the garden. There is no time of year when it looks bad.

I would like to complain of the fastigiate cherry called 'Amanogawa.' It is upright, all right, to the point of absurdity, in its youth. It can be ten feet high and a foot wide, and it is as charming as it is ridiculous when strung with its puffy little flowers. As it ages, however, it thickens out in a fairly alarming way, if one has counted on a shape like an exclamation point. Certain dogs and, I suppose, certain humans, are also a bit disappointing as they mature, so I do not condemn the cherry tree; I merely point out that its slender form is not as permanent as one hopes. Another thing about flowering cherries: nobody seems to dwell on their awful roots. So often I have reflected it would be better if some of those rhapsodists of the cherry tree grew a few of them, for there is nothing like familiarity to dampen one's initial ardor. Cherries have roots as invasive as maples, and it is quite easy to see, beneath old cherry trees, the starved and barren nature of the ground. And yet they are almost supremely beautiful. You would not expect, I know, for a mere garden writer to solve all your terrible anxieties as you weigh the merits and faults of the cherry tribe, but I can assure you that lovely though the trees are, the gardener pays a price in their heavy shade and greedy roots.

Now we come to the Lombardy poplar. This tree is, I suppose, the least fashionable tree in all America at the moment. That is because nurserymen (this is my suspicion) have not found any way to make money on it. It grows from cuttings, or twigs just stuck in the ground. It grows quickly, sometimes four feet a year or so. It abides heavy dampish soil. It was widely "overplanted" a few decades ago, and you used to see it everywhere. It is extremely narrow in outline, or can be (it can also get a middle-aged spread, yet it is the *beau ideal* of the columnar narrow outline in deciduous trees) but of course it has flaws, as what does not? It can get various borers, and the branches can snap off in storms, and sometimes the crown breaks off to ruin the soaring upright line, and so on.

You will notice that fashionable trees (which change with the generations of mankind) never have their faults pointed out; it is only the unfashionable ones that you hear gossip about. But the worst fault of the Lombardy poplar is its root system, which seeks underground drains as the hart the mountain brook. How often is this lovely poplar planted at the end of a garden in a row of five or six, to form a screen (and few things are lovelier). But for yards and yards inside the garden it is virtually impossible to grow anything because of the poplar's roots.

But no matter what you hear or read, I am here to say flatly there is no more exciting or lovely tree in all the world than the Lombardy poplar, and if the gardener is going to lose his head and ruin the roses forever, at least this poplar is a comprehensible infatuation.

The native black locust has a fastigiate form called *Robinia pseudocacia* var. *stricta.* I do not know it, though I have often yearned for it. Locusts have the grand fault of shedding branches in slight winds, for no clear reason. The black locust is also one of the most beautiful of all trees, and its ferny leaves are so delicate that grass will grow right up to the trunk. The narrow, upright variety is a severe temptation.

Among crabapples, the pink flowering 'Strathmore' is said, at least in England, to be reliably columnar. I have often been on the actual verge of ordering it. Another crabapple, the wild *Malus hupehensis* or tea-scented crab (tea crab, it is usually called) from western China, is fragrant and beautiful, blooming with lilacs. It is said to be upright and narrow, but is not. In my youth, when, among other errors, I believed much that I read. I planted it in the corner of an L-shaped building and sure enough it grew straight up, like a Lombardy poplar, for about five years. Then it sort of filled out, which was all right. Then it began to spread on top, and in age it was wider than tall. So much for the tea crab. It is true that the tree was so beautiful I allowed it to spread over the entire roof of the old-fashioned garage. There, it promptly met the spreading branches of *Metasequoia glyptostroboides*, that tree which looks like a bald cypress and which is supposed to be columnar and which is not.

The Dawyck beech is columnar in youth, and fortunately the gardener usually dies before the beech fills out too much, so that fault is rarely seen by the man who plants it. But in maturity it develops a surprising bulge at the base and looks rather like a pear on a stick. There is nothing wrong with that, I merely mention it in case the shape of the Lombardy poplar is insisted on.

The Italian cypress is easily prince of all columnar trees, followed (at some distance) by the Chilean incense cedar, *Libocedrus chilensis*. Neither of them is recommended, but if you are somewhat stubborn, it would not really be crazy of you to try both. Experience in general suggests that the cryptomeria (*C. japonica* and its various forms) is a sounder choice, and nothing can be more beautiful than this tree. Perhaps one should stop saying that of every tree one mentions. The cryptomeria abides light pruning and can be kept columnar even when it wishes to plump out. The same is true of the native red cedar (*Juniperus virginiana*) in its various fastigiate forms—certainly one of the most—but I will not say it.

The English oak has a columnar form (*Quercus robur fastigiata*) occasionally offered for sale. So does the native yellow poplar (*Liriodendron tulipifera*) which I think is fairly rare, since I have not seen it. And so does the English hawthorn (*Crataegus oxyacantha*), which can have ailments as sad as the poplar, not that they will usually tell you that in catalogues.

One alternate plan, if you bog down completely in the matter of columnar trees, is simply to set up a pole and grow a vine on it. Nobody wants to admit it, for some reason, but the common wild Japanese honeysuckle that chokes young trees and fences all over the South is very beautiful and quite evergreen, and it can be kept clipped to a pole to make a fine accent plant. The same is true of the akebia (*Akebia quinata*) and the Carolina jasmine (*Gelsemium sempervirens*), and one can only marvel that gardeners never think of using them as green flowering pillars.

Grand Trees for Great Spaces

A fellow complains too much attention is paid to small gardens in town, to the general neglect of bigger ones, and he'd like comments on trees for large gardens.

Needless to say, the ones for small gardens are eminently suited for gardens of any size, but in addition to them there are many others.

First, if I had a place bigger than 200 feet square, I'd plant a white oak, *Quercus alba*. It is the final summing up of everything splendid in oaks. The only trouble with planting one is that 150 years or 350 years from now, it will break some gardener's heart to see it die.

The ginkgo (*Ginkgo biloba*) is a tree of equal majesty. We often see these ancient trees, dating from the ages when coal was being formed, as somewhat butchered specimens along Washington streets. There is an upright columnar form, and some clonal forms that do not set fruit (the fruit stinks like vomit as it rots). But the run-of-the-mill ginkgo forms an enormous round-headed tree beautiful at all seasons, and none is worthier of space in a large garden. It is fine for a magnificent alley of trees, too, if you have room for such a thing.

A neglected tree—except in Washington, where somebody once had the wits to plant it freely—is the sophora or scholar-tree, *Sophora japonica*. This becomes a large semi-weeping tree that holds its leaves late and its bean-shaped fruits late, and all through the warm weather displays its locustlike ferny foliage. It flowers in late summer, when virtually all other trees have finished.

The Himalayan cedar, *Cedrus deodara*, is to my mind the finest of all large conifers. In the country where I grew up (Tennessee-Mississippi) it was planted too freely, too close to houses, and every fall you could see trash trucks laden with magnificent branches, desperately sawed out in a losing battle to keep the tree under control. A magnificent specimen may be seen at General Lee's house at the end of Memorial Bridge. It is a forest tree, and even more than most other true cedars, its branches are horizontal and drooping.

It does not often occur to people to plant the native ash, though it makes an enormous rounded tree casting soft shade, and it does drop things from time to time, seeds and so on, but this would make no difference in a large place.

I would not grow elms, for the simple reason I not only do not especially like elms but rather actively dislike them, but a number of elms might be grown, despite the unfortunate disease that has ruined so many American elms.

The catalpa is much more widely admired in Europe than here. To me it lacks the quality—though please do not press me to define that word—of the white oak or the other trees mentioned. Still its huge leaves and handsome early-summer candlesticks of white and yellow flowers are gorgeous enough.

You hear many complaints against sugar maples, but if I had the space I would ignore all trifling objections and plant them. I would avoid the Norway maple, but not the sugar.

To me one of the most beautiful trees is the native wild red cedar, *Juniperus virginiana*. Often the rutty lane leading to an old house in the country is lined with these trees, and for the purpose I can think of none better. Some people object to the bronze cast of these junipers in winter, and do not care for the bare peeling trunks. Beauty is a subjective thing, but to me no tree is more beautiful, and its general neglect in the planning of large gardens is nothing more than a foolish contempt for things close at hand.

Various hickories, including pecans, make enormous trees, and the hickories (not the pecans) turn beautiful rich yellow in the fall. I recall one lane through a pine forest studded with hickories, in which the drive was lined with michaelmas daisies, and it was lovely in October with gold and green for background to various shades of blue-lavender.

The common red maple is a poor choice in town gardens because of its greedy roots, heavy shade, and great size, but in a large place nothing is much handsomer in the fall when it turns not only red, but a whole rainbow of yellow-red colors.

The Magnificence of Magnolias

Every year during daffodil season, the rosy chalices of *Magnolia soulangeana* are in bloom all over town. It would not have occurred to me to mention them except for an astounding number of inquiries what they are.

Sometimes people call them "tulip tree," which I dislike for the sound reason I never called them that myself, and it is inherently dumb, as if one were to call a tulip a "magnolia flower."

The pink magnolia is a hybrid, not a wild species. Its parents are the awesomely beautiful wild *M. denudata*, the Yulan of China, and *M. liliflora*, a somewhat pallid lavender magnolia, also Chinese. I do not see either of these in gardens. The Yulan, which may be the most beautiful of all magnolias, is white with a strong sweet lemon fragrance. It is far more beautiful than its pink offspring, and the pink progeny have no scent worth mentioning. It is almost impossible to find the Yulan at nurseries, but that has nothing to do with the fact that it is supremely fine. *M. liliflora* also appears to be missing from common cultivation, and I do not miss it. The ones I used to see were all rather washed out in color. One that you do see often is a dark form of *M. liliflora*, called *M.l. nigra*. It is not black, but dark reddish purple. It makes a smaller tree, a shrub usually, and it blooms late enough to escape the spring freezes that often blacken the flower of the others.

While we're about it, there are two other magnolias that, like all these, bloom in early spring before the leaves appear. The most beautiful of them is *M. stellata*, the star magnolia, which makes a rounded shrub or small tree up to eighteen feet or so, but often much less. Its blooms have twenty little white or blush-colored straps radiating from a center, and they look as much like stars as necessary, no doubt. They are softly and sweetly scented and sometimes on mild damp days you can smell the flowers fifty feet away, possibly the finest scent of all magnolias. And needless to say, this is the greatest magnolia of all for small gardens. Apart from the white form, there is one that is a little deeper than blush pink, and another that is about as deep a pink as the 'Radiance' rose. Neither of the pink forms is readily obtainable so far as I know. It seems to me that in recent years a number of trees of the early white-flowered *M. kobus* have been sawed down or otherwise disappeared from Washington's parks. This tree is not as showy

as the others mentioned. It has rather gray pleasant bark and the flowers are rather small. Still, a large tree in bloom is a fine sight. Most gardeners would not be much interested in it unless they had plenty of woodland, in which odds and ends of trees could be grown for the hell of it.

Our two American magnolias, the best-known ones, are the sweet bay, *M. virginiana*, with neat waxy white-cream flowers once the spring really warms up. They are the size of large walnuts or small tangerines, depending, and the aromatic leaves are perhaps six or eight inches long, maybe no more than four inches (again, depending), and they are half-evergreen. That is, some of them hang on in winter but up here most fall off. They are splendidly fragrant.

The great magnolia of the South is *M. grandiflora*, the bull bay, with flowers ten inches or a foot in diameter, of flawless wax-suede substance and texture, powerfully scented, and the glossy heavy leaves are up to a foot long. This, which is the tree usually meant when one says "magnolia" without any qualifying, is a plant that varies a lot in size of leaf and in other ways. Some have bigger blooms than others, some are more likely to rebloom in October than others, some are nicely felted beneath the leaves with a soft russet fuzz, while others are smooth. All of them are irresistible to starlings, grackles, and anything else that flies, and I myself am by no means as fond of them as a Southerner should be. The leaves dribble down unsteadily throughout the year, but chiefly when you have just swept a lot of them up. Possibly my prejudice against dank forests has shown up before now, but let me say I cannot think of a more awful tree to have against the house. Nothing grows under it, the shade is too dense, and of course sun cannot penetrate its leaves to shine in the windows. It is a marvelous tree, though not showy in flower, at the end of an open sunny garden, and if the place is large enough nothing is quite so glorious as this magnolia with reflections in the water and a certain amount of cut stone and bronze and lead. It is ideal, in other words, for burial grounds. It is also a grand tree for Blanche Dubois-type folk in run-down New Orleans-type ruins with irregular hours and vague means of income. And yet some of my best friends plant these magnolias in city gardens. It takes all kinds.

The big-leaf magnolia, *M. macrophylla*, has light green leaves up to thirty inches or so in length and attractive large fleeting flowers not easily seen unless they are cut. It drops all its leaves in winter, and is a very beautiful tree—the leaves are more often eighteen inches than thirty, by the way.

The cucumber tree, *M. acuminata*, named for the shape of its green fruit, is also native to American deciduous forests. It makes a beautiful tree, architecturally, and its leaves are conspicuously large and fresh looking, though half the size of *M. macrophylla*. It is somewhat neglected, doubtless because its flowers are not showy.

There are many other magnolias uncommonly seen. The one most worth dreaming about is maybe *M. sargentiana robusta*, with great soulangeana-type flowers, only more elegant, which nod down from the branches. I do not recommend it to the general gardener. Alas. Maybe I should point out that *M. soulangeana* includes many named varieties, differing in color, fullness of bloom, time of flowering, and among the most admired of these are 'Alexandrina,' 'Lennei,' and so on.

The mere fact that the wild Yulan is more beautiful than the pink *M. soulangeana* does not mean the pink one is not worth growing. It is exceptionally beautiful, and any garden is the richer for it. It is simply not supremely beautiful. But you will notice nurserymen are far more likely to offer the very good rather than the very best. Sometimes that is because they think popular taste is a bit vulgar. Sometimes because they fear the Yulan, say, would not sell as well as the pinks. Sometimes because it is too much trouble to find and stock the Yulan. Sometimes because they simply do not know any better.

Crabs: Lovely to Behold

The crabapple is the most important—that is, the most popular—flowering tree in America. That is because of the beauty and luxury and rightness of its massive flowering. But it is worth remembering that even the smallest varieties will grow to be larger than a garage, and that many of them are prone to mildew and cedar-apple rust, and viruses, and borers—all too terrible to dwell on. So we do not want just any crab; we want one that is relatively small, with exceptionally beautiful blossoms, brilliant fall foliage, long-lasting fruit that is clear, glowing red, a pleasing shape, and a general, built-in healthiness and disease resistance.

With all this in mind, an expert at the National Arboretum recommends the following sorts: 'Van Esseltine,' 'Henry F. Du-Pont,' atrosanguinea, sargentii, floribunda, 'Dorothea,' 'Katherine,' hupehensis, lemoineii, aldenhamensis, eleyi, and 'Radiant.' The English Royal Horticultural Society recommends purpurea, floribunda, 'Profusion,' hupehensis, and sargentii. My own two choices for my trifling little garden have been the red crab called 'Almey' and the relatively new 'Hillierii,' a deeper pink form of *Malus floribunda*, the Japanese crab.

Perhaps some of this will be helpful for those who do not have a crabapple and want one. But I would not want any gardener to feel disappointed with his own otherwise satisfactory plant of 'Hopa' or some other crab that I have not mentioned. Nothing is more pernicious than the implication that one is not flying right if he does not grow such-and-such. Surely our gardens need more variety, not less.

Going to the Dogwoods

The only catastrophe that would deserve the name is for all the dogwoods of the capital to disappear, and since there is no sign whatever of that, we are in good shape.

It is important, I read somewhere, for us to keep a picture image in our mind of something perfect, just in case there might be bumps, so to speak, along life's highway. Nothing, probably, serves that purpose any better than the dogwood.

It is, incidentally, one of that notable handful of trees (including the magnolias, most notably) that dislikes fall planting, preferring to be shifted in the spring, if it must be shifted at all. There are now a number of named garden varieties in both white and red or rose, and there is nothing wrong with them, necessarily, but I have sometimes reflected that of all the things in a garden that need the plant breeder's attention, the dogwood is not one of them. It comes to us complete and perfect from the wild. There is a weeping, or drooping or semi-pendant kind, that is fairly pleasing. There are variegated sorts, the leaves blotched vaguely yellow, that I would not want myself, but if one wants a variegated dogwood they are probably just the thing. The so-called pink dogwoods, which range through various tints of rawness between diluted beet juice and curdled rose, can be very pretty, though the gardener will discover they do not look so good with many flower colors.

What amazing luck that the common white dogwood (*Cornus florida*) is both so common and so remarkable.

It is no great advantage, that I am aware of, to develop from a lavishly flowering tree a variety with even more flowers, thus converting full splendor to overstuffed extravagance. The Japanese, if one may say so without offense to that nation of superb gardeners, have in some cases turned the flowering cherry into something rather ugly, in its double forms. In wet weather (and of course it rains in the spring) the double sorts turn sodden and as they wither the gardener is presented some days of appalling corruption to look at. I cite those cherries as an example of a garden plant that was much handsomer before the breeders got hold of it and improved it. There is such a thing (as the admirable gardener Gertrude Jekyll once observed of the old white lilac 'Marie LeGraye') as arriving at a perfect beauty and being content to stay there. There may be a fine line between improving garden flowers and making them ugly.

The difficulty arises when real improvement stops and mere flamboyance begins. Many flowers are flamboyant and gorgeous, and nobody objects to the general gorgeousness of a peach tree in full bloom, I think. Nor, for that matter, of a grove of flowering cherries around the Tidal Basin, or a field of sunflowers or a thicket of azaleas.

Ha. Here we are coming close to home. I have a shocking patch of azaleas, fortunately not very large, of pink, three shades of red, and a couple of whites. I like them, but they are dangerously close to grossness, and some of my neighbors do better, I think, with their clumps of fewer colors. I knew it was wrong to add two or three yellow-orange-salmon-tawny deciduous azaleas across the walk from the reds and pinks. But even this sort of garishness is not the flaw that most annoys me when I speak of grossness in "improving" flowers. Instead, I mean things like turning the delicate single cherry blossoms into powder puffs. All of which brings us back to the "improved" and garden varieties of the common dogwood. Here is the end of the matter. It is not evil of gardeners to like double dogwoods or dogwoods with too many flowers on the branches, or to like them with a stew of mottled leaves instead of

God's sweet green. On the other hand, the sane and wholesome gardener has every right to glory in, and to prefer, the plain dogwood of the woodlands, esteeming it the best of all, not because it is common and plentiful—there is no great merit in that, necessarily—and not because it is the easiest to acquire, but simply because it is perfect, and because one is at a loss how it could possibly be improved.

We should keep asking ourselves, when we are tempted by color and display and show, whether it is beautiful as well. The world should not be a nice drab universal gray. But nothing is gained by painting sidewalks orange, either. We will all hit on different balances in our gardens, large or small, and that is what makes them endlessly different. But though we may answer differently we should at least not forget the question, which in gardening will haunt us always, even if we try to duck it. Is it beautiful, that is a great question and the ultimate one. All the rest (is it rare, is it showy, does it hold up well, does it grow easily, etc.) is relevant, but less important.

Up and Down the Garden Path
—Or, Designs for Gardening

Nine. ☐ A garden should be, of course, whatever the gardener can make of it, and this is (as a rule) not much. But it is more important for the gardener to be enchanted than for critics to be pleased. All the same, I have never thought gardening was one of those occupations like painting or music where every few years the past may be smashed without regret and where anything goes.

With this acknowledgment, then, that the gardener should please himself, not me, and with full reprieve and pardon to all those who have odd notions about things, I will jot down a couple of things that work, as far as I am concerned, better than others in the layout of a garden:

Do not concern yourself to conceal the boundaries since that is the wrong way of looking at it. If the garden is twenty-seven feet wide, I cannot see any advantage in making it look wider or narrower than it is. On the other hand, if there is a clump of fine juniper trees on the other side of the alley, and if you have a very conspicuous fence on your side of the alley, then you might clothe the fence with plants to obscure its lines—not because you wish to conceal the lines, but because you wish to let the junipers show up in their beauty without assertive distractions in the foreground.

Most gardens are best rectangular, subdivided down to shapes approaching a square.

Gardens in the "Japanese style" tend to be particularly vulgar and unsuccessful, by the way. As far as that goes, no style of gardening should be aped. The land should be treated instead from the standpoint of what the gardener wants it to do. Has he a passion for cabbages or artichokes? Has he great needs for water lilies? Or is the garden to be chiefly a place to sit in the sun, or drowse in the shade, or to be a background setting for the house, or to have cocktail parties in? The garden layout should "solve" the problems set by the gardener, in terms of the specific piece of land involved.

Walks should be straight, or at lease curved geometrically if they are curved. Or (failing all that) they should look right. What makes a walk look right? Mainly it is a question of appropriateness in proportion, use, texture, light. A polished marble walk six feet wide curving and twisting along the side of a tennis court is going to look stupid because it is stupid. A path of beaten earth twenty inches wide leading up to a baroque doorway is also going to look dumb, because it violates harmonies, switching from one general approach to another, randomly and capriciously.

In general, walks should be paved, at least four feet wide, and if narrower they should relate to other pavements in a way that the brain registers "this is an expanse of pavement." Otherwise the effect will be that of ribbon—insubstantial, stingy, restless, foolish. If a walk does not need to be four feet wide, it should not have any focus on it as a walk, but should be treated like a dirt path, necessary but unimportant.

The scale of the garden should generally be much larger than seems right on paper. There should be fewer "elements" of design than usual, and those few should be larger. Instead of a small lily pool with a sloping rock garden and a wee bog and a bit of moor or prairie, let there be the lily pool period. Bigger than seems right on paper.

Keep the center open. Do not plant bushes and trees merely because one sees that one could jam a crabapple into this space and it would not necessarily die. No, do not do it that way, use bulky plants only where they increase the tone of serenity and rightness, not where they break it.

Never plant anything or build anything without considering, at exhaustive length, the effect on everything else in the garden. This is, of course, the crux of the whole matter, and while none can say (in isolation, and without specific examples) what that rightness is, still one can very accurately say that installing walks, pools, arbors, sheds, flowering trees, or anything else, without dwelling on the complexities of (for example) how the grape vine is going to look, not merely in a two-dimensional picture, but as you move about in the garden—ignoring such matters will result in a garden that does not satisfy the gardener on profound levels.

If a camellia offends thee, pluck it out. Better to sacrifice one treasure than ruin the complete rightness. Of course, I myself could not chop down a large camellia if my life depended on it. But I would either move it, or redesign the garden so it looked right.

Avoid any show of wealth. This is marvelously easy for many of us. Do not permit anything in the garden to be more costly, in material, than is necessary. If wood poles will serve, don't use brick columns. If brick will do, don't use stone. If stone will do, don't use marble.

Sculpture, quite apart from being the most difficult of all fine arts, is a poor team player. It rarely looks like anything but a mess, if required to be part of a larger frame of reference. I do not say sculpture cannot look good in a garden, merely that in practice it never does. I exaggerate, but not much.

Masses, volumes, should be distinct. It may sound nice for things to flow into each other like mists, but it doesn't work. Plan with severe formality, then plant informally within these formal bounds, and nature will tend to the rest, provided you correct your errors as you notice them. Usually with a saw or hatchet.

Do not imagine there is any safety in simplicity; there is not. Color is very complicated, so are outlines and volumes, and most of all light is complicated. They are all going to be present, no matter how you "simplify." So head right in. The point is not to dodge complexity but to master it. This any fool can do if he sets his mind to it. But artful cop-outs (Versailles is the great example) exact the usual price of ignorance, insensitivity, grossness, and defiance of reason: that is, failure.

Your garden will reveal your self. Do not be terrified of that. You have as much right to live as—well, at least one may always say, "nevertheless, here I am."

Gardening is not some sort of game by which one proves his superiority over others, nor is it a marketplace for the display of elegant things that others cannot afford. It is, on the contrary, a growing work of creation, endless in its changing elements. It is not a monument or an achievement, but a sort of traveling, a kind of pilgrimage you might say, often a bit grubby and sweaty though true pilgrims do not mind that. A garden is not a picture, but a language, which is of course the major art of life.

Toward a Painless Garden

The saving of time and labor in the garden is not important if you have an endless supply of both, but many gardeners find themselves unable to keep it all together, as you might say. There is no magic answer, but there are some answers all the same, if the gardener wishes to ask the right questions.

First of all, a large garden requires more sweat than a small one. In cities a garden 60 by 200 feet is thought enormous, and 40 by 100 is thought roomy indeed. It is precisely in gardens of that size, and up to half an acre (100 by 220 feet, say) that ingenuity is called for. In big gardens there simply has to be plenty of labor, and in tiny places, 30 by 30 feet, there is nothing to absorb the gardener's energies except raccoons, neighbors, and cats. The problem in Georgetown, for example, is to find something to do. But in the small place up to a half-acre, the gardener is usually tempted to have a border of flowers, a few roses, a bit of lawn, a small greenhouse, a couple of coldframes, perhaps a small swimming pool, a badminton court, and the Lord only knows what else. A place to cook—I forgot people are forever wanting a place to cook.

Here are my suggestions for such a place, where the owner has to do it all himself:

If there is lawn, do not let the grass run up to the edge of rose beds or any other place where hand-trimming will be necessary for a neat effect. Instead, let the lawn come up a grade-level band of stone or concrete (concrete need not look like a sidewalk, but may be textured, or colored gray or earthcolor) so that on the last lap the mower rests partly on the lawn and partly on the stone.

Have as few edges to things as possible. Narrow beds have a disproportionate amount of edging; therefore a border 14 feet wide and 100 feet long (with stepping stones to get at things) is easier than a number of small beds separated by brick or grass paths.

Have no more paths than truly necessary. One path, six feet wide, is best. If it is brick, it should be set in mortar. If it is flagstone, it should be set in mortar. The inexperienced person has no conception at all how many hours can be spent weeding pavement that is not set in concrete and grouted with mortar, and while on this subject, take pains with the color of the mortar. White mortar between brick, fieldstone, slate, and so on looks awful. (Existing white mortar joints can be toned down by going over them with a coat of fresh mortar colored with oxides of iron or whatever other coloring agent gives the best result). Gravel is absurd. It rarely looks good, is never comfortable, and is ideal for weeds and masochists.

Avoid intensive care projects. Nothing known to man equals a rock garden for labor. Incredibly enough, I have twice seen rock gardens advocated as labor-saving devices, but this only proves that human perversity is boundless. Nothing in all gardening requires so much work for so little return as a rock garden. If the gardener wants lewisias and saxifrages and other rock plants, he should struggle with them in tubs or raised borders, not in a rock garden.

Greenhouses may be nice (usually they are a total mess) but the labor of keeping them up is substantial. They have heating and ventilating systems that somebody has to take care of, and it is rare that today's liberated wife will accept greenhouse chores. A greenhouse can be endlessly rewarding, but the gardener should be certain he really wants one, and if he really does, then it should be as large as possible, not as small as possible.

Avoid plants that necessarily involve many hours' labor a year. Irises and roses, to name two, must be hand weeded and sprayed. No other flowers surpass them in beauty (and indeed no other even equals the iris, I think), but if they are to be grown at all, they should be given ideal sites (they will sulk otherwise) and high culture.

Of course there are many roses as trouble-free as a privet bush, especially the shrub roses and some climbers, though even these require pruning from time to time, which is thorny business. Also, such irises as the Siberians and some of the spurias will clump up and take care of themselves in borders, but the gorgeous, tall bearded irises will not, requiring the very best of everything, including air space around them and total absence of weeds. Even an iris fanatic like me will admit that peonies, daffodils, daylilies, and even true lilies are much less demanding than irises and roses. If labor is short, therefore, it makes sense to choose flowers that require a tenth as much time to care for.

Wide borders with shrubs (smoke bushes, fringe trees, small plums, pink locusts, mahonias, nandinas, photinias, small junipers or yews or box, hybrid rugosa roses, Japanese maples, azaleas, blueberries, viburnums) and clumps of bulbs like daffodils and tulips, perennials like peonies, Japanese anemones, baptisias, artemisias, poppies, and so on and on, are less work than borders of annuals or borders of those numerous perennials that must be staked, lifted, replanted every year or two. Hostas, yuccas, and wormwoods of various sorts are also superb, trouble-free creatures. Before planting anything, ask yourself if you will need to stake it, tie it, prune it, spray it, and weigh its beauty against your real commitment to it. Often, one would really prefer peonies.

Gravitate always to plants that have good foliage when not in bloom. Irises, for example, have terrible foliage in summer. The handsomer the foliage of a plant, the less work in making the garden look good.

If you need a lawn mower, try to store it where you don't have to lug it half a block before you use it. A small shed, with good outdoor electrical plugs, can be worth the hassle of building permits, electrician's bills, and the loss of the space it occupies. Lawn mowers were invented by the devil and fiends love them.

When possible, store tools, fertilizers, stakes, etc., in the center of the garden or at both ends, rather than at one extremity. Clearly I do not mean to store oil drums of bone meal in the center of the main walk, but often a little thought will show how to cut down on general lugging of tools and supplies.

Consider a water-lily pool as large as possible. (In all such projects, be certain to check zoning and building-permit regulations first, not last.) Dollar for dollar and hour for hour of maintenance, the garden lily pool is the best investment of all. But never start such projects without reading books. Sheer ignorance accounts for much wasted money. There are ways to build pools that will result in decades of delight. There are other ways that cost virtually as much, and which will be a constant source of repair and anxiety.

The smaller the garden and the less labor available, the more important the architecture. I do not mean marble temples with gold flames sticking out the top. I do mean a wood bench of first-rate honesty and solidity, and I do mean plain arbors of sturdy lumber, given three or four coats of expensive paint, the beams and posts mortised, and so on. Such things cost dollars, because good material is not cheap, but good proportion, solid construction (as distinct from meaningless gewgaws that seduce the innocent), are worth far more than their dollar cost. A good place to sit in the garden is worth having, and it will count strongly in the design, far more than the frumpy ornaments sometimes acquired.

On the matter of furniture outdoors, it should be weatherproof. If the chair cushions cannot take rain and sun, to hell with them. If the glass table top has to be polished every time you set a cup or a paw on it, to hell with it. Which of the large staff of servants do we think is going to store the chair every night, or at every cloudburst, and who is going to clean the glass top? Iron, teak, redwood, steel mesh, plastics are materials that work. I personally dislike things that look as if the Department of Interior designed them for the use of grizzly bears, but no matter whether it is oafish or elegant, at least let it be weatherproof and practical. I have been all over town and have seen excellent things at stores, reasonably priced, that will neither blow over in the first wind nor, on the other hand, look as if they came from the Black Forest via oxcart.

Keep all outlines bold, over-scaled, plain, rectangular, and keep to gray, black, earth color, except in chairs, if you like to spend fifty hours a year painting them. White leaps out in the garden, but if you like the effect (and in other people's gardens it can look great) of white fences, white furniture, be prepared to paint.

The Crowded Gardener

One of the worst problems of gardening is the spacing of major plants and since there is no perfect solution, it is important to know which errors are the safest.

The most dangerous error (to start at the most common fault) is to refuse to acknowledge the plain facts of a plant's size. Often the gardener will want a tree. It means little, apparently, for him to learn an oak will reach seventy-five feet. "Not in my time," he will say. And true, it does not reach seventy-five feet in his time, but it reaches forty-seven feet, and he starts muttering and whining about his roses or dahlias or all those other things that will not take shade.

The normal height for crabapples is twenty-five feet. Let us think of them for a second, since some gardeners are very proud of themselves for choosing a "small" tree. But what they do, since crabs are small trees, is decide they can squeeze one in "over near the fence" and they think how splendid it will look in April, wreathed with flowers, and they flat shut down their brains and refuse to contemplate what a bulk twenty feet high and twenty feet broad will look like in a few years.

As a general rule, it works best to plant a dogwood, sourwood, persimmon, crab, sassafras, or Oriental magnolia wherever you want a "big" tree, and are thinking in terms of oaks, sycamores, beeches, yellow poplars, and the like. That is because "small" trees like the crabs and dogwoods will reach the roof of a two-story house and are as big as you probably have in mind for an oak.

Also, when you find yourself thinking in terms of a small tree like a dogwood, you will sometimes do better to forget it and settle for a shrub. "Shrub" for some reason suggests a nice little bush the size of a couple of bean baskets or washtubs. In reality, of course, the smoke bush reaches fifteen feet, the height of two stories in a modern house, and many viburnums, though shrubs, are as large as the gardener's notion of a "small tree."

In short, unless you have much experience and discipline (as distinct from wishful dreams) in judging volumes, always choose a plant smaller than you think you have room for.

Not to bog down on details, we should remember that large trees should have at least fifty feet between them, small trees twenty-five feet, shrubs at least six feet (in practice fifteen feet is more like it), and even vigorous hybrid teas, if they are to be grown as rounded bushes, should have four feet between them, or at a minimum, three feet.

Now what happens on a small lot when you find there is nothing growing on it, and you want to start planting? First, decide what size tree, and how many, you want. If it is a fifty-foot lot, all you have to do is get out a yardstick and measure the bulk a crabapple will reach. But the four-foot little tree you plant will seem awfully small and insignificant. Gardeners cannot be expected just

to sit there admiring the tiny crabapple for ten years while visual-
izing its ultimate size. To get any kind of furnished look, plants
will go in thicker than can be allowed once they approach maturity. You will simply have to compromise. It is possible, after all,
to fill in the youthful gaps between small trees with brooms, spi-
reas, forsythias, roses, and so forth, knowing that when the trees
gain bulk, you will simply chop down the fillers.

There is no such thing as laying out a garden from scratch that
will look all right in three years and also look all right in fifteen
years. It is a continuing process of digging out and chopping down.
Do not—for here is the tragedy—plant some noble treasure like
the Alexandrian laurel (*Danae racemosa*) just where it will have
to be removed within ten years when it is reaching its own beauty.
Instead, use plants that you know you will have the heart to get
rid of when the time comes. This boils down to thinking clearly
which plants you want in the garden "forever," and then planting
so that whatever else comes and goes, they will have room to develop.

Now, nobody likes to address himself to this point we now
come to: what if you change your mind? Then change it and start
anew. But not lightly.

Permanent plants—plants that require years to show their true
beauty—should not be planted in the first place unless you are
convinced you cannot live without them. It is a cruel thing to stick
in a little magnolia and let it develop for ten or twelve years and
then have to face the crisis of whether you keep the magnolia
(which of course has grown faster than you were counting on) or
the double-flowered pink plum (which has also quite surpassed
itself). You should have planted them twenty-five feet apart in the
first place and put in a couple of lesser things to take care of the
first few years.

No, even in great gardens planned with reference to a century
or two and planned with every resource of knowledge and money
at hand—even in those gardens there is constant renewal. If we
think it hard to chop down a fine old mock orange that must go,
think of the agony of chopping down an exceedingly rare Indian
rhododendron or other treasure. But the point is, we should keep
our sorrows to a minimum and plant less (not more) than we
think we have room for. I do not necessarily follow this good rule.

What to Plant Where?

Garden plans on paper are all very well, but the lay of the land dictates almost everything. Therefore, no precise decisions should be made about the placement of important plants without an intimate knowledge of the land itself.

I don't mean you have to know all about the soil and fertilizers and all that—a great deal of time is wasted by amateur gardeners playing chemist and pseudo-scientist. By and large, whatever soil you have will grow anything it occurs to you to grow (and a great deal more) without your doing anything beyond letting in some sunlight and digging in some humus. I was horrified only this week to hear a fellow tell me how many pounds of lime he had sprinkled about his place on the recommendation of somebody at the Department of Agriculture, and for what? To grow (if you please) some grass. It is quite remarkable, when you think of it, that if you tell somebody to buy something and dump it on or squirt it on, he will almost certainly do it, after a fashion. But if you suggest that he observe something or think about something or learn about something, he almost certainly will not. Yet those gardens we admire are never the result of dumping and squirting: they are always the result of muddling things about in the brain and the eye.

The land—to get on with it—has such a presence, such an authority, with its wonderful diversity of contour and exposure, that no plan out of a book will work just as it is, but will have to be adapted. These somewhat lofty reflections are brought about by the observation that garden plans should not be judged as if they were two-dimensional drawings. A plan that looks loose or spotty or overbalanced here and there may be a good plan indeed; whereas a plan that makes a nice appearance on the printed page may be totally lifeless in the three-dimensional reality of the living garden. What we are really talking about here is the great question, "How do you know which plant to place where?" and it is the controlling question of gardening.

You often notice that so-called great gardens seem to go to pieces when the original gardener leaves, succeeded (as he so often is) by an institution, or by some state agency, or (in nongreat gardens) a new owner. The reason for the deterioration is not far to seek: not many people have the sympathy that the original gardener did for his own garden. Decisions about how far to prune the holly, or where to stick in the crocuses, are no longer made the same way as formerly. Unlike stone structures, which merely decay slowly, a garden requires the continuing presence of somebody who cares a good bit about just such details.

It would be a terrible thing if anybody got the notion that a dandy garden is difficult and that if one makes a garden he lays himself open to the possibility of making an ass of himself. That is not the way it is, at all. On the contrary, the gardens that look most right are usually small "yards" presided over for some years by a gardener who is not even thinking very much of design, in any abstract or formal way, but who is exercised over how to grow his favorite plants as well as he can. Such a gardener, without even intending it, cannot help learning how big his plants get, and over the years he potters about, moving this plant or that because "it got in the way of the strawberries" or some such thing.

What has in fact occurred, in such gardens, is that quite subtle shifts and adjustments have been made—things that "got in the way" or "didn't look so good" have gone. But what grew well, and what did look good, remains; and if the gardener is enthusiastic and also cramped for space (the chronic situation of all gardeners) he soon has to bite the bullet, as you might say, and make hard decisions. He is either going to have his row of camellias or not—and if he does, then the other things he might just as easily have grown cannot be grown in that space. And his roses—let us say he is wild about roses, as many people appear to be. He very soon learns that if he acquires, say, 'Tropicana,' then some other rose has to yield its place. The garden, in relatively little time, shows the results of such decisions, and the interesting and comforting point for amateurs like myself is that such gardens are generally pleasant. Nobody should be uneasy, then, or fearful to set out planting whatever he likes all over the place.

It may be that later it will dawn on him that if he had made it his business to see more in the beginning, he would have been choosier about the things he planted. But no matter what he plants, he will make changes as the years go by, and as he is tempted by this rhododendron and that tulip (temptation is the mother of excellence, I have noticed) his garden will start bearing his own imprint.

Now, nobody imagines his modest little patch is going to be the greatest thing since copper bracelets, no. But it will be personal, and it will be fascinating, because there is no such thing as dullness when the gardener is going full steam ahead and damn the torpedoes, as it were.

All this, you may argue (for readers often have bad habits and appear not to be improving much) has little to do with where you dig the hole for your new apple tree. The truth is, however, that where you plant the apple tree depends, or should depend, on how its rounded shape and considerable bulk—an apple tree is roughly the size of a garage—will consort best with the other shapes of the garden. It should be planted where its undistinguished foliage is assisted by the far more interesting foliage of, say, low spiny plants or fleshy fat-leaved plants, or sheaves of spikes like yuccas, or emerald green or acid green hummocks, or tufts of white-gray mealy things or billows of bronzy or purple things.

Wherever the apple tree is, the eye should be able to see fairly startling contrasts of shape and texture near it. Experiment will show (gardeners stoutly refuse to take anybody else's word for these things) that contrasts of shape and texture (spike against billow, fuzz against polish) are far more pleasurable than contrasts of color (red against blue). But violent contrasts, even of foliage (such as purple basil against gray-white lavender cotton) are soon self-defeating. Refinement eventually results, not because any human is really delicate and refined and pure and noble, but because it is learned that violent (and presumably exciting) contrasts soon start canceling each other out.

Excitement and drama are possible only with control; thus, a field of scarlet and orange flowers soon palls and the eye is soon bored with it, but a touch of vermilion or russet with a patch of blue-gray will prove quite heady, and so will a little raspberry with sulfur, sky-blue, and white. At the same time, anything approaching red, white, and blue will usually fail in the garden, not because there is anything wrong with the colors in themselves but because they are insistent, obvious, high-voltage, uncompromising, and easily exhausted: once you've looked, you've seen it all.

Fortunately, nature has not known how to design plants of really bad design or really hideous color, so that even if our own taste is deplorable we are often saved by the subtlety and grace of the plants we use. Thus even a mass of red, white, and blue is often less revolting than we hoped it would be because nature (unlike paint companies) does not so easily provide us the means to be blatant or altogether coarse and gross. We begin, often enough, by hoping to knock the neighbors' eyes out with the largest mass of color since the lions ate the Christians, but usually we cannot help noticing (amid the gore) some especially happy effect we did not plan. We repeat that happiness, and by easy stages we give up the neon, as you might say, only because we find effects that please us more.

It is a great joy the day we discover that we can learn things without actually having to make the mistake ourselves. The gardener learns what works and what doesn't—the mistakes have time enough to be discarded or corrected.

There is, so far as I can learn, no substitute for that process; though much wear and tear is saved by thinking first, and learning a little first, instead of racing about with sacks of lime because some bureaucrat thought that was the quickest way to shut the questioner up and send him off happy.

The one part of the process that cannot be skimped is the active planting of various things—no garden was ever yet made by just thinking about it (except those gorgeous gardens of dreams). And the second thing that cannot be skimped is the question, when you see the results of your planting, "Does this really delight me, does this charge me up like mad?" What is there about it I don't like—if it's blah, is it because there is too little variety? Too much?"

And so on. Dig those holes, tote that bale, ask those questions, and the seasons as they toddle along will do the rest.

"Minor" Bulbs—Major Joys

Winter Aconite and Naples Cyclamen

Ten. ☐ September is the time to plant two of the "minor" bulbs that will give enormous pleasure, the winter aconite and the Naples cyclamen.

You will often read in books, if you have a taste for rambling garden chats, that the best way to acquire these two bulbs is to move a block of them while they're in full growth. Just lift a sod of them. Surely (the books always say) you have a friend who can get you started. I have never, in all my years dabbling about the garden, known or heard of anybody who had a friend who could get me or anybody else started with these two bulbs.

Once I did succeed in getting a nice patch of the wild cyclamen established and discreetly seeding beneath a willow oak. All that was necessary was to buy fifty corms, of which about half grew and flourished. Within a few years the whole patch of formerly bare earth (not counting the half-hearted ivy that struggled about here and there) was covered from September until April with the beautiful cyclamen leaves. These endure the hardiest weather in the open air. They are broadly halberd shaped, half the size of a lady's palm, and are soft olive to moss green, marbled with soft gray and almost white. It is said no two leaves have the same patterning, and I can vouch for it that no leaf is less than beautiful.

In late July or August or early September, the flowers appear, without leaves, or else with the leaves just barely poking through the earth. Blooms are like ordinary florist's cyclamen, except they are only six inches high and proportionately small. They are a soft rose bengal (that is, a pink with a bit of blue in it—a great color for cyclamen, phloxes, camellias, and azaleas, to say nothing of roses) and lovely, though scentless.

How few plants there are with fresh leaves all fall and winter. I had mine by a brick walk under the oak, in a sort of tiny clearing in the cleyeras, azaleas, and sarcococcas. You saw them as you came down the front steps of cypress planks, just before you made a sharp turn into the driveway. At least, most people saw them. I had a few friends who persisted in walking straight ahead and not turning, and for a while I threatened to put an iron railing around the cyclamen, but never did, of course.

Anyhow, if anybody had come over with a spade and said he wanted to "get started" with a sod of those cyclamen, I should have said, ha, indeed.

We are reduced, I am afraid, to buying our corms of this cyclamen from bulb dealers and waiting a few years for them to thicken into fat clumps. As you probably know, the older the corm gets the fatter it grows. Eventually, an old corm will produce a hundred flowers or so in the season, and if you have a number of old corms you have quite a pleasant sea of flowers.

This is the sort of flower, blooming when nothing else of great interest does, that is worthy of close attention (it will not do to plant them 300 feet away, but rather where you will see them, coming and going). The leaves are wonderful for picking, during the winter, but of course I never let my wife pick any, though I would have "once they are really established" which would be roughly the year after I ceased gardening.

The other great little bulb is the winter aconite, *Eranthis hyemalis*, which heaves up flat gold flowers the size of dollars or a bit larger in the winter—January to March.

Last fall I planted six tubers—they cost about a nickel each, as I remember, at a local garden center—which is not what I recommend to anybody else. Always plant a hundred or so for starters. At the time, however, I had only a few cents change. They bloomed in early March, about ten days before the fat brassy crocus that you see everywhere and which is so permanent and so well worth growing. The trouble with this aconite is that the tubers dry out terribly, and fatally, and thus you never quite know if they're going to sprout or not. Sometimes I have planted them and hardly any came up. This time all six bloomed. They looked very foolish in the lily of the valley bed all by themselves and gave me considerable delight. I do not say, however, they were worth a cross-country trip to see. They would be well worth a pilgrimage if there were a few tens of thousands of them, however, and if it is happy, this aconite will seed cheerfully about.

Whereas the cyclamen likes to snuggle up to an old oak, the aconites like to be bone-dry all summer and moist and sunny all winter. They will thrive in such unlikely places as the shade of beech and hemlock, that awful tree beneath which hardly anything will grow. A famous planting of the aconite in England exists beneath a grove of horse chestnuts, where the south sun reaches them in the winter but where it is dry in summer and so shady that no other plant even tries to grow there. This wonderful gift of thriving beneath horse chestnuts means the aconite is not so happy in more favored positions where it is damp in the summer.

It is always worthwhile to have a handful, just to reassure you spring is coming (they are even earlier than snowdrops and are finished by the time daffodils bloom) but if you happen to have a grove of horse chestnuts you should consider planting them by the tens of thousands. Or, at least, planting as many as you can and letting them seed.

The reason these two wonderful minor bulbs are so little seen is simply that they should be planted in September, no later, they are both a little fussy about settling down, and, finally, they do not make a great show like a bucket full of tulips or a mop full of dahlias. Neither would be esteemed so much, except for their season of bloom and, in the case of the cyclamen, the foliage, which is hugely ornamental. Garden columnists are always scared to death of these two bulbs, because you can't buy them just everywhere and a happy issue does not always follow their planting. They are both hardy as rocks, and the only trick is to plant them and get them started, resigning oneself to losing perhaps a third of them, but recouping magnificently as the years pass and they increase.

The cyclamen, alas, is no longer to be bought by the hundred —it is now 50 cents each in one catalogue, I notice—but even six are a start. You will not call them "minor" bulbs at all when they bloom.

Dutch Crocuses

Let us have no more talk about "fat Dutch crocuses" or "fat Dutch hyacinths"—as if the better sort of gardener loved only the slender, elegant wild crocuses and hyacinths unfed, unbred, and untouched by the Dutch. The truth is that nothing is more sprightly to see than patches of fat Dutch crocuses in March, coming as they do to lift our spirits and amaze the young and simple.

Though I have only a tiny yard I have given a place of honor to the grand Dutch crocuses, not only because I love them myself, but because I know few flowers are so attractive to children. I do not expect to see many flowers; I expect the children to pick them. For this reason I have planted them conveniently near the sidewalk. When children pick flowers, I do not like the word "steal," and the quickest possible route to hell, it has been said, is to growl at a child for picking crocuses. The child should be gently taught the curious customs of our society, that he should not pick flowers without permission, but it is intolerable to think of a child's excitement over these wonderful sweet gaudy flowers all ruined by harsh reproaches. Now of course if the child gets into *Lilium langkongense* or the irises, well, that is something else again, and a tub of boiling oil is recommended.

But crocuses—why, I have often been tempted to pick a few myself. The Dutch varieties are very large, the individual flowers perhaps three inches or even five inches tall. I know that some are theoretically much better than others, so I have grown a number of varieties. Unfortunately, I have not been able to find any I thought unworthy. This is partly because the Dutch seem to offer only good kinds now. The great striped 'Pickwick,' which is whitish with bold violet stripes and golden stigma (the little column in the middle of the flower), is larger than small tulips. 'Remembrance' is a grand purple, but then so are 'Purpurea Grandiflora' and 'Paulus Potter.' 'Little Dorrit,' a soft silvery lilac, is cleverly named to deceive the gardener: it is perhaps as large as any crocus in cultivation. ('Ruby Giant,' on the other hand, is a much smaller crocus, a hybrid of the wild *C. tomasinianus*, I believe, and a much-valued dark form of that fine species though, alas, blooming a little later.) 'Dutch Yellow' or 'Dutch Yellow Mammoth' or 'Aureus' are all likely to be the same thing, the same wonderful thing, a flower of great brilliance and dignity, altogether weatherproof and often permanent in gardens. It usually blooms ahead of the other Dutch crocuses, but last year they bloomed together permitting a fine vulgar show of rich purple and gold and white and striped sorts, all mixed up together. Other varieties are just as good, and the intending planter (as one of my favorite journals sometimes calls the baffled gardener unsure what to plant) will find all varieties quite satisfactory unless he is choosier than your humble servant here.

Top-sized bulbs, at about eight cents apiece (if you buy 100) are a better buy than smaller bulbs at six cents apiece, but there is nothing wrong with the smaller size bulbs (or corms, as they may be correctly called) and since they produce fewer and smaller flowers, they are even better for refined places where you don't want the biggest crocus you ever saw.

But the ones by the sidewalk are the biggest ones I could get. Children, as we well know, are inherently vulgar in their taste, and prefer the biggest always. The biggest crocuses are also excellent for gardeners who fear they are themselves getting almost too refined to breathe. They will find much refreshment in the general flauntery of these crocuses, though admittedly there is something absurd in choosing small flowers like crocuses in the largest varieties possible.

Squirrels sometimes eat crocuses, but often leave them alone. English sparrows and some other birds are fond of crocuses, but they do much more damage to crocuses abroad than in this country. English sparrows here have not generally discovered that the crocus flower buds are good eating, and one may hope they do not pick up this information from some international seminar of birds.

Snowdrops

A small bulb rarely or never eaten by rodents is the snowdrop, *Galanthus nivalis.* I grow a few other kinds (and let me say there is no such thing as a bad snowdrop) but finally decided none is prettier than the commonest one, *G. nivalis.* Snowdrops have gotten very expensive lately, about fifteen cents apiece as I remember, but if you get a windfall you could do worse than go hog wild for snowdrops. They are grand on shady banks under trees, at the edge of woodlands (or shrubs), and other places that get a bit of sun in early spring but none in summer.

Scilla tubergeniana

It is easy to be unfair to *Scilla tubergeniana*. More than once I have heard gardeners say, "Oh, that."

Like most early (late February or early March) blooming scillas, it should be planted thickly. A dozen bulbs should occupy the space of a butter plate, to give you an idea. Unlike some other scillas, this one is pale blue, almost white. It lacks the sharp gentian-blue good looks of *Scilla sibirica*, for example. It is so pale, and it blooms so short—right on the ground; if there are five or six small, thimble-like flowers on the stem, the bottom one does not even clear the earth.

It is the easiest plant in the world to pass by, if you see it cut in a vase, or in a small pot at a flower show. But its virtues are not all seen at first glance. It makes a patch of pale blue (later virtually white) that starts off right on the ground but gradually rises to perhaps six inches. It blooms for several weeks, in bad weather. It starts with the early *Crocus chrysanthus* flowers, and lasts well past the snowdrops and *Iris reticulata*. It continues along with the early cyclamineus hybrid daffodils, and persists up to the time *Tulipa clusiana* begins to bloom.

Like many valued things in gardens, it is esteemed not because it knocks anyone's eyes out, but because it is pretty, because it increases and thickens moderately, because it makes a little bridge of color between the flowering of so many early blooms among the small bulbs, and because its texture (the texture of its bristly little clump of color) is different from, and adds interest for, the other flowers of late winter. It is planted in September or October, and is not expensive. Even a dozen bulbs will make a pleasant small show. I mention it now because I find myself consistently underrating it; and yet I know if it disappeared, I would be considerably disappointed. Add it to your list of things to get around to.

Local garden centers nowadays have better selections of small bulbs: eranthis, galanthus, tritelia, crocus, narcissus, erythronium (some really fine ones like 'Pagoda' and 'White Beauty'), wild tulips, brodiaeas, and so on. One such place has a fellow who told me they are trying a lot of varieties new to them, and I assured him they were good sorts indeed. I think he was surprised to notice he sold out almost immediately (before I got there, I was annoyed to notice) of the little *C. chrysanthus* variety 'Gypsy Queen.' I had to content myself with several equally lovely, equally desirable kinds. This is grand progress. In the past it has often been difficult to find these small spring bulbs. Gardeners will certainly plant them, once they are aware of them.

May I intrude a suggestion that when you see a small, inexpensive bulb of some flower you never heard of and which has a suspiciously un-American name, you buy one or a few just out of sheer curiosity or bravado? You can't lose much, and if they were not beautiful, the bulb growers wouldn't grow them.

Autumn Crocus and Meadow Saffron

Summer is the time to order bulbs of two fall-blooming flowers, the lavender-blue wild crocus and the violet-mauve meadow saffrons. They will be planted outdoors toward the end of August and will bloom handsomely in October. Needless to say, the fall-blooming *Crocus speciosus* (which strikes almost everybody as the best of the fall-blooming sorts) is not the same as the crocuses that bloom in February, March, or April. Once somebody asked me what I did to make my crocuses bloom in October, not realizing they were a different sort entirely from the spring types, and thinking some way had been found to make the poor things bloom twice a year.

The little corms, or bulbs as we usually call them, are similar to the late winter-blooming crocuses, and should be covered with two inches of earth. They like sun or half-shade—an ordinary garden border suits them; they do not flourish in heavy shade. The bulbs should be watered well, once, after they are planted. The books say plant them by August 15, but often you can't get them that early, so plant them when you can, usually the very end of August or shortly after Labor Day.

There are perhaps half a dozen minor variations in *C. speciosus*, the most notable being a white form called *C. speciosus alba*. There is variation in the regular lavender-blue sort, however, and some are larger, some are bluer, some bloom a bit later than others. I have seen many rather distinct variations, but in the past I have had little success getting them by name from bulb dealers. My advice is to order the plain *C. speciosus* or *C. speciosus alba*, and enjoy the variations.

These fall crocuses sit there several weeks, then send up pale shoots like thick white toothpicks. These fatten out in two or three days, and the flowers emerge. If the bulbs are planted two inches apart and in great quantity, the effect is beautiful. If space or money or both are on the short side, however, do not hesitate to plant only a dozen. Too often in the past it has been said these crocuses should only be planted by the hundreds or thousands, and while that is fine, it would be a shame for the gardener to suppose that a dozen is "not worth growing." If they are happy they will seed, but do not count on that. In deep shade they will gradually peter out, but in ordinary borders they multiply steadily over the years.

The flowers are born naked, without leaves, but these begin to grow as the flowers fade, and reach perhaps a foot in length, like blades of grass, by spring; then they die away during daffodil season and nothing happens until next year the welcome white toothpicks appear again in September or October.

Even showier in the individual flower is the meadow saffron, *Colchicum autumnale*. There are several forms of this; also, there are a number of other colchicums. Once, in a fit of madness, I ordered two hundred of them—they are relatively expensive, compared to crocuses—and learned the hard way that they should be planted in the earth promptly, not left to sit about, if there is any dampness. These bulbs vary in size, but perhaps the size of a nectarine is average. The blooms look like crocuses, only they are the size of rain lilies or smallish tulips sitting right on the ground. They are nice in thin grass where it is not so dense in a woodland, or, of course, in full sun.

The variety called *C. autumnale major* is the one I notice most often, and it is very pretty in rosy lilac. Like the crocuses, the flowers come naked, but the leaves shoot up in the spring. They are maybe fifteen inches long and tongue-like, and when they start to ripen and die off in late spring, they turn various ghastly shades of yellow and appear to be in agony. This does not bother me, since my thyme and rue more or less ameliorate, or at least obscure, these goings on, but plant colchicums where the ripening foliage does not bother you.

One thing I have sometimes noticed: where the colchicum leaves die down, the earth retains a sort of funnel shape—a hole where the sheaf of leaves used to be. It struck me that water might collect in such a place, but no, these hollow channels (which in heavy soil seem almost to be baked in a kiln) are said to make it easy for the flowers to emerge in September, so perhaps we should not worry. A number of flowers come from each bulb for a period of two or three weeks, it seems to me, and in my own garden I have only four bulbs. I mention this to suggest, again, that while a whole meadow full would be nice, it is amply comforting to have even a very few.

Many plants—sometimes I think most plants—are poisonous, and colchicums are. It is from the bulbs that the drug colchicine is made. Children should be taught early not to sample the leaves, bulbs, flowers, or fruit of any plant they do not know to be edible (and of course they should not eat the edible ones either, if the idea is to ornament the garden with them). Some people get upset about poisonous plants, yet those of us who are not forever gnawing on flowers need not be deterred. It is startling that people accept that war, automobiles, and power mowers are ordinary hazards, but begin to fidget if there is a colchicum somewhere, as if it might attack or poison one while dozing.

Marigold Madness—Or,
Color in the Garden

Colorful Conifers

Eleven. ☐ If I had a lot of space I suppose I would go berserk for conifers—conifer collections have often ruined the gardens of the rich, giving them a funereal and ponderous air—but fortunately I have room for scarcely any, and I mention them only because of color.

They change in color. Of course everyone knows that, yet I find upon checking that very few books mention it. Hardly any book points out that oaks and maples are bare of leaves in the winter; presumably any fool knows that. In the same way, it is assumed everybody has noticed that conifers change colors with the season, too.

And yet even so eminent a gardener as the late Gertrude Jekyll was caught by the yews. She wanted a background of almost black, and wisely chose the somber dusky intense yew. But to her horror (she wrote) the new growth of the yews sprouted just as her irises were in bloom, and the new growth of yew is the most wonderful brilliant yellow-green that asserts itself like a neon marquee. Far from providing the dark sober background she wanted, the yews were so brilliant in the coloring of their new growth that she barely noticed the irises in bloom.

There is no point belaboring the obvious, but various junipers turn a soft lavender in winter, and other junipers (which were selected for their intense blue-white color in the summer) turn soft sage green. In all cases the effect is perfection itself—God did very well indeed in designing and coloring conifers—unless, of

course, you were counting on a different color. It is well, therefore, to see the conifers in winter (a fine collection at the National
Arboretum) before getting schemes fixed in your head.

I mention conifers because of all plants they are most constant, yet even they have a greater range of seasonal color than
the gardener is likely to think. Here in December, I have been
looking at a dwarf arborvitae. I planted it so I would have a globe
of rich bottle green in the border in the winter. It has turned a
rich bronze, instead. It reserves its dark green for warmer weather. I should have known—after all, I have often seen the various
dwarf forms of the occidental arborvitae in other gardens, and I
suppose I must often have seen it in the winter. But I never noticed its color change until I planted it myself.

And what is to be said of spring and summer, the seasons
when color is most apparent? Only this: the gardener must experiment until the result excites him, then leave it alone.

It is no good to say scarlet and yellow are garish together. It
depends. They can look marvelous together. It is no good saying,
"Magenta is evil." Magenta can be the most rewarding color in
the world. It depends. It depends on what else there is, and how
much of one color there is in relation to other colors.

My own suggestion, which is worth little and for that matter
is worth nothing if you see the matter differently, is as follows:

Colors of roughly the same intensity go fairly well together.
Full yellow and full red generally please one better than full yellow and pink. Pale purple and pale sulphur or straw color and
pale rose will usually look better by themselves, with perhaps a
dash of strong raspberry, than the same colors with a strong blue.

No color is "safe" and no color is "dangerous." More gardens
are rendered dull by timidity than are rendered vulgar by exces-
sive daring. Be bold.

Be simple. Use large enough patches of color to make the point.
It is good of me to say this truth, since my instinct is to jam in a
great many things, instead of choosing a few things and giving
them plenty of space to show their character and color.

Pay far more attention than seems reasonable to foliage color
and texture. Such plants as lamb's ears, wormwoods, lavender cot-
tons, certain mulleins—these are worth their weight in vermilion

though all are gray. Gray is a color hardly any garden has enough of. Another color too rarely used is blue-gray—the color you find on plums, grapes, and cabbages, a fine glaucous powder that makes the surface look blue.

There is no substitute for dark green. Do not ignore the holly, the box, the yew. There is no substitute for such fine textures as we find in the yew, the tamarisk, the juniper. There is no substitute for things like bamboo, in which the light penetrates deeply.

It is terrible, I know, to reflect that with a little thought one could "get in five more peonies" or "if we took out those junipers we could have a patch of roses for cutting" and so on. All these temptations, so heady, so irresistible to the young gardener, must be weighed. Perhaps I should append a rule or two, not because they are good rules but because they may correct giddy allurements:

If you are not aghast at how much space you have given evergreens—conifers, camellias, hollies, etc.—you do not have enough, and should saw down the roses and plant more green.

If your main walk is less than four feet wide, and if it is white concrete, then widen it, no matter what has to be sacrificed (oh, we could allow exceptions), and resurface it with brick, stone, or something less glaring and dull. Three flowers against a good-looking pavement will do more for you than thirty flowers against white concrete.

Do not be afraid of black. It is the best color to paint many things, including outbuildings and sometimes fences. It depends. But pay no attention to those who think everything should be white.

Give space to reflecting water. Even if it means giving up flowers (which of course it necessarily does). Less color and more lily pool are better than more color and less lily pool.

Marigolds and Mass Madness

Marigolds are bright and beautiful if, like cousins, you don't have too many of them at once.

Hardly any flower makes sense when bedded by the thousands, though that is the way you commonly see flowers used in parks. Nobody expects much imagination or thought in public plantings, however; and the theory—as I understand it—is that if you're driving along at seventy miles an hour, it makes no great difference what the flowers are or how they are grouped.

But in home gardens, needless to say, there is no reason to mass flowers of the same kind endlessly—there is no reason to have solid beds or (here I commence to meddle) for that matter solid edgings of a single brassy flower. The mere fact that you get a lot of seeds in a packet doesn't mean you have to plant all of them. They keep quite nicely for next year. A handful of marigolds, stuck in here and there among violet or blue or yellow petunias, can be festive, whereas a solid mass of marigolds, apart from being overwhelming, looks dull.

It is the principle of the skyrocket, of course, that applies here. Rockets seize all eyes when they burst in gold rain against a dark sky. But if you make the sky solid with gold (as the sun does at noon) then you rather lose the effect of skyrockets. Similarly, a touch of scarlet is one thing in a necktie, but something else again when shirt, pants, socks, shoes are all vermilion. Without further laboring the point, therefore, let me respectfully command you to plant your marigolds for brilliant accents, not for masses.

One can never say that some particular way of using color is "right" and other ways are "wrong." Rather it is a fact that drama and delight are lost by using colors some ways, and enhanced by other ways. Now I have a friend who would be happy if all the world were turned purple, and that person actively dislikes all yellows. Strange. But then people are. And who would wish to argue with somebody strangely constituted colorwise? Such persons should go right ahead with color arrangements that please them, however odd. But relatively normal gardeners usually respond with the greatest pleasure when colors are used not necessarily sparingly, but rather carefully. In general, the more brilliant the color the less of it you need. Or, put another way, the more brilliant it is, the sooner you have a belly full of it.

This does not mean (as the timid suppose) that the garden should have nothing but gray and puce in it. Quiet colors can be notably boring. I have a gang of dark violet petunias in pots. When I group these all together they are fairly dull, however safe from the reproach of vulgarity. But these dark petunias are wonderfully alive if two pots of raw brilliant pink petunias are stuck in among them. The pink is assertive and loud and restless, but when used sparingly with dark purple it is magical and splendid.

Among roses you can hardly help noticing that whole family of neon-electric vermilion-orange-pink. There is nothing wrong with the color as a color—it is clear, brilliant, sparkling, and if it makes you rather sick it is because too much of it is used. If there is a paved walk in the garden, it is possible to set up poles near the end of it, covered with vines, a shady bower with the walk continuing through it. If there is a garage, as there often is at the back of a garden, try covering the walk with vines (up in the air, of course) so that you see the walk in blazing sun, then dark under the vines, then (at the far end) in brilliant sun again. At that far end, you can have good effects from roses of the most day-glow brilliance. They are set off by the dark bower in front of them. There such a rose as 'Tropicana' may show itself off. It can be handsome with purple-leaf plants around it, or with plenty of gray leaves. But it seems to me a mistake (the rose itself is a mistake, as far as I am concerned, because I have no aptitude for these neon colors in roses, but there they are) to use such a color in beds of rose and pink and crimson and yellow roses, for there the strident color wars with and dominates everything within sight.

Dark crimsons, by the way, and intensely rich violets and mahogany and bronze—what sumptuous colors they are. And yet in a garden they invariably give a heavy dull effect when used by themselves, and what is strangest of all they become invisible at thirty feet. You discover, after a bit, that, rich as those colors are, they do not give rich effects, except when used with other colors. Straw yellow—a color that hardly anybody starts off admiring— is one of the most useful of all colors, as you will quickly see if you try it with the rich bronzes and crimsons. It makes them come alive, and so does fairly pale magenta.

Yellow irises (to give an example here) are great favorites of mine, and once I thought they would look fine contrasted only with sky-blue and white irises. Theoretically they should have looked good, since the colors were all pure and sparkling. To my surprise, the effect (which I feared might be too brassy, contrasting the yellow and blue) was distinctly tame and yawnworthy.

"I warned you to use plenty of wisteria lavender and sweet-pea pink," said an experienced gardener at the time, surveying my dull effect and quite pleased (for gardeners are not angels, let me tell you) to see it had worked out as badly as she had predicted.

As it happens, that mauve-magenta-sweet-pea pink is a color I cordially dislike. But the next year I included the lavenders and off-pinks, as instructed by my friend, and over my dead body of course. Needless to say, the same yellows and blues came brilliantly alive.

One of the most glorious of all colors is royal purple, and fortunately you find it in irises as in no other flower. I have noticed that men tend to go hog-wild with it, as I have so often done, and then wonder (as I did) why the effect was not as opulent as they thought it would be. One of the great disappointments of my life was the discovery that rich purple loses its effect unless used very sparingly. A few blobs of rich purple is fine—but if planted as freely as I would like, it becomes lifeless, however gorgeous the color may seem in an individual flower.

Thus experience forces us to learn a little, and after years of muddling about we usually discover (often late in life) what "everybody" has always known:

Soft and non-brilliant yellows and soft unspectacular lavenders and grayed blues and clear but not aggressive pinks are endlessly satisfying. Then you add extremely little deep purple, virtually no mahogany red, virtually no bronze (though it is beyond any gardener's strength to omit them entirely) and the result suddenly becomes marvelous.

White is commonly recommended—by the blind, I have often suspected—as a great pacifier of warring colors. I find it eggs on the warriors rather than reconciles them. White can behave like a spotlight, throwing everything else out of key. Of course there are many whites, some on the yellow side, some on the blue side, and the yellowish whites are the easiest to live with.

No harm at all is done if the colors don't seem quite right to you at first. Simply move the plants around until you like them better. When you shift things about you get a good many surprises, and commonly one partner of an especially satisfying color group will promptly die, or else grow out of bounds. That sort of thing we all know very well. No matter. We just keep at it, and presumably we will get it all worked out the year after we die.

But along the way we really do learn that marigolds gain enormously in impact when used as sparingly as ultimatums. We learn the pitfalls of too much brilliance, in which the gorgeous ones cancel each other out. In colors, as in humans, we learn there is much to be said for the modest, the pure, and (God save us all) the relatively dull.

Red, Red, and Still More Red

You never know, of course, what crazy notions lurk in the tangled minds of your friends, though after a few years very little will surprise you. Thus, I was not astonished when a gentleman associated with one of our major cultural institutions confessed to a love of nothing but red flowers.

I say "confessed," but he did not seem to feel guilty about it. Since he is rather ignorant of flowers (most persons with determined color prejudices are awed by the complexity of the world) a very elementary treatment of red flowers is indicated, especially since he does not read garden notes or, come to think of it, anything else actually written in the vulgar tongue. He will most likely wind up with red petunias, red zinnias, and red salvias, acquired all on some desperate day at some curbside garden center. And I for one wish him joy. And yet we know, do we not, that great joy is hardly to be found without exertion, thought, etc.?

The first really vulgar and effective flash of red that I can think of, as we proceed through the calendar, occurs in mid-April with the flowering of the 'Red Emperor' tulip. This tulip grows well, often persists for years without attention, and boasts a red-orange-hinting-vermilion color as intense as anything in the organic kingdom. If it were rare (and it was, until quite recent years) it would well be worth many dollars per bulb instead of its current moderate price. Let me suggest that 100 bulbs of this tulip in a space 30 by 50 feet (in clumps of three to seven bulbs sprinkled about wherever visual shocks seem called for) will produce a very considerable impression of redness.

The next outburst occurs in mid-May with the flowering of Oriental poppies. Here, in this flower, scarcely matched for silken texture, one may achieve heights of gaudiness undreamed of outside a flag factory. The basic wild color of the wild plant has not been improved upon, or at least my friend would not think so, as it is an orange red (it is plain red, but there is a hint of orange in it) that can be seen as far as there is daylight. There are also crimson and madder rose and soft orange and white Oriental poppies, some with big black center blotches and some without, and there are rose-lavender kinds too, but my friend would wish to stick closely to the fiery reds, I feel. Certainly there is no other flower in which it is easier to hew to his scarlet faith, so to speak.

Also in May the roses commence. I would especially call to his attention the brilliant mass-flowering floribunda called 'Sarabande' which will give entire satisfaction. There must be at least several hundred red roses currently in commerce. Who does not love the old black-red 'Ami Quinard' or the crimson 'Etoile de Hollande' or, for that matter, the older 'Grüss an Teplitz' and 'Louis Phillippe,' to say nothing of the dozens of modern reds?

Without going into it all, however, I suggest to my friend that he try 'Sarabande' and for a climbing rose the single 'Dortmund.' 'Dortmund,' one of those modern German roses, is sufficiently brilliant to kill the color of any iris yet known to man. I discovered this by the simple expedient of growing it once in my former iris garden. 'Dortmund' is a repeat-flowering rose, extremely vigorous, with good dark foliage. It has nice hips or pods in the fall, as well. It has something of the assertive quality of a bougainvillea.

Another climbing rose which does not bloom except in the spring is 'Climbing Christopher Stone,' and for some reason this is not seen so much. It is more scarlet than crimson, and of course it is a double hybrid tea—a florist-type rose, in other words. The dark red climbing rose 'Guinée' is rarely seen—it is more crimson than scarlet, as I recall it, and I suspect it is a bit on the tender side, though it should do well enough in Washington. It is, I guess, the most gorgeous red climber I have ever seen.

As far as that goes, 'Paul's Scarlet Climber,' which grows everywhere, is a fine color. My only objection to it is the blooms are small, not fragrant, and the vine does not repeat its bloom to speak of; and one may get weary of seeing it all over the place. Yet it is a fine rose in many respects and well suited to gardeners too lazy to track down better ones.

Next come red daylilies, the end of June and in July. I mention them not because I like them very much, but because some gardeners are unaware there are dozens of varieties of daylily now available in various shades of red. 'Alan' is a good early-blooming sort, and I confess to a fondness for the later-blooming 'Holiday Mood.' It is usually listed as a bicolor, but it is simply red with a yellow stripe and without arguing the merits of red day-lilies I can recommend that one to the red-struck gardener without reservation.

Gladioli, which bloom about three months after you plant them (and thus flower from June to October depending on when you get them in and how large the corms are, since the large corms or bulbs bloom soonest) are good sources of red flowers. Some years ago I used to enjoy the miniature red 'Atom,' which I do not see listed much anymore; doubtless there are improved varieties of it. You know, probably, as I did not, that "miniature" gladioli are usually three feet high and the standard large sorts sometimes run to shoulder height. Anyhow, there are many reds, all of them chronicled with varying degrees of ecstasy or drunkenness in catalogues.

The same is true of dahlias, which are great for color in September and October. Such varieties as 'Bishop of Llandaff' and 'Rocquencourt' not only have red flowers but bronzy foliage.

We have not considered red tulips for May, but it might as well be noted that following the April-flowering 'Red Emperor' there are dozens of other reds, some of them quite hideously showy and therefore suitable for my friend.

Nor have we contemplated peonies. These provide reds of various tone and the rash gazer will wipe an eye for some of the early hybrid peonies that flower before the main-season Chinese peonies. The single Japanese peonies, with bosses of yellow stamens feathered out to resemble small petals, should not be overlooked either.

The mere fact that most people prefer red as a jewel-like accent (nothing is lovelier than the early spring silenes like fiery scattered stars, for example, or the summer-blooming *Lobelia cardinalis* in a little green bog) is no reason the gardener should not have masses of solid red, of course.

How can we have forgotten phloxes? The red 'Starfire' is typical of the more fiery sorts, and there are many others less flaming and working their way into magenta. These follow daylilies and precede dahlias.

Then there are chrysanthemums (no really fiery red ones, but some nice mahogany-reds for fall) and of course nothing has been said of red azaleas or hibiscus or erythrinums (hardier than gardeners think) or wild horse chestnuts or any other woody plants, though treasuries of red are found therein.

If my friend would like to get red out of his system once and for all—or perhaps rejoice himself fully for once in his life—he should concentrate on the month of May and plant the following: Roses as previously cited; peonies 'Chocolate Soldier,' 'Philippe Rivoire,' 'Red Charm,' 'Pfeiffer's Red Triumph,' 'Big Ben,' 'Richard Carvel,' 'The Mighty Mo,' 'Dandy Dan,' 'Lustrous,' 'Mrs. Wilder Bancroft,' 'Red Star,' and 'Sword Dance.' Also red Russell lupines, red heucheras or coral bells, a good assortment of red Oriental poppies, and the irises 'Martel,' 'Donnybrook,' 'Fire Chief,' and 'Flaming Dragon.' None of the irises is really red—one is a rich magenta blend, one is orange, etc.—but I dare say they will suffice. All these things will bloom more or less together during May and should answer any complaints that one has "never really had enough red flowers at once." Needless to say, friends with weak hearts should be warned not to drop in during that month. And it probably would be prudent to call the fire department about the end of April.

True Blue Blues

Blue is a color that pleases me best when used just for itself—what some people would call an accent—as if it were some remarkable new auk worth contemplation just for itself. I have tried, just once, using blue in a great mass, as children sometimes dream of ten pounds of chocolate cherries, and found it indigestible and oppressive. But I notice that without thinking of it consciously, I wind up giving blue the place of honor over the years, and I mention it not to advance any claim to being descended from bees (whose favorite color it is) but because I never ran into a gardener who did not like blue.

You might think the same thing could be said of red or yellow or purple, and I do not want to make any large deal of it; but I mention the subject of blue flowers because I suspect there is indeed some numinous aspect to blue and that other gardeners sense it as much as I do.

Last fall I bought a number of pansies at a Beltsville nursery, glad to see the plants superbly grown and perfect for planting out in October. During the winter two-thirds of them died, a phenomenon I have come to expect in winters up here. But of the survivors, two-thirds were a blue pansy called 'Azure Blue,' and if God gives me strength and memory, I will plant a lot more of it next fall. I have it here and there, but most handsomely in a half whiskey barrel that contains a twisted willow. The willow is that electric green, both sharp and melting, that has pleased gardeners for some aeons, and the surface of the dirt is pretty solid now with the blue pansies.

I have a Siberian iris now in glory that owes its beauty to the uncommonly graceful placement of its stalks and its elegantly recurved leaves, more than to the perfection of its flowers. It is supposed to be the old 'Perry's Blue' but I doubt it, since not even a catalogue writer could call it sky blue, which is what Perry's iris is supposed to be. Mine is blue-violet, and you would never think of calling it blue at all, unless you are color blind (as an infinitude of people are, especially fanciers of irises). It is very elegant, all the same, with its little white patch at the throat. Some Siberians bloom with the stems jammed together like a Roman fascia, as if they had gone rather berserk, but it is worth poking about to get Siberians that have grace as well as mass.

When I first grew the hardy geranium 'Johnson's Blue,' which is a cranesbill and not a greenhouse geranium, I was annoyed that it was almost red in its purple coloring. But the hotter the season got the bluer it got until it was finally an intense and seemingly pure blue. I now regard it with considerable patience in May, knowing that in June it will be true blue. A moral there, probably.

One of the pretty forget-me-nots is called *Myosotis scorpioides* —and some day I must investigate the name, but can say now it does not have any scorpions in it. Once I was stung on the chest by a scorpion and it was unpleasant but no worse than a wasp sting. And there were no forget-me-nots on that island, either. Anyway, this particular plant likes to have an inch or two of water over its earth at all times, so of course I do not provide it. It sits in a half-barrel that is primarily sacred to the violet-stemmed taro, which sulks in a dishpan in my bathroom all winter and moves out in May. This tub also has a quill-leafed rush from seed borne by the wind, and in the summer it also will have a tremendous papyrus of the Nile, one of the most beautiful of sedges. And the forget-me-not is supposed to run around the base of all these and spill over the edge. I do not keep these plants under water, as they would prefer, since the water would not be deep enough for fish, and without fish there would be mosquitoes. So I keep the dirt saturated, but not covered, with water, and they make do.

There is no such thing as a blue rose, but various roses are violet or dusty-slaty-gray violet leaning either toward blue or toward red. The old 'Cardinal de Richelieu' is, in bloom, blue-violet, and 'Reine des Violettes' red-violet that fades off. My wife dislikes all of them, so they eke out an undignified existence back of the shed where I can go and admire them without rude comments from others.

We have wandered a trifle from the topic of blue flowers as crown jewels, perhaps, so I shall sign off with a salute to the false indigo, *Baptisia australis*, which has spikes of pea flowers like a lupine or a thermopsis only lavender-blue, and you would call it blue rather than lavender, I think. It has glaucous handsome leaves, a little like a meadow rue, and it rarely needs staking. It is handsome with pink Japanese peonies and yard-wide clumps of hosta, especially the glaucous-leaved *H. sieboldiana*. Or anything else.

Blossom Time—
A Miscellany of Flowering Plants

Dicentra

Twelve. ☐ Whether a plant seems beautiful or "showy" depends on the eyes of the gardener, and some do not see much merit in anything less solid with flamboyant color than a large plot of azaleas. Others, however, get carried away by little weeds from a remote crag—plants that if you look carefully you can see ah, yes, it is indeed in flower.

Between the bonfires and the gnats, as you might say, blooms many a plant conspicuous enough to please the nearly blind, but elegant enough (in foliage texture, growth habit, articulation of flower shape, delicacy of color) to please the fastidious.

And a perfect example of a perfect plant is the bleeding heart, *Dicentra spectabilis*, also known as Dutchman's breeches and lady-in-the-bath. More about that later.

In about early April, we may expect to see these plants, in cans, on sale at garden centers—I bought a splendid one a couple of years ago from the plant stand at Washington Cathedral—usually in bud or bloom. If planted outdoors in a half-shaded spot and well watered, the creature will never know it has been moved.

It is a shock, to those unfamiliar with the plant, to see it turn yellowish and die away completely in the summer. This does not mean you went wrong somewhere. Pay no attention. In early spring there will again be signs of life, and in April there will be the usual sheaves of leaf and flower, better as the years go by.

The plant forms a substantial clump of leaves, eventually knee-high, of soft blue-green leaflets, halfway between a maidenhair

fern and celery or meadow rue in general appearance. Above
them, in little wobbly arcs (arching forth, but often turning up a
bit at the ends), come sprays of flower, eight or ten inches long.
All along this bloomstalk hang little rosy hearts, like valentines
hung up to dry. They are up to an inch in length. The color is
clear cherry mixed with cream, wonderfully clean and pure,
though various tints are found in each flower. The color is like
that of *Clematis texensis,* if you know that marvelous plant, and
has much the softness and clarity of certain sweet peas. (This may
be a good place to complain to Providence that this coloring is a
great favorite of mine and extremely few flowers possess it.) The
result of this lovely color in little arcs over the blue-green leaves is
a picture of high elegance combined with vigor. Everything about
it is reasonable, but highly imaginative also. Some plants—by no
means all, or even a great many—manage to arrive at a flawless
balance between showiness and restraint, between coarseness and
oversubtlety.

It depends, as I say, on the gardener's way of looking at plants,
but I would always be willing to be counted a great friend of the
bleeding heart.

Now about that bath with the lady. If you take an individual
flower and turn it upside down and pull on the two side places,
they open up to disclose a lady (a very pale one) in a boat or tub,
and there is a fitness about the name, lady-in-a-bath, because the
whole thing looks so clean and rosy and innocent. Wholesome,
with a dash of the erotic.

There are other dicentras (a yellow one from the West that
I have not seen, but which is worth investigating, I imagine)
including various named varieties such as 'Bountiful' and 'Luxuriant' and a couple of wild forms, too, from our own country.
Attractive as they are, and some of them have the merit of a
longer blooming season than the bleeding heart we have been discussing, none is so beautiful, to my mind, as the lady-in-a-bath,
D. spectabilis. The others are smaller plants, and the flowers are
not borne so gracefully, and the colors tend toward madder, and
in general they manage to miss the perfection of *D. spectabilis,*
although they are by no means to be despised. I have grown them,
two or three of them, in the past with great pleasure.

A further word on just where to put the big bleeding heart,

which winds up the size of a young peony clump. Suppose there is a bed on the north side of the house, with maybe a hydrangea and a couple of camellias. It is a good place for the bleeding heart. The soil ideally should be fairly light—sand and leaf mold—and rich—occasional top dressings of rotted manure. This does not mean the bleeding heart sulks in gardens with heavy clay loams. It does mean that it appreciates some lightening of the clay with leaf mold and sand.

Over the years it strikes me the plant is attractive to dogs, but that may be only because I have always grown it in some place of great interest to dogs, such as the kitchen steps. With me, they are forever stepping on it, until I get around to putting up a little barrier.

You should not imagine that the plant is happy only near a north wall. It has grown since 1816 (the year of its introduction from Japan) very contentedly in regular garden borders, where it consorts well with lavender and primrose-colored tulips, to give an example. In such borders you should keep in mind that from the Fourth of July on, there will be a gap until next spring. Neighboring plants that flop over a bit are called for. You would not dig right down into its dormant crown to plant a gladiolus, of course, but you might let some artemisias or forget-me-nots or any such plant sprawl over the top of the aestivating bleeding heart. (Such plants of course die back in winter, leaving the space free for the emerging bleeding heart in the spring.)

I have never investigated this but suspect a clump of bleeding hearts might last in a garden for thirty years or so. If the clump gets too enormous, it can be divided in early spring, shortly after it sprouts out, but no time should be lost getting it back into the ground, of course. One would not want the lady's bath water to get cold or, God forbid, dry out.

Waist High in Gladioli

Last year we had no gladiolus blooms at all, because of thrips, those barely visible insects that drain the vital juices out so the flowers never open from the healthy looking buds. But this year, from the same batch of corms or bulbs that failed last year, we have excellent flowers. The stems are five to six feet high, normal for the large-flowered gladiolus. I remember one year I was upset at a large assortment of "miniature" gladiolus, all of which were a bit above waist high. Some of the large sorts go to seven feet or so.

The corms were rather cheap ones from Holland that I picked up at a grocery store. Last October, after they failed to bloom, I dug the corms, let them sit a couple of weeks to dry, then cleaned them, cutting the old stalks right down to the corm. I just set them in a cardboard box, and since I have no place to store them cool, they spent the winter in the furnace room, the only warm room in the house, though I do not mean to complain.

In March I soaked the corms for three hours to kill thrips. In a plastic pail I used 1½ tablespoons of Lysol per gallon of water. I took them out after the three hours and set them to dry in the air, and a day or so afterwards I planted them six inches deep outdoors. This was about March 17.

I have never liked gladioli in the house very much, and consider them poor cut flowers, since of course the bottom flowers wither before the top ones open. The top ones never do open, and even when you cut off the dead ones at the bottom the stalks look ratty, and give the impression they have been scavenged from a florist's garbage can.

Gladioli are not, in any case, my favorite flower. In the garden I admire them, but as everybody knows they flop unless staked or supported in some way. Books sometimes say that if you plant them deep, they do not need support. That is nonsense. Man and boy for fifty years I have grown and observed gladiolus, and if they do not flop, then they lean, which is worse. And yet I do not like stakes much. Once I used stakes that rose five or six feet above ground, one for each gladiolus, and that was good, because the varieties were huge sorts, and the stakes had three coats of dark green paint. But what a nuisance.

This year I planted the gladioli in a rectangular band around a bed in which I set tomato cages, those useful but not especially lovely five-feet-high cylinders of steel reinforcing mesh, used to strengthen concrete. The idea was to get the gladioli in by mid-March so their foliage and blooms would obscure the cages where the tomatoes (raised from seed but not set outdoors until May 10) were growing. For two or three weeks from June 20 on, the gladioli are pretty, and you do not notice the cages. As the gladiolus stalks reach five feet, just before the flowers open, I tie the stalks to the wire mesh. Then when it storms, the stalks do not start falling down or leaning at odd angles. When they wither, I cut the stalks out, leaving the gladiolus foliage. The tomatoes by this time are growing admirably, and conceal the cages themselves. Then in October, I shall dig up the corms once more, take down the cages, cut down the tomato vines, and set out pansy plants for the spring.

Having a Passion for the Plumbago

The plumbago or blue leadwort is a plant that would be reckoned among the most valuable in all the flowery kingdom if there were any justice or true sense of proportion in the world. When it is in bloom, seething with cobalt and smartly attacking the eye with its brilliance, not even gentians surpass it in its color, and in addition to that it has assorted merits so great that any one of them entitles it to attention.

It grows about a foot high with leaves somewhat like a periwinkle's, and in the late spring (it sprouts its leaves only after spring has really come) it starts sitting there looking like a small broadleaf evergreen. It is not an evergreen and it is not woody, it dies back every winter, and yet if you didn't know better, you might think it was a vinca or a small andromeda. All summer it sits there biding its time and going from strength to strength in a controlled, sturdy way. It is not one of those things that has raced five feet off from where you planted it. No, it spreads reasonably but knows nothing about how to become a weed.

Then, in late July, or in August, an occasional nickel-sized flower will appear at the tip of a shoot and these burst forth with increasing energy in September and continue, slowing down a bit, until late October. The buds appear in densely packed clusters at the end of the shoots and open in succession, though often with half a dozen or so open at once in each cluster.

In any case, it is not the individual flower that one admires so much as the carpet sprigged all over with deep and highly charged blue. You either go to pieces over blue or you don't, but most gardeners do. Even azure and violet are not to be sneezed at, since there are so few flowers that can rightly be called blue. But this leadwort is blue. It has, like most blues that make you blink, a good bit of unexpressed red in it. The little bracts at the base of the flowers are rosy bronze or even purplish. Usually you don't consciously notice them but I think they have something to do with the general effect of brilliance.

After the flowers are all gone, the reddish bracts remain for a bit, and the foliage of the plant itself often (almost always) turns to rich bronze and red. So even when the fall turns cold the plant is handsome in its modest way, which is the best way for anything to be handsome, as we know.

The great Victorian authority on everything in gardens was William Robinson, to whom gardeners owe all. He was only moderately awed by the leadwort, partly because he went mad for asters, which bloom at the same time. Perhaps he found it hard to admit that no aster rivals the leadwort for color. And, unlike asters, there is nothing weedy or second-rate or make-do about the leadwort, which is an aristocrat.

This plant used to be called *Plumbago larpentiae* but has now advanced to *Ceratostigma plumbaginoides*. Most nurseries have not heard of the new name, which I think has been in effect only the past fifty years, or else I suppose that like me they like the old one better. The plant is Chinese, by the way.

It creeps a little or flops. It builds up and then lies down. It does not exactly sprawl. If there is something for it to lean against or wander among (such as low junipers or cotoneasters or a pile of stone) it gets up as high as two feet. If you had a horse-trough, for example, and ran some wire fencing a couple of inches out from it, and planted the leadwort at the bottom, it would lean up and lean through and lean out and it could be clipped back, so that at the last you would have something like the effect of ivy on a wall, covered with blue. The usual way to use the plant, however, is at the top of a very low stone wall, where it will work its way down if the stones are an inch or two apart. At Washington Cathedral in the Bishop's Garden they use it as a ground cover, very prettily, with old box bushes at the back. It likes sun, a light soil, and a bit of freedom to spread out. It happily accepts the sort of half-shade of gardens, but it will sulk if you try to make it grow in heavy shade under such dismal trees as maples. It does not like woodlands, not even oaks, unless there is some sun and unless it is watered to make up for the tree roots guzzling all the natural rainfall. It is by no means a difficult plant, and anybody who has even "a little bed of flowers" can just stick it in with every certainty of success.

It is soundly perennial, no fear of losing it over the winter.

There is another leadwort that is sky blue with much bigger clusters of flowers, but it is a plant for the cool greenhouse, though handy for setting out in the summer. They used to use it a lot in Berlin and, for that matter, Memphis and New Orleans. It is a beautiful creature, but it is not cobalt and it is not hardy.

I do not want to oversell the leadwort, which is merely a minor ornament of gardens along with being, I suppose, utterly all a plant ever needs to be.

Hollyhocks

Some hollyhocks have spikes of single flowers, like funnels, set all along their six-foot stalks, and these are the ones you find bees in at night. Others are double, almost like floral balls, and I never see bees trapped in them when the flowers close at night—there is not room for a bee, the petals are so thick, no doubt. But then there is yet another structure in which the center of the flower is double like a pompon sitting on a flat ruff of single petals—the kind of bloom called anemone-flowered when you find the same type of flower among camellias or peonies. These seem to me the best looking, the ones with the flat ruff centered by the large boss of petals of the same color.

All these hollyhocks, of whatever floral shape, come in crimson, purplish red, rose pink, ivory, primrose, and tints intermediate between white and pink. I used to have one that was very pale flesh or blush colored that was pretty, and sometimes you see them with dark veins against a pale petal color.

There are two theories about the bees. One is that they get chilled from staying out too late in the evening and die in the hollyhock flowers. Since one often finds them alive and buzzing when the hollyhocks open the next morning, I find that theory hard to accept. Another theory is that something in the pollen or nectar of hollyhocks causes the bee to zonk out, as it were. In any case, I approach all hollyhocks with the same caution I approach

grape vines, thyme, thistles, mulleins, musk roses, and virtually
everything else, since I seem to have accidentally enticed the visiting hives of every beekeeper within ten miles.

Hollyhocks get red spider mites sometimes, which causes the
flat salad-plate-type leaves to become pale and mottled, as if a good
bit had been drained from them by the daily hassles of this world.
I do not spray against the mites, but rather try to keep the hollyhocks out in the open (not against walls or under eaves) where
the rains hit full. Mites are rarely a problem unless there is a dry
spell. Hollyhocks also get rust, of which I am very proud to say I
am ignorant.

Anyone can raise hollyhocks from seed, planted in July, for
example. This allows the young plants to get a good bit of strength
and vigor by late October, and they pass admirably through the
winter without any protection, dying back more or less (in mild
winters they are almost evergreen) and ready to send up fine
flower spikes in late May, flowering off and on through the summer but mainly in late June and in July.

One year, in a former garden, we had a nest of brown thrash-
ers in a hollyhock clump, only a few inches off the ground. The
nestlings all did very well and in time flew off, though it was important in the early stages not to let the dog investigate them as
much as he was keen to do.

The alleys of Washington are much improved by clumps of
hollyhocks, certainly, and one is pleased in those neighborhoods
where sensible people have let them spring up unmolested. Sometimes one sees hollyhocks eight feet high in such places, snuggled
up against wire fences before you come to the garbage cans. The
more open and sunny the spot, the less likely the hollyhock is to
need staking. Often they hold themselves up neatly, at least for
other people, though unless one stakes them it will generally be
found that the stalks begin to lean this way and that when the
spike is in full heavy bloom.

Mulleins I Have Known

Most gardeners, I notice, are quite fond of mulleins, once they
get used to them, but you almost never see them.

In the past I grew two or three kinds but they did not persist.
Almost all verbascums (to use the botanical name of this dandy

plant) are biennials. You plant the seed and they make a nice rosette of leaves that sit on the ground. They sit there all through the winter, and then the next spring, about the time garden irises are in bloom, the mulleins send up a fuzzy stalk several feet high (up to twelve feet, I have read, though more usually it is shoulder or head-high) with bright little flowers like yellow nickels all along the stem.

Some mulleins, like the old 'Cotswold' series of hybrids, come in "pink," if you want to be charitable, or madder diluted with white clay. Some are light magenta, not very intense or brilliant, and some are buff or straw color getting on toward primrose. The hybrids are sterile, and since they are biennials at heart (though some may prove perennial for a time, and come back several years in a row) you lose them before long. The garden hybrids, which are rarely offered for sale, are propagated from root cuttings, but I must say my occasional efforts to propagate them that way were complete failures. There are also—and even much more rare— dwarf mulleins and hybrids with a related genus, but to tell the truth I cannot imagine why anybody wants a dwarf mullein, since the whole point of growing them is for their rather startling height.

But it is the tall mullein we contemplate today, and O for a lute of fire to sing their merits. They do not look like much, you understand, as floral spectacles, and will never wrest the palm from the iris, the rose, the carnation, no.

But so often people come back from England and babble on about gardens there and say what a pity we cannot grow the things they do. We can, of course, grow virtually everything they do and a vast deal more, but our gardens will never look very good if we insist that every plant in it have a flower the size of a melon, the color of a hallucinated upset of the head, and a perpetuity of bloom to rival death and taxes.

Then why grow mulleins if, as I say, the flowers are not all that exciting? And the answer is, for beauty and drama, which are by no means the same as a floral riot. Form and texture, out-line and habit of growth, these are every bit as important as those blobs of brightness you see at rose shows. Elegance is not neces-sarily translatable to billboards or neon signs, and high drama is not always able to be rendered in a form suitable for comic books.

Mulleins are among those glorious plants that are almost but not altogether entirely weeds. They have the vigor, the easiness of strength, that we all must admire when we (rarely) see it.

The one most familiar to us is *Verbascum thapsus*, a weed from Europe long naturalized along highway cuts in hilly country, and also (less picturesquely) almost everywhere else. It is said that cows do not eat mulleins, and you often see them in pastures. (This may be the place to record that I have personally seen a cow eat one in a pasture near Shepherdstown, West Virginia, however. Few generalities are absolute.) That kind of mullein has fuzzy green leaves, greenish-gray but mainly green, and in June it sends up an unbranched stalk to ten feet—I have seen them that high. It opens a few of its yellow flowers—there must be hundreds all told—each day, and this goes on for some weeks. Formerly the thrifty goodwife used to cut the stems and store them dry for winter, for if soaked in tallow they make good torches. I have never tried that, since our very small house has little use for torches in its baronial halls, but it is worth knowing this formerly practical use for the plant. My own favorite of the mulleins I know is called *V. bombyciferum*, which possibly means "carrying a bomb," though my Latin was never very good. It is well suited to the modern garden. Last July I planted some seed (from Park Seed Co.) and it came up looking exactly like some ordinary weed, with smooth green leaves, and I thought, alas, this cannot be the great bombyciferous mullein at all. But within a few weeks the plants developed a gratifying fuzz and by winter had many rosettes more than two feet across.

They like a sunny spot and good drainage. They must have quick free drainage or they will die. The side of any dry bank will do, along the alley would be nice, or in any other part of the garden where the soil dries out reasonably fast after a rain. They will take the shade of an open woodland, but give them full sun if you can.

The glory of this mullein is that it has the whitest leaf of the entire family. The mealy finish of the leaves is so conspicuous that the leaves often appear to be painted white, and they are at least as white as lamb's ears (*Stachys lanata*) and if anything they are even softer to the touch. We have a friend who is forever trying to steal our mullein leaves to rub against her face, and of course that could not be permitted when the leaves are few and young.

By flowering time in May and June (it varies according to how strong the plant is) the rosettes may be a yard across. The stems on mine are only six feet, but I shall persist in the hope of growing them some day to a height of fifteen feet. They are wonderful looking, to me, even before they bloom, but they do have the bad habit of taking up a good bit of space, and you need not expect any little plant within a yard or so of them to endure the suffocation of those great mullein leaves on the ground. This mullein is said to come from Bulgaria. After its bloom season is over I shall let the seed ripen and hope it comes up all over the place, and I shall save some in an envelope for next year's crop as well.

Portulaca

One of the most beautiful flowers, somewhat neglected because it is simple and any fool can grow it, is the portulaca, *P. grandiflora*. It is called sun rose, rock rose, rose moss, and moss rose, and all those names annoy me a good bit, but there they are. This annual comes from Brazil or Chile, depending on which authority you like, and was introduced to gardens about 1827. It creeps modestly, and is six inches high, and throughout the warm season it is bravely studded with silky flowers the size of nickels or half-dollars, depending on variety and soil richness.

The trouble with it, if it is not churlish to find fault with so innocent and bright a creature, is that it opens only in the sunlight, and closes in the afternoon. I think it has its own notions. Sometimes it is not open, though the sun is brilliant, and sometimes it is open though the sun is not shining. I have never quite satisfied myself in this business, except to notice that books are commonly wrong about it, since something more than merely sunshine causes its flowers to unfurl.

Years ago I noticed it growing in small boxes stuck in the window sills along a narrow and wretched street in some dismal town in the south of France. What a difference these small taffeta explosions made when they opened scarlet, magenta, lemon, primrose, white, salmon, and rose in the mornings.

It was also, in my own country along the Mississippi, a great favorite of tenant farmers who grew it in washpans and other ingenious containers on the sagging wood porches of their shacks, commonly flanked with hounds who woke up occasionally to snap at bees. I knew it first a half-century ago, where my Aunt Marie Trigg grew it in big stone troughs on her porch, overhung with elms, but it made no difference since the sun in those parts is so fierce that sun-loving flowers do well enough in the shade. It sowed itself every year, tending to the fine rich magenta that must be its basic color, though even after many generations there was a sprinkling of other colors.

This year I found myself possessed of some half-barrels of oak, in which whiskey had aged, and while mulling over the wonderful things that could be grown in them, the season was going right ahead. I filled them with very sandy soil, and a few lavender and rosemary plants, and sprinkled a few portulaca seeds about. The portulaca, which does not care much for strong rich clay, goes mad for quite sandy loam.

It is wonderful on hot mornings to see them. About the time the tall lilies steam to death in the heat (or, if it is dry, shrivel to paper) the portulaca hits its stride.

In one place I sowed some seeds of the white-leaf mullein, *Verbascum bombyciferum* (that name is irresistible), in pots and tubs, not because it needs such coddling, but because it gets too big if grown in heavy soil. Around the mulleins I planted some more portulaca, and the effect has pleased me no end.

Nowadays you can get portulaca in named varieties, as indeed you used to be able to do in Victorian times, but ordinary seed packets from garden centers and hardware stores produce results as fine as any. The blooms are usually double, but single-flowered sorts come up too, and as the great authority William Robinson used to say, it is hard to know which is more beautiful than another. It is an ideal flower for big pots around swimming pools, or on balconies that bake all afternoon. There is only one common reason for failure: planting the seed too deep. Just scratch it in on the surface.

It has always been a mystery to me why people keep planting beds of red geraniums, since I find the globs of color oppressive and boring, when for less money and trouble they could have portulaca instead. Of course, even if a plant is quite perfect in beauty, like the portulaca, its elegance rules it out for certain gardeners who require a flower to be gross.

It is a good bit handsomer, by the way, than the tuberous begonias gardeners love to fail with (they abhor hot muggy summers and strong sun) and I like to think gardeners of wholesome and innocent and sensible natures will turn, next April, to a pack of portulaca seed for a change, and experience the novel sensation that life can be beautiful and success easy.

Poppies

Poppies like full sun, plenty of room to spread out, and a nice sandy loam with a reasonable amount of humus in it.

You will see, therefore, they are not ideally suited to heavy acid clay overhung with a virtual forest canopy. If the gardener possesses the usual dank shady strip so common to this capital, with acid soil laced with maple roots, then the poppy will be of no help whatever.

If people wish to live in a forest, there is no reason they shouldn't, and I believe it took millions of years for certain apes to move from a forest darkness into the light, so I do not expect the human fondness for dense shade to alter any time soon in favor of sunlight.

Those who garden in shade should visit any woodland where they may see ferns, hepaticas, etc., and this sort of growth can be quite pleasant in a city garden. Such exotics as pieris, skimmia, many azaleas and rhododendrons, and various Asian maples can be added, along with a carpet of small bulbs to bloom in late winter. Such a garden, especially if contrasted with stone, brick, hewn wood, and a good-sized pool, if possible, can be beautiful.

It is just at this point—having achieved a delightful woodland glade—that the gardener decides he wants roses, peonies, irises, daylilies, chrysanthemums, and poppies.

It will save time and confusion all around to say the gardener cannot have everything, and where there are fine oaks and maples and elms the gardener may as well dismiss the chief garden flowers from his mind and not waste effort and money trying to make them grow.

I saw an exhibit called Vegetables for Shade, and I have seen

many articles titled "You Can Have Flowers in Shade," and when you get down to it they all boil down to this: you cannot.

Of course, if you want to call a spot that gets five and a half hours of sun a day a shady spot (and the duplicity of some garden writers is breathtaking) then you can grow a great deal in the "shade," including many flowers that require full sun.

But the poppies, to get back to them, are not going to live in a thicket of laurel underneath some oaks even if, at 6:10 P.M. on June 20, you get a shaft of sunlight.

The Oriental poppy, which I have never been able to resist, is a perennial that requires not only sun but also the space of a bushel basket (or larger) to flop about in. It is in a glory of bloom for perhaps three weeks from May to June, at which time its silky cups, six or eight inches in diameter and borne on hairy stems two to four feet high, are as spectacular as anything in the garden.

The best ones are red. I have some called 'Prince of Orange,' which are orange, and I trot out to admire them extravagantly, and there are plenty of rose or watermelon-colored sorts, and some whites that are not terribly pure white, and all of them are dazzling enough, but the crimson reds seem to me the handsomest.

It is hard to believe that a plant as complacent and opulent as the Oriental poppy in full bloom can be miffy. But it often takes them three years to settle down in the garden. The first year they often do not bloom at all, and the second year not much. During this period in which the poppy is getting itself entrenched the gardener will be sorely tempted to stick in a few other things—a peony here, a redwood there—since the poppy is not occupying as much room as the gardener thought. No. And it never will, either, if we start plopping in other plants over it. We all understand the merits of simplicity and boldness, but few gardeners can be trusted to give the poppy a thirty-inch circle. Period.

Once the poppy is really established, however, it is fairly tenacious. It is a commonplace of life that no sooner does the gardener get his Oriental poppy blazing along like a California canyon than he decides it would look better somewhere else, and moves it. Often it fails to move and the transplanted creature dies, but a whole tribe of poppies shoots up in the old spot, having grown from fragments of the old root. Some of the best displays of this poppy are in gardens where the good husbandman keeps digging up his plants to put them somewhere else, and every year he does this, more grow from roots he has missed.

This poppy starts to die down as soon as it finishes blooming for the year, taking several weeks to retire. In the usual hurly-burly life of the average sunny garden, I do not think the withering and temporary disappearance of the Oriental poppy in June and July is as ugly as some say it is. I would not, however, plant an Oriental poppy against the Venus de Milo or all along the edge of your marble basin full of comet-tailed shubunkins, where the poppy's ripening (withering) and the resultant bare space would be an eyesore. But among peonies, box bushes, roses, daylilies, and the like the poppy's retirement will hardly be detected.

It is best planted from dormant roots in the month of August. Most gardeners are in no mood for planting anything in August, and wait until spring, ordering poppies in April and setting them out when the plants are in full growth. The poppy, which does not like being transplanted in the first place, reacts often by dying outright or, more commonly, by sulking for an extra year. Plant them, therefore, in August or September if you can. They make a growth of leaves in the fall, then die down during the winter, shooting up with vigor in April and dying down again in June.

Where there is space for them they provide an air of unstudied fatness and richness that no other late-spring flower provides, not even the peony. If there are sunny bays between shrub roses, the Oriental poppy will quite overwhelm the gardener in late May. I need hardly point out that the fiery colors and enormous size of the blooms do not do a great deal for the effect of tall irises, which have soft colors. But one or two of these poppies—not too many— will clash well even with pink roses, so one should not be too timid.

The field poppy, a splendid weed of grain fields in Europe and known to us for its association with Armistice Day, is an annual. Some succeed with it as readily as cornflowers, and in the same sort of sunny spot, and it can be planted (from seed) in late summer, fall, or in February, where it is to bloom. I have planted it at various times without any success, probably because I got busy and did several other things with the land before the poppies got going.

The Shirley poppy is a garden strain that specializes in clear pastels. My Aunt Marie used to fling Shirley poppy seeds along the south side of a shed attached to her garage and they always did well there. She used them for cutting and never saw them except when she went round to gather a bunch. They would be nice in a narrow strip outside the fence in the alley itself, if sun permitted, since often the soil there is gritty.

The Iceland poppies are perennial, usually treated as biennials, planted in August for bloom the next May. These come in soft bright yellows and oranges.

The opium poppy is most often seen in a sort of dusty rose inclining to lavender. It grows to four feet where happy. Often it is troublesome to start, but once it flowers and seeds, it may be around for years without further planting. It likes to come up between stones or at the edge of a lawn and in a grand variety of places the gardener does not want it. Usually a few can be left, anyway, even in unlikely spots, where they present an air of inspired carelessness. This poppy is either single, like a teacup nodding on its stem, or double, as double as a peony. It is handsome long before it blooms, with its nodding buds, and the seed pods that follow are also beautiful and ingenious little architectural follies.

The main reason we do not see more poppies, even in sunny cottage-type gardens, is simply that we think of them in the spring, which is too late to plant either seeds or roots. Let us think of them in June, the correct time, and prepare a small bed—or a large one—that can be very lightly scratched in August, and the seed sown.

The seeds are sown almost on top of the soil. Just barely covered. When they behave well, as they sometimes do, nothing is more silky, bright, innocent, brave, or festive in the early summer.

Camellias

Every gardener should have a camellia and this capital would be the better for it if all business stopped until every gardener got one planted.

But we may as well address ourselves to the plain truth of the business: every year we shall go through a period from January to April when we do not know, and cannot well predict, whether the camellias will be beautiful or a total loss. This is the time of year, I well know, that tries the camellia's soul. Gray foggy days, a bit above freezing, are grand weather for camellias, but the gardener trembles during those spells when the temperature is in the 60s and the sun comes out. There comes a point when the flower buds, which camellias form in July, swell to the point of no return. Once they reach a certain condition and size, they show color and begin to open. It is at that critical time that endless damage can be done by snow, ice, or a drop to 14 degrees.

Last March, to cite a rather disgusting example, the camellias never looked better. Then there was a two-day period at the end of the month, as the flowers were beginning to color, in which we had sleet. For most gardeners, not a single camellia plant bloomed decently last year. Sleet, incidentally, is the worst five-letter four-letter word I know.

In spite of the terrible weather (it was ironic that non-garden-ers scarcely even noticed it) and in spite of other inevitable dis-appointments with camellias in years to come, I think it may be flatly said that the camellia must rank as one of the preeminent ornaments of Southern gardens as far north as Washington. Even last year some camellias bloomed almost normally. That is because through some accident or quirk of microclimate or interior plant chemistry these camellias were a little behind the others—their buds were not so far advanced.

No culture, no care in siting the plants, can entirely prevent bitter disappointments with camellias this far north. So much the greater reason, then, to do everything we can to choose varieties most likely to succeed, and to give them every advantage in their actual siting in the garden. First, it is critical to plant hardy va-rieties. Today we shall think only of *Camellia japonica* varieties since these are the camellias most people think of when "camellia" is said. What is required for a camellia at the northern fringe of its possible culture in the outdoor garden is a robust cold-hardy plant that sets buds that do not open in warm spells. The National Arboretum has experimented for years with many varieties—the collection there numbers more than one hundred japonica sorts—and can vouch for the following varieties. Others may be as good or better, but these at least have proved their practical outdoor-garden worth here in the capital, and a beginner should give the list some weight:

Red—'Arejishi,' 'Blood of China,' 'Governor Mouton,' 'Mathotiana,' and 'Tricolor Sieboldi.'

White—'Finlandia,' 'Leucantha,' and 'White Queen.'

Variegated (white and red or pink)—'Donckelarii,' 'Elegans,' 'Lady Vansittart,' and 'Ville de Nantes.'

Light Pink—'Berenice Boddy,' 'Dr. Tinsley,' 'Magnoliaeflora,' 'Marjorie Magnificent,' and 'Pink Perfection.' (I personally have the gravest doubts about 'Pink Perfection,' but they say it does well outdoors here.)

Deep Pink or Rose—'Kumasake' and 'Lady Clare.'

My own suggestion would be to start with any of the pink or rose sorts. 'Magnoliaeflora,' for example, is semi-double, flesh pink with deeper flushes, and it blooms so heavily that a good-sized bush will invariably stop traffic. But then the same is true of the others, too.

In the garden it is important to remember the warm spells that can occur at any time from January on. For this reason, the camellia should be planted out from a north wall, or in high woodland (if you have any high woodland on your thirty-foot lot) where it gets no winter sun and where it is not stimulated to start into growth at every warm spell. Often gardeners think they should give camellias a "protected" place like the corner of a southeast wall. Nothing could be worse, and in such a location the camellias will often or usually be ruined. They do want protection, but not that kind. Pine branches forty feet above them and shelter from the winter sun—that is the kind of protection camellias appreciate here.

The plants are easy to grow. Give them woodland conditions when you can. Failing that, give them a soil well laced with leaf mold or peat moss. They grow in the same kind of soil Kurume azaleas do, and anybody going about Washington has noticed that those azaleas grow extremely well here. When possible, get thick, bushy plants about knee high to waist high. Failing that, get the plants that seem thriftiest and most compact, not the rangiest. It must be admitted that many camellias are leggy when young, however. They appreciate normal moisture. Supplemental watering in July and August is often necessary, but do not imagine these plants are temperamental or fussy or require any special skill to grow. Give the plant a mulch of pine needles. Do not mulch with peat moss, which packs down. Peat moss well mixed into the planting soil, however, is excellent. Plant the camellias outdoors in March or April, before the soft new growth begins. You'll be glad.

The Tulip Connection

Thirteen. ☐ Sometimes the gardener takes it into his head to have a good batch of tulips of all colors. Nothing is easier to achieve, but as with everything else you have to think what you are doing and be wary of words. I should say that often the gardener planting the tulips says, in November, that he will grow them "for cutting," so his Assistant (greatly given to luxurious ways) can have jugs of them sitting about the house. Indeed, if money is a bit short, the gardener will find the expenditure is received with better grace if he or she announces, "Well, the tulip bulbs don't cost anything like as much as tulips at the flower shop," and usually the non-gardener will agree.

When the tulips bloom, of course, it usually turns out they brighten the garden sufficiently that the gardener sulks if they are cut. "It is sort of dumb," the gardener may say, for example, "to strip the garden for a few bowls of flowers anybody can get in a shop." I have even heard of gardeners who got downright disagreeable. "Here," the gardener says, "is three bucks. Go buy some from the florist." Three bucks does not buy a great many, and usually the Assistant never goes off and buys any but is greatly inhibited from cutting tulips on a large scale.

But, to get back, it is often written that tulips for cutting may be grown in an unused part of the vegetable garden, a good sunny loamy place that in past years has been generously treated to cow manure. The truth is, I have never known anybody who had "an unused part of the vegetable garden," and the tulips must therefore be planted wherever room can be found for them. Often a foot or two can be stolen at the edge of shrubs, say in front of low junipers. And yet it is a rare gardener who has not already appropriated pretty much every square foot already for something else. A common ruse is to narrow the grass walk on the theory that it doesn't have to be all that wide and a few clumps of tulips will help things a lot. That is not a good thing to do, but since I have more than once done it, I will say it certainly is one way to get space for tulips.

As far as I am concerned there is no right or wrong way to group tulips. One year Woodward & Lothrop's Chevy Chase store had a spectacular display in a flower bed out front composed entirely of tulips in every color imaginable, all mixed up together. It was much handsomer than those blocks of tulips in one color such as they use in parks, where often the main pleasure people get from them is discovering one yellow tulip in a bed of five hundred red ones. Growing tulips in great blocks of solid color derives, no doubt, from the practice of Dutch growers, who have to keep the varieties separate in their commercial fields. Those who perpetuate it are probably dull sorts who worry a great deal about colors clashing, and about doing the wrong thing. The wholesome, ebullient gardener need not emulate it. If he has room for only a few dozen bulbs and loves many dozen varieties, he should plant one of each. If his garden is enormous, of course it makes sense to have a great number of one variety planted solid together. Also, if there is a long wide border for flowers (say 100 by 14 feet) it is agreeable to plant tulips in clumps of six or a dozen in separate colors, since there will be room for many colors as the clumps proceed down the border.

But it is not true that one tulip alone looks like nothing. One year I gave a friend one bulb each of fifteen varieties we were unfamiliar with. That gardener planted each bulb several feet distant from the next, and I was astonished to see how well they looked. Tulips look least well, perhaps, when planted single file in ribbon edgings, but if the effect pleases the gardener then why not?

One pitfall, if one wants a bed of all colors, is that tulips sold as "mixed" usually have only a few varieties included in the mixture. Once I bought 100 mixed Hybrid Darwins, and there were only three varieties in the mixture. I have read of gardeners finding only one variety in a mixture. A better word than "mixed" would be "unlabeled," with the note that one should not expect a complete sampling of tulip colors.

Sometimes it is feasible (I have done it) to keep an eye on bulb sales at local garden shops. Grand assortments can be made, a few bulbs of many different kinds, and in that way one knows he will get all the colors he likes, in just the proportions he likes.

Satisfying Your Wildest Desires

Wild tulips, unlike their domesticated cousins, are not the plants to make a big splash in the garden, but they are charming nonetheless, reminiscent of brisk terriers, except better behaved.

For years these small tulips were rare and costly; now that everything is costly, they seem cheap, and even if they never bloomed they would be worth getting merely for the high delight of examining the bulbs. Nothing is neater in the entire world than these small bulbs, often smaller than a butterbean, wrapped in their natural skin or tunic which is sometimes like satin, sometimes like a russet pear, and sometimes lined with a soft yellow-brown fur that sticks out the top of the bulb a trifle.

All the wild tulips I have tried bloom roughly with the daffodils, April being their great month. They are best planted in the first half of November, but often the bulb merchants sell out before then, so I like to get them as soon as I can, especially since it is so agreeable to peer at the different shapes in the few weeks before they must be planted outdoors.

It must be remembered that they come from various parts of the Middle East and Central Asia, and the ideal site for them is a sunny slope to the south or west, and if it bakes hard all summer, fine. They are not at all suited to shady woodlands; they have nothing to do with deep woodsy peaty soil that suits camellias. Sometimes people have a bleak, sunny bare place near a garage or by a back-door step, and such sites are good for the tulips, although life in an ordinary border suits them well enough if it's not too damp in summer. They do not care much for having luxuriant plants flop over the earth where they are planted, even when their own leaves have died in May. They do not mind golden thyme or other modest plants crawling over them, and portulaca does well since it flowers all summer when the tulips are gone and only comes back from self-sown seeds when the tulip foliage is passing off in May.

Too great an issue has been made in the past of the cultural requirements of wild tulips, so the novice might think they were difficult. They are not. When bulbs are rare, people always suppose they are difficult to grow, and of course the English, with their frightful climate and general failure of sunlight, would have more trouble with bulbs from sunny lands than we. Since the English are the world's best gardeners and garden writers, their well-publicized disappointments with some of the tulips frightened many gardeners of sunny regions who in fact never had any reason for alarm.

They are ideal in rock gardens—if anyone is still so reckless and extravagant as to possess one—and they do not mind clay. Often I work a couple of handfuls of sand into heavy clay loam when I plant.

The best-known wild tulip is *Tulipa clusiana*, which has narrow bluish-gray leaves and a slender stalk fourteen inches high, holding the flower which seems broadly striped vertically because its petals alternate cherry and white. On warm days the flower opens flat and is all white inside, but like other tulips it closes at night, again showing the soft color of its outer petals. Once I grew a patch the size of a bathroom rug with this tulip, planted seven inches deep, and over the tops of those bulbs a batch of hoop-petticoat daffodils, about four inches deep, and over those a gang of crocuses (*C. chrysanthus*) about two inches deep. Over the years, the crocuses objected, dying out here and there but marshaling their forces toward the edge of the patch. The wild daffodils diminished slightly in the first four years, then held steady. The tulips did not increase much, but never dwindled.

T. clusiana, which according to a Royal Horticultural Society article is sterile, commonly seeds (doubtless the result of our sunnier climate) and I had a friend who was startled to see this tulip blooming all along the edges of a small drainage trough in a border of irises. The tulips seeds floated down with the rains, and in a few years (perhaps four) began to bloom. I mention this to show that we need not panic for our wild tulips every time it rains.

Another curious tulip is *T. acuminata*, which for some reason I have never grown. When I was a young gardener this tulip was costly, and the petals were said to look like the fingernails of Chinese ladies. Perhaps the price and the description turned me against the flower. Now the bulbs are quite reasonable. The flowers suggest a Santa Barbara girl who gave up tennis for macrame, that is, they look a bit odd, as if they had tried drugs and lived in Tangiers awhile, yet they are interesting.

I used to wonder why anybody would fool with *T. tarda*. It is only two or three inches high and its flowers are star-shaped and green outside but yellow and white inside. First of all, it sometimes grows to six inches instead of two, but mainly this is a fine example of a modest plant whose virtues are never quite captured in print. I first grew it only to try to comprehend why merchants kept selling it. Now I know. It is one of those plants you never want to be without. It is as exuberant and vigorous as it is small. It costs only a few cents, and looks fine against cobblestones.

Now, *T. batalinii* is five inches high and slightly balloon-shaped, of soft yellow a bit deeper than primrose, sometimes flushed with a madder-type rose. The long-rare *T. urumiensis* is somewhat similar, a bit more bronzed, as I remember it dimly.

T. kaufmanniana and its endless hybrids bloom with the hyacinths, early in the daffodil season, and it comes in many patterns of rose-madder, cherry, red, ivory, sulphur, and gold, opening out flat (as wild tulips generally do) in the sun. Its flowers are relatively large and suggest water lilies against a nest of leaves. The early tulips at the northwest corner of the National Geographic Building in recent years have been varieties of this tulip and *T. greigii*, which has leaves striped and mottled with madder-maroon.

There are a number of other wildlings, every one desirable to try: *T. praestans* has clusters of vermilion blooms, shocking in brilliance and clarity. *T. pulchella violacea* is short, relatively big in bloom, and an amazing rich soft magenta. *T. eichleri* is a bit fatter than *T. praestans* and blooms a bit later and its vermilion is not quite so brilliant, though it would still make a fire engine seem pale.

One of my favorite flowers is *T. chrysantha*, almond-shaped, ten inches high, soft yellow with alternate petals soft red on the outside. Most gardeners like it, of course, and then go on to the next thing, but I practically faint dead away every spring when it blooms.

Please do not sneer at any wild tulip unmentioned here, or assume it is less good than those I have named. Few indulgences are so painless or so relatively wholesome as an assortment of wild tulip bulbs. For a modest sum you can get quite a few, and they last for some years, many of them more than ten or fifteen years, without lifting the bulbs or spraying or even fertilizing.

Taming the Tulip

Tulips started showing up in Western gardens in the reign of Elizabeth—I don't recall Shakespeare's mentioning them, but then he was a garden snob, preferring wild meadow flowers—and ever since, they have been correctly regarded as major treasures. It has always been the Dutch who were the great masters of their cultivation (coming from the Middle East and Central Asia as they do, it is remarkable that tulips can be made to grow in Holland at all, much less to thrive there). I have muttered and grumbled in the past about the Dutch taste in daffodils, comparing it as unfavorably as possible with that of the English and Irish daffodil breeders, but I humbly acknowledge the Dutch preeminence in tulips. Not only have they raised this flower to quite undreamed-of heights of beauty, they have also improved its weak constitution past recognition, mastered to perfection the mass growing of the bulbs, and pioneered and still lead in the area of bulb curing and storage, and they do all this so efficiently that their tulips are marketed throughout the world at reasonable prices.

At this moment, however, I want to take into consideration one particular—and startlingly valuable—achievement: their development of the Darwin Hybrids. In order to do this, it is necessary to say a little about the history of the tulip in general. For almost three centuries the tulips favored in western gardens were "broken"; that is, the basic color of the flowers was interrupted by flames and streaks of another color, giving quite rich and bizarre effects. The time came, however, when it occurred to gardeners that tulips need not be grown merely for the bizarre and flamed patterns of the individual flower, but were even handsomer when the color was solid and unbroken. So there was a little flurry to collect or retrieve the old solid-color tulips, at the time in actual danger of dying out, and from them emerged the old Darwin tulips in the nineteenth century.

The flowers of the Darwins had a squared-off look at the base instead of being curved and cuplike, and their stems were sturdy, not pliable and curved like the old Cottage varieties. Blooms of the Cottages are more cup-shaped, and come in bright, sparkling colors. Both types are late April and early May-flowering, as are Breeders, which run to purple and fawn combinations or rose flushed with gold—rich and often sweet-scented.

But now the Darwin Hybrids are something quite different. They result from crosses between the Darwins and the wild vermilion *Tulipa fosteriana*. (This may be the place to say that it was rather discouraging to the Dutch, after three and a half centuries of breeding garden tulips, to discover in the wild a tulip larger, more richly colored, and more dazzling than any in cultivation. The tulip we commonly grow in gardens as 'Red Emperor' is nothing more than a selection from the wild stock of *T. fosteriana*. It has no garden blood in it; it is a pure wildling.)

The Dutch took one look at the wild *T. fosteriana*, and determined to breed its size, its remarkable constitution, its flamboyance into the garden tulips that already existed. They crossed the Darwins with it, and the race is called Darwin Hybrids, but the critical parent is not the Darwin but the fosteriana.

In Darwin Hybrids you find a very special combination of traits: enormous flowers (compared to most garden tulips) that bloom with the midseason or late daffodils, some days before most older garden tulips do, but later than 'Red Emperor,' and a reasonable and good color range of primrose, canary-mustard, and (the glory of the tribe) scarlets. Even in damp Washington, I have had some of these Darwin Hybrids produce enormous flowers from bulbs planted outdoors and left untouched for five years.

I have not grown all of the Darwin Hybrids, but perhaps twelve sorts over a period of years, and can say that my favorite is 'Jewel of Spring.' This is an ivory yellow, yellow but not brilliant like a teen-ager's Mustang, of colossal size on stems nearly waist high. (Officially 26 inches, but often taller.) The petals are edged with a thread of red so slight it is not noticed at the distance of a few feet, and for all practical purposes the tulip is solid buff-primrose. It is just the color that blends beautifully with any other. My first acquaintance with it some years ago, and its enthusiastic reception by those who plan the flowers of London parks, and the unmistakable affection with which it was referred to in the beginning by some of the Dutch tulip authorities, all led me to suspect it was a tulip among tulips, and the years have only increased my admiration.

'Jewel of Spring' is a sport—a mere (and wonderful) mutation of color—of the Darwin Hybrid 'Gudoshnik,' which is a creamy peach flecked and nutmegged with rose. I like 'Gudoshnik' very much, but it is a variable flower, yellow inside, and sometimes rather light, sometimes dark. This upsets some gardeners who call it unstable, but I find it very beautiful, and it has every good quality a tulip can have, and unlike most tulips it can last in beauty outdoors for a full three weeks.

A fine scarlet is 'Apeldoorn,' one of the first varieties put on the market. A great authority on these flowers observed several years ago that he still thought it his favorite of the Darwin Hybrid scarlets, standing up to weather uncommonly well. 'Golden Apeldoorn' is a deep yellow sport from it, and 'Beauty of Apeldoorn' is another sport, yellow, prettily stippled with carmine. 'President Kennedy' is a full, rich yellow, sometimes flushed scarlet but usually not.

Among the older scarlets are 'Dover,' 'Lefeber's Favorite,' 'Oxford,' 'General Eisenhower,' and 'Holland's Glory,' all of them fine. Indeed, I have never seen any Darwin Hybrid on the market that was not worthy of a place in the most select garden. But if you cannot grow them all, at least try five or six bulbs each of the great wild fosteriana, 'Red Emperor,' and its soft yellow descendant, the Darwin Hybrid 'Jewel of Spring.'

There was one year that I somehow lost track of which bulbs I was ordering from which grower, and then picked up a few more here and there at various garden centers around town. The following spring I ended up with about three hundred gaudy fosterianas on my forty-foot lot. Frankly, I would not have needed so many. But then, as I pointed out to my wife, one does not want to come up short, and with as many as three hundred on the premises I might even be able to spare a few to cut for the house.

Reflections on Gardening

Expect Not the Impossible, But Revel in the Magical

Fourteen. □ A fellow reproaches me for mentioning too many plants he's never heard of and not enough of the ones he has.

Marigold, marigold, marigold. So much for that.

It's important, isn't it, to think of the garden as a wonderful place to be, full of wonders (not necessarily rarities) and enchantments at all seasons. Some mischief has been done, probably, by calling the garden an "outdoor living room," as if any living room in the world had such wonderful things in it as a garden has. And as for "plant material," that is one of the supremely vulgar phrases of this language, and I hope if anybody has been using it, he will stop immediately. It is a barbarism. Plants are not "material." The phrase is commonly used by people of careless habits, indifferent brains, and, I suspect, no morals whatever. We do not want, therefore, any "plant materials" in any "outdoor living room," but we do want bushes, herbs, flowers, water-plants, and so on, and while we all have sense enough not to expect the impossible, we have a right to expect the magical.

The first lesson we might learn is that the point of the garden is to be wonderful, yet almost any gardener at first does not think that way. He thinks instead of maximal floral tissue, how to jam as much flowering flesh as possible into the gaudy day. He is on the right track, wanting all those flowers, but he will be forced by experience and his own disappointment to change his view a little, because the truth is that too much beauty (or what the gardener first thinks is beauty) simply defeats itself. The garden will not give the effect the gardener wants if it is planted solid with, say, zinnias. There are too many months of the year when zinnias do not bloom, and even when they do bloom, they are tiresome if the place is solid with them.

Sooner or later the gardener sees something somewhere that he thinks looks splendid, and he does well to stop to see exactly what is growing there that makes him happy to see it. In almost every case, the eye will go to some wonderful color or shape—it may be a sensational spread of scarlet roses against a white wall— and he says ha, it's the roses against the white wall. But often that is not the secret of the garden. The sober green yews, the twining Carolina jasmine, the tropical foliage of the grape vine, the misty gray-white clump of Russian sage (and not one of these in flower or fruit at the time of the roses) are the true reason the rose against the wall looks so wonderful.

Plain solid masonry, plain sturdy wood, plain expanses of water (fountains are almost always a disappointment to those who try them), and plenty of plants that are beautiful (not necessarily showy)—these are the components of the garden.

Even if the gardener is a nut for some particular plant—rose, iris, lily, poppy, chrysanthemum—even then, some thought might be given to what the garden looks like in January, or August.

The main space and the best space may well be devoted to the favorite flower, but it will look all the better in its transient season—and let me emphasize how transient the season of full bloom is, no matter what the flower—if such things as yews, junipers, kerrias, hostas, rosemarys, pinks, sedums, grasses, and honeysuckles are part of the general plan. Not one of them is startlingly beautiful in bloom, yet no gardener who has ever experienced the richness that modest plants give a garden will ever willingly revert to a solid fence-to-fence tangle of marigolds, irises, azaleas, peonies, or anything else.

Do not hold it against a plant if it flowers only once a year, or suppose that a variety that flowers repeatedly is somehow better. A repeat-blooming rose like 'Blaze' is hardly any rival of supremely beautiful roses like 'Silver Moon' or 'Mme. Gregoire Staechelin' which bloom only in May. What is the point of perpetual flowering or sumptuous color if the result falls short of the very magic the gardener is looking for? Think of the lilac. It has no color to boast of, no admirable foliage, no lengthy season. It is not even a very good-looking plant, yet it has its place, for its scent and its modest unassertive charm. Would the lilac really be better if the trusses were thirty inches long and scarlet?

A garden, to my mind, ought to be rich in plants. I could never be satisfied with something like Versailles or the Villa d'Este or Union Station. Most gardeners, alas, share my fault of wanting one (maybe we could work in half a dozen?) of everything. Even so, we can minimize our fault, I think, by choosing some plant like the grape vine and using a great deal of it in different ways (on wires, over arbors, on walls, on garlanded chains, in trees) to give some sort of unity.

The whole trouble, needless to say, is that there is no easy formula. We want lots of color but we also want repose and calmness. We want richness, but we do not want giddiness. We want good proportions—yet the size of plants is constantly changing. We do not want so many evergreens that the place looks like a setting for a memorial to General Patton; on the other hand, we do not want such masses of raging colors that the eye is sated and bored, or confused.

Things must work together. We can spend our lives venturing enough so that we make mistakes (mistakes in the sense that we do not like the result, that we had thought was going to be so fine) and then working out of them.

If we persist, I do not doubt that by age 96 or so we will all have gardens we are pleased with, more or less.

In the meantime, we usually learn that modesty, charm, reliability, freshness, calmness, are as satisfying in a garden as anywhere else. And in plugging right along, patience, and freedom from fretting, are supreme gardening virtues.

A Matter of Scale and Passion

Young gardeners (those who do not think of themselves as old gardeners) often have trouble with "indispensable" plants. I mean by this that we are always being told some plant or other is utterly necessary for the garden. Somewhere recently I saw *Lonicera fragrantissima* recommended as an absolute necessity for the winter garden. True, it blooms (or can bloom) in January when not many shrubs are in flower; and it has a truly ravishing scent, like the [much-despised] Japanese honeysuckle of our woods, which we usually regard as native and therefore worthless. But it is not quite so sweet as to deserve "fragrantissima." Surely "fragrans" would have been sufficient. It can make a great rounded shrub twelve feet high, like a great bun or loaf of bread. It is halfheartedly evergreen—it drops its leaves in the fall but perhaps a third of them hang on, somewhat discolored. The flowers come at the leaf axils. They are not ugly. On the other hand, they are not very beautiful, either. They are off-white, or non-color.

All my life I have loved this shrub, but not excessively, and not to the point of folly.

If I had a woodland, then this shrub might well go in toward the edge of it somewhere, because its fragrance is splendid on mild, damp, late-winter days. It is also good to cut big branches of for the house, if you happen to like branches of shrubs in the house. (It looks less shabby if you pull off all the leaves of any cut branches before setting them in jars or vases.)

But my point is this: a shrub that might do very well if you had plenty of room, may not do at all if you have only a very small garden. And please consider this, too: if this particular shrub brought back happier memories for you than any other, then you might well wish to plant it; also, if for reasons peculiar to yourself the shrub seems just wonderful in its beauty, then of course you should grow it. But I was thinking of normal gardeners.

It is not enough for a plant to do something unique. All plants do something unique. That is how you tell them from other plants. So no, this shrub honeysuckle will not get in this garden merely by shouting it is one of those extremely rare plants that gives fragrant flowers in winter. The box and the yew do not have scented flowers even in the spring, let alone the winter; and yet I say to you that they are a good bit more exciting, and even a good bit more comforting, in the winter than the gawky shrub honeysuckle is.

Do not be swept off your feet by the claims of a plant, however heady they may sound at first. Hold on. Ask it, "Apart from your so-called marvelous performance in winter, how do you do in spring, fall, summer? And apart from your flowers, which of course are all very well, how is your general air and average appearance through the year? Do you enhance other plants, or detract?"

No need to lash the honeysuckle, of course. No plant is perfect. On the other hand, no need to value it excessively for its uniqueness. Every snowflake is unique, but you don't see gardeners running up and down the alleys about it.

In judging plants for the small garden, please follow this scale which I have spent some years perfecting and which is now correct:

• Personal passion. If a plant is one you cannot live without, it is often well to plant it.

• Beauty. This is a complex matter, consisting of the balance between color, shape, texture of blossom and structure, texture, bark, and so on, apart from blossom. If we are to understand beauty, or at least recognize it, it is necessary to pay attention.

• Feasibility. Let me merely say that almost all plants turn out feasible if the gardener is sold on their beauty.

Magenta Azaleas Are OK

People are forever coming up to ask, "Is it all right if I have a magenta azalea?"

And I always answer, "Yes."

This relieves them only a little, and with great wistfulness they always say, "But I only have a cruddy modern house—it's got (gulp) modern bricks in it."

"Even so," I invariably respond, "you go right ahead and have your magenta azalea. And what is more, you may plant red tulips in front of it."

Some go on their way rejoicing when they hear this. But others, beaten down by too many years of being pontificated at, turn away sorrowing, because they have read that only lemon-colored azaleas are okay and even they are vulgar except in front of seventeenth-century wood houses in Old Pottebelle, Vermont. One can do only so much to assist such gardeners, and I know they will probably settle for ferns or a nomocharis or a romneya (nomocharises and romneyas are okay because common gardeners don't have them).

I should like to give thanks to whoever invented magenta azaleas. There is nothing more gorgeous in the vegetable kingdom.

As far as that goes, no color is more magnificent than a good firm determined magenta. Nothing more royal. Of all magenta flowers (there are many) none excels the azalea for giving one a really good eyeful of it.

In England they have no sunlight or heat of a natural sunny sort, as indeed their gardeners are forever complaining. They make do—their gardens are the loveliest in the world today, largely because of the almost insurmountable challenge of the gray climate. There is nothing like impossibility for getting a gardener's energies up. Knowing that by nature they cannot (and do not) have anything, they have set themselves with zeal to the task of making gardens in the very face of the devil and the North Sea.

But their triumph is hard won. They do not care so much in bleak places for magenta azaleas because they have learned that in the pale light of their unfavorably situated islands anything more assertive than a snowdrop tends to look like Baghdad in flames.

This brave land, by contrast, has a climate the English would give their right arm for with its sunlight and skies and felicitous warmths of summer. In its strong light, a certain boldness of color —stronger than shadblow pink, say—does not come amiss.

But suppose it did. Suppose it were judged, even by the high authorities here, that magenta azaleas were a trifle vulgar or a *soupçon* gross. Even so (or especially so) I would remind the gardener that his yearning for this gorgeous color and this gorgeous plant is a far more authoritative arbiter of correctness in his own garden than anything he might read. Not that we decry gardening ruminations in print. Far from it. But a garden is somewhat exalted above ordinary notions of correctness. A garden is more than a matter of the right fish fork, as it were.

On the contrary, a garden is (for the gardener) not so much a picture that will please the faint-eyed, but a cycle of wheeling life, encompassing more than trifling designs of color which (if that's what you're after) may so easily be had in pastry tarts. So *floreat liliorum*, as they say at one of the schools, or (in the vernacular) let the magenta azaleas be everywhere.

eave Your Plants Alone

f of mankind permits many great
rt, such as trudging about on the
od quality it has its dark side.
n bent for never leaving anything alone
ction of plants from all over the world and
gnificent gardens in places where nature did
to grow so much as a single tree. Or—converse-
s in places like our own eastern coast where na-
reat lack of imagination, could devise nothing better
gloomy forest from pole to pole.
ort, there is much to be said for the human determina-
be forever fiddling with things that were perfectly ade-
te to start with.

The trouble arises when this poking and prodding and sampling is precisely the wrong thing for a plant subjected to it. How
difficult it is for us to remember that plants are totally unhuman
and that they exist in quite different rhythms from us. They are
not geared for action, if you stop and think of it, in the way that
we are, and they would be much better off if we stopped pestering
them all the time.

The current fad for talking and singing to plants and telling
them we love them will probably result in nothing more impressive than a vastly increased rate of plant mortality—as gardeners
proceed farther and farther down the foolish road of what they
presume to be utter communion.

People who would blush to defend, intellectually, the notion
of plant consciousness, nevertheless assume that plants are human
—we say, after all, that anemones abhor drafty positions, that pin
oaks prefer a deep soil with more than usual moisture, that rhododendrons despise lime, and so forth. Such is the power of words
that we soon get to expect that plants will behave like people, and
some gardeners become indignant when a camellia, say, behaves
rudely in spite of much kindness on our part.

Before the whole concept goes too far and kills off the vegetable kingdom, let me remind you there are times when the greatest kindness you can do a plant is to leave it strictly alone. And
this should be the easier for us to do, since there is hardly any-

thing to be done for a sick plant; and if the plant i̶
health, then we do well not to upset things by poking ̶

Peonies, as everybody knows, have a curious wa̶
sprouting all at the same time in the spring, especially
spring after they have been planted. Everybody knows,
easily imagine, that when the tender new growths begin
the ground (and they are wonderfully brittle then) it is dang̶
to poke in the dirt around them. And yet, if one peony out o̶
fails to sprout above the ground when "it should," there is pr̶
ably not one gardener in this capital who will not be out the̶
"gently" removing some of the earth over that peony to "se̶
what's the matter." This results, of course, in snapping off the
brittle growth bud in roughly 100 out of 100 cases of investiga-
tion. It wouldn't make any difference except that a new plant may
have only three such growth buds. If the gardener snaps off one,
and the dog sits on the second, and botrytis blight gets the third,
then there is no peony.

Lilies are also killed by the million through our attentions. We
may be too lazy, or too cheap, to provide them with a three-foot-
deep bed of leaf mold (preferring to whine away the decades as
the lilies consistently refuse to flourish) but there is no gardener
alive who lacks the energy to get out there in March and see why
L. auratum is not coming up next to its stake. Like many lilies,
auratum often wanders about underground, its stem resembling a
snake, and it is a very lucky auratum indeed that escapes being
speared by the exploratory gardener. The moral, as everybody has
always known, is to leave lilies strictly alone in late winter, but
like most moral precepts it doesn't do much good merely to know it.

Every mild fall we may expect vast deaths among spring bulbs,
not because the winter is going to bother them, but because gardeners will. By Christmas many daffodils, hyacinths, and tulips
will be showing their noses above the earth. This will certainly
result in Emergency Measures by the gardener who will assume
(nobody knows why he assumes this, but he invariably does) that
these plants cannot bear cold and will be frozen if he doesn't do
something. Although it is very naughty of bulbs to sprout in December, nothing is accomplished by fussing with them. Do not
cover them, do not do anything to make them grow more than
they already have.

Another asinine project greatly favored by us gardeners is the application of heat to outdoor plants. The gardener acquires a camellia, plants it out in September, comprehends it is perfectly hardy, and is well content until the middle of February. At that point, reading that the temperature will drop to 8 degrees, he starts to panic. Usually he or his wife has a friend who suggests the electric light treatment, which consists of running an outdoor light on a cord to a box hastily placed over the plant. The possibilities of damage are, of course, almost endless.

The true time to assist a plant that can be hurt by cold is before you plant it. A well-drained site, a soil extremely rich in humus, protection from overhanging tree branches at least twenty feet above the ground, a position untouched by the morning sun—all these directions for siting camellias have been given for decades, and if they are followed the results are dandy. No later nonsense about lights and boxes will make up for basic indifference and skimpiness.

But suppose the gardener is honest enough (and I have known two or three) to acknowledge that he is far too lazy to do anything really right, because it involves more labor or money than he is prepared to spend. What then, when some crisis arises, such as the tulips sprouting too early or the peonies too late, or the camellias faced with a freeze?

One of the few ways I could really be helpful to any gardener is precisely at this point, because this is something I know with every atom of bone and blood:

DON'T DO ANYTHING AT ALL.

At least give nature a chance, give the plant a fighting chance to survive. Tulips come from some of the bleakest climates of this world—they have great powers of survival if left alone; but no plant has a chance if the one wrong and disastrous thing is done, and that wrong way is invariably the way we gardeners choose.

Man and boy I have snapped off peony buds for nigh on to half a century, and it depresses me to think how many fritillaries I have investigated to death, and the blood of many little cork oaks and *Parthenocissus henryana* and *Pieris forresti* and I don't know how many pretty rarities is on my hands, because I could not leave them alone and give them a chance. If a shrub is frozen to the ground, it may be several months before a new shoot emerges—time after time after time the gardener (who knows all that) starts digging just two weeks short of the plant's recovery, and the plant dies (it will often make only the one effort) when it would have lived if left strictly alone. This is especially true of rather tender shrubs, already on the extreme border of hardiness. Always, always, the rule is to give them a full year or so after they have been killed back.

Not many gardeners will confess right out that they have snapped off many a peony in their busyness and folly, but the most valuable of all lessons for the gardener is that if we are not quite sure what we are doing (which is almost all the time) it is infinitely better to do nothing than to guess. In this way, as in many others, gardening differs from examination papers or business or politics.

Dig It!

I never saw any point in perfectionism for its own sake, such as carving the eyelashes of angels on top of church towers a hundred feet in the air—such exercises are mere busyness and fussiness. And there is no sense, either, in seeing how much labor we can dream up in the garden; there is enough in the nature of the task to suit any reasonable man's sweat.

There is, moreover, the danger that perfectionism easily becomes an excuse for doing nothing at all, so we find gardeners who will not plant things because they know perfectly well they have no intention of digging to China first, and incorporating truckloads of humus: they have been severely frightened or intimidated by too-stern lectures on Soil Preparation. And we must admit that sometimes we get the notion (if we read) that gardening is a burdensome task to which we are expected to devote our lives, our fortunes, and our sacred sacroiliacs.

Fortunately, I am myself as lazy a man as ever lived and you are in no danger whatever of reading here that you should stand on your head and bow thrice before planting basil in the full moon's paralactical ecliptical balderdash the third hour after the fifth rain in March. All the same, some work has to be done or— I guess I should phrase it to avoid the word "work"—some operations are desirable in gardening.

To be very plain with you, I seem to have failed to make it clear that a certain amount of digging is absolutely necessary. Let me give one example. If you happen to be gardening in an open field that has been in cultivation for several years, following a century of pasture grass upon it, and if the soil is such that you can easily dig down three feet without using any pressure to speak of from your back, then all you have to do (to plant a climbing rose, say) is open up the earth to stick the roots of the plant beneath the surface. There is no need to excavate vastly, or add a bushel of leaf mold or anything else. Just get the roots beneath the soil, in dry weather, and firm the soil with your feet when the plant is in, water well, and sit back to enjoy a felicitous result.

The trouble arises (and the occasion of work) when for some reason you do not happen to have a loamy field in full sun, but instead have the usual compound of rock, tenacious clay, scrap lumber, rusted snuff cans, etc., or, in other words, the typical soil of American city gardens.

Sometimes you will wonder, if you have much time to waste, how it is possible for humans to occupy land for upwards of two centuries without improving it. But when the reverie is done, it will still be necessary to begin.

To plant the same climbing rose in your small garden (we are now moving away from the example of the loamy field) it will not do at all merely to get the roots under the surface. Something more is required. Not because some drudge says so, but because the rose will not grow—I repeat, it will not grow—if you just scrape away the grass and chop a hole into which the roots may (with some ingenuity and pushing) be jammed. I know because I repeatedly tried it, before I saw the light.

The hole for the plant should be at least twenty inches wide by twenty inches deep, and the earth with which the hole is filled must be full of humus and friable. This is accomplished by working in a bushel or two of peat moss, digging it into the original dirt, until it is uniform in texture. Then you proceed just as if you were planting in the loamy field.

Now this is a very different thing from saying you must dig the entire garden forty inches deep and lay drain tiles, and put a twelve-inch layer of two-year-old cow manure at the bottom and have the soil tested and zub, zub, zub. Any gardener who wishes to carry on in a grand manner is free to do so, but in the example of the rose plant I am saying merely what seems to me absolutely necessary if the plant is to have a chance.

Even if you are lazy, as I am, you will quickly see the difference between extravagant carryings on and minimal preparation of the site which is to contain the living rose.

The shocking thing, and a measure of failure that haunts me on bad nights, is the number of people who seem surprised or hurt when informed of the very minimum for a rose. Surprised or not, hurt or not, I could assure them that if I say "this much is really necessary" then it really is, because I am not one to labor for general amusement.

It is true (and this makes me sympathetic) there are pressures from all sides on the gardener to buy this and buy that. The message that gets through is that if you acquire enough fertilizer, enough tools, enough plants, then you have done your bit, and are entitled to a dandy garden. But that is nonsense, when you examine it. The plant does not care whether you bought anything at all, and it will not be nice to you merely because you spent the children's lunch money for your garden equipment.

No, the plant requires no more (and no less) than the chance to grow and flourish, and this may be quite independent of anything you buy. Consider the rhododendrons of the forest—nobody carried on about them to get them planted. Nevertheless, you will never find them except in those places naturally suited to their requirements.

Of all the techniques of gardening which are aimed to promote the general flourishing of plants, allow me to say what I personally believe is the truth, that nothing else is quite so important as digging, and giving the plant an earth of good texture to get started in.

This blessing cannot, alas, be bought for a dollar at a store, but must come from your labor. No, not necessarily your labor—but from somebody's labor. To break this news as gently as I can, I am showing you a little illustration of a frog with a spade. It is from the late Dean Hole's book on gardening, from the last century. He trained his frogs to do the digging. And if you can do the same, you may safely forget this whole sermon.

Avoid the Bare-Earth Policy

Bare earth bothers me because nature leaves nothing bare that will support life. Often I have reflected this is why men worry about baldness. In any case, ground in the garden that is not planted solid with ornamental plants will soon be solid with weeds, so the point is to cover the ground. Also, there are many places in which one wants the calm effect of a large mass of one sort of plant. Often under trees, where grass will not flourish, the Japanese pachysandra makes a rich dark glossy evergreen cover, requiring hardly any maintenance and giving a neat and finished appearance to earth that would otherwise be sparsely furnished with a few struggling weeds.

The common ivy, and its endless varieties, is a beautiful ground cover, though it should be clipped over every year or two so it does not get too dense. When rank, it is susceptible to bacterial leaf blight, and it then loses its leaves, but if the gardener is patient (or even if he is not) it soon revives and sends out new growth.

Often one does not want a dense solid cover like ivy or pachysandra, however, but clumps of foliage strong enough to take care of themselves under trees, with open spaces left for such spring flowers as Spanish scillas and the tougher sorts of daffodils. The barrenworts, or epimediums, are very good. The common yellow one has foliage good all the year, as handsome as a maidenhair fern, almost, but its root is tough and it will hold on even in a woodland laced with tree roots.

The plantain lilies or hostas are not quite as fond of dense shade as most gardeners think, and flourish best in a rich border

shaded a bit from full sun. But under thick woodland conditions the hostas will grow if the gardener can devise some way of keeping them supplied with water. The huge-leaf one usually called *H. subcordata grandiflora*, with ribbed leaves the size of cantaloupes, is good along a shady walk if well treated. If left to struggle without coddling, its great leaves are small as a hand, but even then they are handsome and the highly scented white trumpet flowers in August and September are welcome.

On sunny banks the prostrate junipers are beautiful, especially the ones that turn violet in winter. Most of these will reach three feet if not trained as young plants. I once watched the tamarisk-leaf juniper proceed over a bank with increasing vigor, reaching knee height in a couple of years. I did not know it had to be clipped and encouraged to hug the ground. Those who want it low will find it can be kept to a foot and treated like a lawn—a very prickly lawn that will not take any wear and tear, of course.

This may be the place to remind the innocent that vines and creepers (including roses) can be a poor choice for ground cover. One of my favorite plants is Hall's Japanese honeysuckle, a plant of exceptional merit though widely despised by snobs who rarely have any judgment in assessing beauty and who cannot abide plants that grow nicely along alleys and ditches. But this honeysuckle will climb up any young tree and ruin it, of course, and if not clipped back occasionally it mounds itself up to three or four feet. Any number of creatures, including wasps, like the shelter it affords. It is an extremely dangerous choice, therefore, for covering a bank. It is not dense enough to retard weeds, by the way. It has a merry way of flinging out runners on the ground, which must be watched for, or they will wander for twenty-five feet and then start climbing up something. Equally dangerous, and by no means so beautiful, is the bittersweet with orange berries in the fall.

On the Necessity
of Keeping Garden Records

On or about April 9, I had occasion to check on the tadpoles of our native American toad. This essay is not going to be about toads, but you doubtless have noticed the toad tadpoles are extremely early this year. Last year it was end of the first week in

May that I noticed the tadpoles around Great Falls. This year, in deference to the warm February that so pleased us all, I supposed the tadpoles might be three weeks ahead of last year. Sure enough, they had just hatched out at Great Falls, both in the rock pools and in the shallowest parts of the Chesapeake and Ohio Canal itself.

If I had not made a note last year of the date of tadpoles, I would not have been able this year to estimate their probable arrival time.

This is a plea for the keeping of garden records and weather records, not because it is really important to anybody else, but because the person who keeps the records gets so much pleasure from it. Also, records reassure us (or have thus far) that the world is not going to fall utterly apart. It is those who know least about weather who get most upset at what they presume is Communist interference with atoms, or some such nonsense. I have never myself lived through a particularly amazing year as far as weather is concerned—except perhaps two great floods of the Lower Mississippi (well within the range of normal river behavior) and the great Dust Bowl droughts of the West in the 1930s. I spent a summer in Montana and found the drought astonishing enough. And yet we have always known that rainfall sooner or later will fail in those regions, and it is always a gamble to use prairie lands for things other than grass. The fact that nothing but grass grew there to begin with is a clue that they will not support oak forests, or crops that require much water.

The point is, if we keep up with the tadpoles for some years, we soon learn the range of dates within which we can always count on finding them. We will not be surprised, then, to find them in early April one year or early May another, for we will know these variations are normal in nature.

Thomas Jefferson was a great weather buff, at Monticello and while far distant from it, too. He wrote his daughter on March 9, 1791 (for example), from Philadelphia to say he had heard frogs for the first time that year on March 7. He asked when she had first heard them at Monticello, and (knowing how bad she was about paying strict attention to such things) admonished her to be lazy no more, but to keep records. The poor girl never quite got into the spirit of jotting down all the statistics Jefferson was interested in. Once she said she had been so busy with the chickens, trying to hatch them out and raise them, that she had had no time at all to notice the martins, etc.

But Jefferson, despite the inconveniences of absence from home and the sad failure of Maria to keep an eye on everything, eventually compiled enough records to establish a picture of the climate near Charlottesville. The red maple, he noted in his Garden Book, began to bloom as early as February 18 or (in other years) as late as March 27. The shadbush (amelanchier tree) bloomed beginning March 28 or beginning as late as April 18. The dogwood, he noticed, bloomed from April 3 in an early year to April 23 in a late spring.

Here in Washington, the dogwood, I would say, bloomed April 8 this year—depending, of course, on what part of the city we are talking of, since the advent of spring can vary a number of weeks within just a few miles here at the Fall Line. But if we know that April 3—April 23 is the usual spread of time for dogwoods to come into bloom at Charlottesville, then we are not likely to be surprised at their blooming April 8 this year in Washington. We will not say (as the ignorant do) that there never was such a spring as this, or that the flowers never have been so early here. They are quite within their usual blooming season, we see, thanks to our records. Or, to be truthful, thanks to Jefferson's.

One thing the gardener might enjoy doing, at least for a few years, until the seasons no longer surprise him, is to keep a record of a few key things, such as the date the red maples bloom; the date that Rock Creek Park first gets that feathery hazy look with the new growth of trees; the date of the first daffodils, the first peonies, the length of the blooming season for several particular plants of the same genus.

The daffodil 'Spellbinder' sometimes stays in bloom for me (and doubtless for everybody else) a whole four weeks. I enjoy noticing that 'Spellbinder' is in bloom a full week before 'Red Rascal' opens, then remains in bloom a good ten days after 'Red Rascal' has withered. Such observations teach us things we do not learn merely from examining a cut bloom at a flower show, or even from seeing the plants in bloom in a garden. It is only by noticing the dates that we see some daffodils last in beauty a great deal longer than others, and this is like having twice as many flowers, if they last twice as long.

For Jefferson (I am sorry I cannot find his dates for the appearance of tadpoles at Monticello) the first lightning bugs appeared in the garden May 8. He did not record another date for them. I am sorry to say I have never noticed when the lightning bugs appear here. Wouldn't it add a bit to the general interest of life if we knew? I do not say it makes any great difference, but suppose we kept records for sixty years and always recorded the first lightning bugs about May 6, and then one year the first ones turned up March 31—we would know enough to be startled then, and would be on our guard that extraordinary weather might be at hand generally.

It is only after the gardener has kept such records a couple of years that he begins to get special kicks. In my new garden the old and not very worthwhile (I am fond of it, I must say) daylily 'Lady Bountiful' has twice begun its bloom season on May 16. This year, as you can see, I will be quite interested in this daylily to see if it blooms on the same date. I would not care at all, if I had not noticed in the past.

Surely the point need not be labored further. A gardener profits from the return of the seasons, and profits from small trifling facts, and the more of them he has observed, the more resonant, the richer, his (or, needless to say, her) enjoyment becomes. It is one thing for tadpoles to be seen April 8. It is quite another thing to have observed, say, that this is the sixth April 8 of this century that they have appeared on that date. It is not the fact that is important, but the gardener's awareness that a fact is being beheld.

Jefferson never was quite able to convince some people of that.

Living without a Lawn

There is something to be said for lawns, but it does strike me as obvious that lawns are work and that several million blades of grass all together can be monotonous.

These things are subject to fashion, of course, and not reason. The other day I was reading an old account of a man who said his lawn had been chopped down to an acre and a half from its former expanse. In the old days (before World War II), people sometimes lived in large houses on large lots, and lawns were pretty inevitable. You can't, after all, plant irises or roses solid for a city block, or at least that is not the idea of a garden for most people. But similarly it is also true that in tiny forty- and fifty-foot lots, to say nothing of those minuscule little warrens of Georgetown and Capitol Hill, a lawn can be rather silly, in terms of labor versus final effect.

The genteel tradition, which died about 1910 among the advanced sector of the population, still has its little strongholds, and none is more apparent than the continuing notion that all the best people have lawns. I can remember quite well when all the best people had cows—Mrs. Taft, as you know, had her cow brought up every day from Foggy Bottom to graze on the White House grass—and before that all the best people had deer parks. All I am saying is that you don't have to grow grass if you don't want to, and in many cases, especially on small lots, it makes more sense to eschew it.

What, then, are we to do with the space around the house if we do not put it in lawn?

Just here we may take a good lesson from the Spanish, who are not thought of as great plantsmen, but who at least never spend all weekend mowing grass. They have used paving, pools, and small beds of plants cultivated intensively (or tubs or pots) and in this way they have saved money on water, which is of course expensive in arid regions. In California, Arizona, and such other deserts, the Americans lost no time starting lawns, a very foolish thing to do, instead of following the excellent Spanish precedent of no grass at all. In the East, on the other hand, we live in what will once again be a forest, once the cities collapse, and the style of arid gardens (those of Egypt, Greece, Spain, for instance) is not imposed on us by any shortage of water. On the contrary, the natural style of garden for here is the woodland garden.

But on tiny lots, though we might have a tiny woodland or a tiny lawn, it often makes more sense to treat the outdoor space as simply an extension of the house, and to pave some of it or most of it, and to wind up with what is really no more than an outdoor room furnished with plants instead of tables and chests.

A lawn 17 by 20 feet is just fine, if you think a lawnless life is not worth living, but I hate to see anybody badgered and shamed by unholy pressures into growing grass simply because everybody else does.

Often we may see tiny lots overhung with enormous trees, beneath which the poor humans (far more industrious than the ant or honey bee, which only stirs because life itself is at stake (dart fitfully about with loud machines and later creep on all fours to trim here and there. From time to time they may be seen sprinkling grass seed, fertilizer, and other gold out of sacks, and they continue this for as long as God grants them energy to move around. If this provides pleasure—it certainly keeps them off the streets—then all to the good, but reason would dictate something other than a lawn in such a site. Why not azaleas and camellias, with a little clearing (covered with duff of the forest floor) sprinkled about with Virginia bluebells, lilies of the valley, Solomon's seal, veratrums (if it were damp), and grand little bulbous things like anemones, crocuses, and the like? The number of shrubs that enjoy light woodland conditions is vast and, while nothing is labor-proof, still it is more more satisfying to care for camellias, viburnums, and so on, grown to perfection, than to work like the devil for a scraggly patch of lawn. The Cryptomeria Glade of the National Arboretum is a beautiful example of shrubs and trees in beautiful harmony without, I am happy to say, a blade of grass in sight. Or, if the site is not overhung with trees but is in full sun, what could be more delightful than a large lily pool with a terrace on which to spend much time observing the fishes, toads, water lilies, and other treasures of such installations. Back of that could be roses or vegetables or what you preferred, and there would be no need for a lawn. I am speaking, still, of tiny plots.

Obviously, if you want the effect of a million blades of grass shorn uniformly, only shorn grass will produce that effect. But I suspect many gardeners would do well to think of something besides grass and the little noisy juggernauts you cut with.

Iris

Fifteen. ☐ Thanks to careful and scientific planning, I am able to look out my window on the irises and roses even in bad weather, and from the comfortable security of a dining chair I can observe whatever happens to be in bloom at the moment getting bashed in by storms.

This is not, however, an entire delight.

As gardeners, surely we have done our duty once we have registered our disapproval at the general arrangement of the universe, with complaints of special sharpness directed toward the clumsiness—indeed, sloth—with which wind and rains are scheduled. It is all that can be expected of us. The rest is the full responsibility of the heavens and need not, therefore, concern us. It does seem to me odd, nevertheless, that this "Nature," which is supposed to be so wonderful, so rarely lets anything come to full perfection. It is all designed on the frog in the well principle, two hops forward and one backward until a certain level is reached, then the whole thing collapses. That is all anybody needs to know about nature.

Now, before the thunderstorm of May 22, when two inches of rain fell in half an hour (not that it stopped at that) things were going fairly well in the garden, considering nobody but Providence was in charge. As late as 5:30 P.M. of that day the irises were in full bloom. I have one bed of them 4 feet by 15 feet which had produced about two hundred stalks of bloom. This is only accomplished by jamming them in and very carefully fertilizing them with a teaspoon here and a teaspoon there through the year. The idea is to feed, cultivate, and water them within an inch of their lives, stopping just short of making them so lush they rot—which they will do en masse if you go too far. (Always err on the side of too little rather than too much pampering, if you must err; but it is better to hit it precisely right. Light feedings—a teaspoon of 5–10–5 chemical fertilizer on March 20, April 23, July 10, and August 3, for each clump of seven fans of leaves, is about right at my place—are better than one gross feeding, in my experience. This presupposes, of course, that the irises were planted in July in beds dug eighteen inches or so, with plenty of leaf mold or its nearest equivalent mixed in and allowed to settle before the rhizomes were planted, and of course you sprinkled about one good single handful of 5–10–5 per square yard before you started your digging.)

In this particular bed of irises I was handicapped by not knowing what the varieties were, the labels having got lost in two previous shifts from other gardens, but I did know they were all irises I liked and the colors, I trusted, would clash well, as a wit once put it. Imagine my amazement, when they started blooming well on May 16, to see the colors flawlessly balanced and arranged as well as I could have done it if I had known which iris was which when they were planted.

There is room for personal preference and taste in the disposition of iris colors, and the gardener should (needless to say) suit himself, but over the forty years I have grown these flowers—unchallenged princes of the vegetable kingdom, one might say—I have discovered what suits me best:

• Between a third and a half of the plants should be some tint of yellow, from pale straw through ivory-primrose, sharp lemon, full sulfur, to yellow verging on (but not falling into) orange.

• A sixth of the plants may be dark, chiefly violet-blue or darkish rose-violet or velvety black, but navy blue (a color not found in irises) is what I am after.

• A sixth may be blends, or irises in which several colors produce the effect, but for me these blends should not look much like blends, but should look like orange, though blended of apricot, pink, tangerine, and so forth.

• A sixth may be pinks, orchids, whites, clear magentas.

• The colors should be more or less mixed up; blues should be here and there throughout the bed, for example, rather than in one great glob.

• Whenever there is any doubt, plant light yellow.

• Do not plant any reds, do not plant any browns, do not plant any bicolors (unless they are soft, not startling, in effect, such as 'Arpege' or 'Sunset Blues' which are soft blue violet with very pale off-white or pale violet tops). Do not plant any deep rich blends, nor any red and yellow variegates. These are incredibly seductive, but try to be strong.

• Ignore the common warning against whites and deep yellows. These blend perfectly. Do not be afraid of them.

• Avoid plicatas, as a rule—those glorious flowers of white or yellow, stippled and etched about the edges of the petals with darker color. They are extremely beautiful, as all irises tend to be, but they do not work as well as one hopes in a mixed bed. All these banned or excluded types are grown elsewhere in the garden.

Following these precepts, then, you cultivate them off and on throughout the year with repeated light scratchings, going no deeper than an inch or so, except that two or three times a year I use the trowel (or an old broken knife does nicely) as a knife, jabbing vertically, straight down for two inches, then straight out. This is only done when the plants are established for a year, and needless to say it is not done directly at the back of the base of the fan of leaves, lest the roots be chopped off.

However one does the cultivating there should be no weeds, simply because the iris when well fed tends to rot, and needs to air out and dry out as soon as possible after rains and dews.

Having done this all more or less faithfully, you will be rewarded by spectacular blooms in May. The iris is one of those plants that may as well be spectacularly well grown as not. Properly done—and it is at least as easy as growing tomatoes or corn or roses or things of that sort—the bloom will be so thick you cannot believe it at all, and the colors will be so sparkling and fresh you will jump (as it were) up and down.

They will be, as a rule, in total perfection by May 22, or whenever the year's major hail and thunderstorm is scheduled.

Cheap Thrills:
Japanese Iris from Seed

Japanese irises are opulent beyond almost any other flower, but they are not showy in the garden and you have to gaze at them as individuals to enjoy them.

Often I fidget in my head to think of flowers suitable for small town gardens, which are mainly brick with a couple of chairs and a few treasured plants, and I thought the Japanese irises might do. So thirteen months ago I got a packet of seeds from Park's and resolved to see how they turned out. Everybody knows those twenty-five-gallon half-barrels of oak that used to hold whiskey. They are about 24 inches wide and maybe 18 inches deep. I got one and filled it with fairly good ordinary garden dirt to within two inches of the top. There are no holes in the bottom for drainage, and I did not drill any, because I wanted something that stayed on the soggy-boggy side.

The iris seeds planted in May all came up like radishes in a few days; and I planted about twenty-four of them in the barrel, giving them their permanent positions when they were about two inches high. Usually one plants the seeds outdoors in October and they emerge in April. During the summer I kept them watered— a bucket or so every week, perhaps—and pulled the tiny weeds out as they appeared, but in a very short time the irises grew large enough to prevent any new weeds from sprouting.

By fall the irises were maybe fifteen inches tall, and two or three fans of leaves had formed for each little plant. About Christmas time I gave them a two-inch mulch of horse manure.

The leaves all died down into a colorless mush for the winter, but in spring they began to grow strongly; and the iris flowers started appearing the end of the first week in June. You will understand that twenty-four clumps (for each plant has about four sheaves of leaves now) of iris in a tub only twenty-four inches in diameter is more than enough, and I was not sure they would bloom very well when so crowded.

From April on, I kept the tub soaked. Virtually every plant produced flower stalks; and while the flowers are not as large as they would be if given more space, still they are bigger than the palm of my hand—and that is big enough.

I began to notice twenty years ago that no matter what the books and specialists sometimes say, there is much of a muchness about Japanese irises. I used to buy named varieties with such impressive stylings as 'Moon over the Tortoise Cat's Ear' and 'Shimmering Brocade of July Charcoal Pit' and so on, though I forget them exactly, and they were nice enough. Then one day I was in a garden where they had raised the irises from seed and I said, "Ha, you have 'Glory of Titmouse Nest' doing extremely well," and they said, "Oh no, they are just a batch from seed." Well. I saw that my named varieties at $10 each were not any better than theirs from seed that cost less than a penny.

In theory, the fine named sorts have greater substance, better poise, etc. In my experience, however, none of them stands up to wind or heat or rain very well—you would not really expect it in a flower as large and flat as a pancake.

It is a good idea, needless to say, to get good seeds to begin with, and I have been utterly pleased with what I got, called the Higo Strain. I think I paid 75 cents for them.

Today there are six plants in bloom, all different. One is milky white with a flush of blue. Another is solid white except for a flush of yellow. One is pale blue with dark blue veins and a violet center. One is pale lilac-rose with a touch of yellow, and another is rich mulberry with some white veins, and one is violet-blue with black veins and a central boss of red-purple. These are standard colors and patterns in Japanese irises, and nothing in the vegetable kingdom is richer, more luxurious, or even more noble than these flowers. The three great, broad, almost circular petals are flat, drooping a bit at the edges, with three small, upright petals in the center. At the center, and extending variously onto the petals, are three little flashes of yellow. There are only two flower buds on a stalk, and the second one flowers a few days after the first. I suppose the tub will have flowers for three weeks. Some bloom only eighteen or twenty inches above the earth, while others are three or four feet tall. The foliage, like very narrow swords, is completely upright, and from a distance you think they are some attractive neat water rush.

In Japan they sometimes grow these irises in individual pots, which are set in shallow pools a few weeks before blooming. Another thing they do is grow the irises in rows like vegetables and by means of little dikes they flood the bed in the spring, keeping a couple of inches of water standing over the plants till after flowering, when they let the water off. Yet again they grow them in large clumps in fish pools (the water only two to four inches over the crowns) so that when the irises are in bloom you can watch the colored fishes swimming among them.

These irises grow and bloom perfectly well in ordinary garden borders in the sort of site you would give a tomato plant or a rose bush, and I have grown good ones without giving them any supplemental water at any time during the year. It is important to keep lime away from them. Our natural soil, so strongly acid that we need not do anything at all to grow fine azaleas and rhododendrons, suits them perfectly. They are gross feeders, as the books say, meaning simply that they appreciate mulches of rotted manure. I used fresh horse manure in December, and it did well. Ordinary chemical fertilizers of common formula (5–10–5 and so on) will do well, but the plants will die with wonderful speed if anything alkaline gets near them.

On a sunny terrace I think these irises in a half-barrel justify their space. Even apart from the gorgeous flowers, the foliage is pleasant and vigorous in itself.

The color range, you will notice, is white through mulberry and deep violet. The "blue" ones are not especially blue and there are no yellows. These irises will never make a flamboyant mass of color like the tall bearded irises. Even if the Japanese iris colors were brilliant—and they are not brilliant at all, but subdued and rich and soft—they are not produced in masses. Needless to say, they will never produce the color in a tub that is so easily provided by geraniums, petunias, lantanas, fuchsias, and so on. And you have the flowers three weeks instead of four and one-half months. So they are no flower for those who want a blob of gorgeous color in an otherwise leafy green and paved town garden.

Maybe if there is room for only one tub, then the annuals mentioned (plus verbenas, nicotianas, heliotrope, snapdragons) would give more pleasure during their very long flowering season. But often there could be several tubs, and the Japanese irises would not only contrast with the bright annuals, their distinguished foliage giving greater dignity to the tumbling petunias, but would provide in their brief season of flower something to look forward to, more than the ceaseless geraniums.

My Wild Iris Grows

Once on the Bayou Vermilion I noticed an iris with uncommonly small leaves and took a small piece of it home. It had been starved, and promptly began to grow all over the place in its new and lusher pasture. It was merely the wild *I. brevicaulis*, with slightly grayed sky-blue flowers on its zigzag stalk. Another time I spotted a tiny iris with leaves only two inches high and brought it back, wondering what in the world it could be. It too began to grow like a weed and turned into the four-foot-high *Iris giganticoerulea*, with electric deep gentian-blue flowers. On a third occasion I noticed an iris in a damp meadow beside an Arkansas road. It was the terra-cotta-colored *Iris fulva*, but I had not expected to see it growing where I in fact found it. All three are so-called "Louisiana irises" and by crossing the three species back and forth a great assortment of colors—blues, pinks, yellows, blends—are now to be found.

For several years I was amazed at the beauty of these wild irises, and I still think the flowers as lovely as anything in the vegetable kingdom, but they have a lot of faults as a garden plant. The rootstocks run about, for one thing, and you do not get as many flowers per square yard as you do from many other irises. For another thing, the stalks often lean about instead of standing up straight and, worst of all, the foliage is not very good in many of them. They start blooming towards the end of the tall bearded-iris season and bridge the interval before the Japanese irises start.

At first I erred in giving them what I thought was a replica of their natural conditions, that is, lots of water in spring, hard baking in summer, and dry in the fall. But later it struck me they did better in ordinary—ordinary, my eye—rich sunny beds with plenty of humus. Although you may see them baked like a rock along the top of bayou banks, I think that is only because they seeded there and have no way of moving off. They certainly do not object to high life if they can find it. I now think those irises are not so well worth space as many others, but they are admittedly glorious in flower.

I notice that the one I miss most, from my former garden, is the plain *I. fulva*, a muted red-tawny flower about the size of a lemon slice or a bit larger. It is always conceivable that a gardener will have a low place, say a foot or two lower than the surrounding ground, in full sun. I had such a spot where a stone terrace drained. I had tried various things there, but nothing was really happy until I planted *Iris fulva*, and it was in heaven. Admittedly, the fine sheaves of thin sword leaves flopped in the summer, but they were vigorous and straight in the spring, and nobody's perfect. These wild creatures are sold by iris specialists especially in Louisiana and there are ads in garden magazines.

I was checking to see how my palmetto came through the winter (alive and outraged) and something about the low area a couple of feet distant made me think of the wild red iris. Maybe I will never grow it again, maybe I will. Garden plants are interesting, in that so many of them almost obsess you at one point in your life, and then you let them go without any special pangs. Except that once in a great while you see something that reminds you forcibly of the time you grew them and the memory becomes surprisingly intense.

Some gardeners are surprised to discover the wild Louisiana irises are hardy in New England. Even in England, where they have no sun and no heat, many of the Louisianas can be grown—and they bloom there, although somewhat grudgingly. Near the Gulf of Mexico people grow them madly. Up here I suspect they will appreciate full sun, though they do not require it in the Deep South, and up here I would give them the sort of good soil you would give roses and other garden irises, and although it does not require water standing over it, from time to time *I. fulva* would probably appreciate it. Its color is unique among all the flowers I know, and curious gardeners will probably fall for it. It is nothing like as showy as the average tall bearded or German iris, but when it is in bloom in late May, the gardener will not think of that.

Roses

Thinking about Roses

Sixteen. ☐ Mid-January to mid-March is the season for choosing roses. There is no earthly point in thinking about them in June, at the height of their bloom. That only results in a hasty trip to the nearest store that sells roses (and some very strange places do, nowadays) and a quick conference with the pleasant teenage clerk who has, in most cases at least, learned to tell a rose from a juniper, and a long trip home involving a detour to visit Uncle Will in Bluefield, West Virginia. Then the rose plant, which was not the right one to begin with, is commonly left sitting about the garage for several days further, until the weather is not nice enough for tennis but too nice to clean out the gutters, and (at last) is finally entombed in raw clay. Let us now repent, and choose a rose sensibly, so that all who come after us will marvel.

First, there is no rose in commerce that is totally worthless. I cannot think of anything more distasteful, or really evil, than for some gardener to choose a rose he likes and then read somewhere it is "not worth growing." Be sure of this: your labor is not in vain no matter what you choose. Any rose that delights you (and one of the most endearing qualities of gardeners, though it makes their gardens worse, is this faculty of being too easily delighted) is a rose you may plant with good conscience, no matter what anybody else thinks of that rose. Second, a number of "great" roses are called great merely because (a) they behave extremely well in rose nurseries, or (b) they are sufficiently death-defiant that even gardeners cannot kill them, or (c) they have some showy feature, usually blatant color or freak size, that endears them to people who can see nothing unless it is inescapably obvious. Third, there are some very wonderful roses that you don't hear much about. Please keep this firmly in mind. It is as with everything else—the greatest pleasures and the happiest discoveries are not necessarily the first ones you see.

'Paul's Scarlet Climber' is a famous rose, despite the fact that it has undistinguished foliage, does not repeat its bloom, lacks fragrance, is susceptible to blackspot, frequently dies back if kept too dry, and has flowers of ordinary shape with no particular beauty. It has two things, however; it has rich, magnificent color (which will war with most other colors in the garden, of course, but never mind) and sufficient vigor to persist in unfavorable sites. Another rose, commonly called the rose of this century, perhaps the greatest rose of all time, is 'Peace.' It has no fragrance to speak of, it has huge flowers that should please anybody who has always longed to grow the largest turnip in the world, and it has good foliage indeed. It also has a superb inbuilt healthiness and is a grand flower, except that it has no fragrance and commonly looks gross and bloated. Its color, to give the devil its due, is soft, creamy yellow flushed with madder at the edges. This varies according to weather but is almost always very beautiful. A third sensational rose (and none of them, as you may have guessed, is among roses I greatly admire) is 'Tropicana,' which has fragrance and good constitution and all good qualities, plus a clear, pure, vibrant vermilion color that can be seen a hundred yards away with no difficulty. If you like that color, this is a grand rose.

This brings us up flat to our purpose in growing roses. Everybody would agree (except those who make it a point of honor never to agree with anything) that roses should be healthy, beautiful in individual flower, highly fragrant, constantly in flower during the warm seasons of the year, blessed with ornamental foliage, and possessed of overall grace. The trouble is there are no roses, none, that do not fail in one or more of these desirable qualities. So the choice comes down to this: since no rose is perfect, which imperfections will you accept, and which qualities will you regard as indispensable?

Rose societies, growers, and nurseries may not be much help.

They would not consider, say, 'Mermaid' or 'Alberic Barbier' a great rose, because these two roses possess qualities they do not value (grace, superb foliage, constancy of bloom, freedom from blackspot, delicacy of color, elegance of flower) and lack qualities they esteem (neatness of bush, suitability for bedding, mass of color, massiveness of individual flower, suitability for impressing a cow when cut as a single bloom in a vase). The fact that different people have different uses for roses, then, is perfectly understandable, and if a rose like 'Peace' seems to you a perfect rose, then look no further, and grow it with joy and thanksgiving. But what bothers me is that any standard of judging roses other than the one that results in 'Peace' being described as the rose of the century is dismissed out of hand. A person new to roses may find it difficult to find any other standard to judge by, and may even wrongly conclude, if he is not overcome by the virtues of 'Peace,' that the sort of roses he has in mind do not exist.

In pointing out some of the merits of other roses, as I stoutly propose to do in the following pages, I mean no disrespect to 'Chrysler Imperial,' 'Peace,' and those other plump beauties currently in favor, and I see no reason why anybody should suddenly veer toward my own bent in roses. My particular hangups (grace, perfume, foliage, vigor, constancy of bloom) are no more inherently admirable than those of the average rose grower, only different. So what I thought I would do is say plainly (insofar as my imperfect amateur knowledge permits) what the merits and defects and uses of some roses are, and thus help the gentle reader to see what sorts would best suit his own needs in his own garden.

Three Good Hybrid Teas

Before anyone says, 'Oh, you writer people are always recommending something nobody ever heard of or can get," let me prove that I am not going to be difficult by mentioning three current hybrid teas that have (in my view) every reasonable blessing. These are 'Sutter's Gold,' 'Helen Traubel,' and 'Mojave.'

With flowers, there is such a thing, as that excellent gardener Gertrude Jekyll used to say, as reaching a certain beauty and being content to stay there. In other words, it is not true that if you triple the fragrance, triple the substance, triple the intensity of color, you get a finer flower. No, when a flower is right, there

is a great art to leaving well alone. Not that I consider these three hybrid tea roses any kind of perfection, certainly not. They are just hybrid teas, and it is not in that class that you need seek the most moving beauty of roses. Still, as hybrid teas go, these are very fine ones and very much in commerce. They have high ratings by the rose society, and if anybody wants roses of good color, fine fragrance, robust health, on stems good for cutting, then these can well be chosen.

'Sutter's Gold' is a fairly strong medium yellow brushed with orange-brown, quite fragrant, with a scent that reminds you of 'Marechel Niel' or 'Golden Dawn.' The brushing of bronze is not heavy, and sometimes it is not present, while again it may vary almost to a suffusion of reddish orange. It is not one of those bicolor things, but it is not absolutely pure yellow; that is the point. The blooms may not last as long as some others when cut. The flowers, when they open from quite beautiful buds, are not all that double, and the open blooms are a bit loose, hence this variety is most esteemed in the bud, as indeed most hybrid tea roses are.

'Helen Traubel' is soft clear medium pink, strongly affected by a radiating or underlying yellow. It is never an intense brilliant color, but always rather soft. This rose nods a bit on its stem; the neck is a bit weak. This has never bothered me, but it would be a serious defect in a florist's rose.

'Mojave' is a soft orange, more or less brilliant depending on weather. If you will think of a yellow-orange or tan-orange or buff-orange touched with a suggestion of pink, you will more or less visualize the color, which is lovely. The point is, it is not one of those roses like a lightning bolt going through a stoplight—such roses are often called orange also, and 'Mojave' is not like them.

All three of these roses are notably fine performers in the long weeks of summer, when many other roses are dawdling about growing roots. The combination of grand color, grand fragrance, grand health, grand freedom of bloom, is a nearly impossible combination to ask for, but in my opinion these three varieties come as close as any hybrid teas now being grown.

Another great stager is 'Charlotte Armstrong,' a light red, which has no scent to speak of, but is a glorious performer and very robust. It has a flaw of sometimes being killed back in winter when other hybrid teas are not, but it is a very great rose in its way.

Some gardeners like only red roses, preferably very double. They will doubtless like 'Crimson Glory' and 'Chrysler Imperial,' both of which have heavy good fragrance. 'Chrysler Imperial' is precisely the sort of rose I dislike, with all those petals—when it blooms I always feel I have witnessed an upheaval rather than a flowering. I mention this only to be fair to the rose by confessing my aversion to roses of that type. It is certainly one of the finest roses in commerce if you like a clear red of grand size, heroic stature, and glorious scent. I like the more open, looser form of 'Etoile de Hollande,' which is as beautiful as a red rose needs to be. It is not faultless, mind you—it gets blackspot more than I approve of and its branching and leafage can be a bit gawky and sparse. What we need, of course, is a good public garden of roses, even if it were in the National Arboretum, where gardeners could go and see for themselves. It is all very well to say 'Chrysler Imperial' is a great rose or, on the other hand, that 'Etoile de Hollande' is. The plain fact is that those who greatly admire the style of one will hardly admire the other. Not every writer on roses will honestly say he detests 'Chrysler Imperial' simply because it is large and full. The home gardener may be searching desperately for the largest and fullest available, and therefore would cherish 'Chrysler Imperial' more than any other red. It is much easier simply to go see the roses than to try to glean from the printed page which red you would like best. You would think that in this capital somebody would have got on the ball long before now and come up with a first-rate public rose garden, but nobody has. We are too busy planting dabs of marigolds at bus stops to have fine public gardens as other towns do.

There are probably two hundred hybrid teas well worth growing of those now in commerce, and there is none but has some merit. Of those I happen to be familiar with, and whose performance records I quite certainly have no doubts of, I suggest the three great ones, as most nearly fulfilling the requirements I have for a rose. Thus, I have omitted the great 'Duet' because it lacks scent—but what a glorious garden performer it is—and 'Tiffany' because I dislike its stiffness (but what a grand fragrance it has), and 'Mirandy' because it doesn't bloom enough (but no rose in the world surpasses it for a fragrant dark red) and 'Eiffel Tower'— well, come to think of it, I can't think of a single thing wrong with 'Eiffel Tower,' one of the most robust and elegant of the cool pinks.

I knew this would happen. Now I want to go back and add thirty or forty additional indispensable hybrid teas. And yet, I know that if it came to the crunch of growing only three hybrid teas, those are the three I would choose, so why not just say so. I have no illusion there is anything magical about my personal choices, but they are a beginning. Without further qualification, then, I submit 'Sutter's Gold,' 'Helen Traubel,' and 'Mojave' as the finest of hybrid teas. Grow them.

A Collection of Climbers

This may be a good time to say a word about climbing roses, of which there are, after all, a great many I approve of and would gladly grow myself if I had room.

First there are the wichuraiana climbers, at least those of the group that repeat their bloom through the season. Preeminent among them is 'New Dawn,' soft, cool pink, fragrant, on a plant of grand shiny foliage, healthy, and almost constantly in bloom. It is ubiquitous and deserves to be. Indeed, on those days I think the Republic is quite gone to the dogs, I think of this rose and say, "Well, as a nation we had wits to see the unusual merits of this rose, at least." It makes a large plant, perhaps twenty-five feet. Two other repeat-blooming pink climbers (half of whose genes are identical to those of 'New Dawn') are 'Dream Girl' and 'Inspiration.' The first makes a smaller plant, a restrained climber to perhaps ten feet, very fragrant and very reliable for repeat bloom. Its flower is extremely double and quartered (the petals are so full they fall into folds, as if the bloom had been lightly indented with a pie knife into four or five generous servings). It nods a little on its stem. So distinguished a rose fancier as G. S. Thomas considered it the best of everblooming pink climbers. 'Inspiration' is a looser flower, not so insistently double ("blowsy," some would say), highly perfumed and very constant in bloom. Those who grow it swear by it, and I have myself been rather impressed by it in one Washington garden. For an everblooming pink rose to grow on a city garden fence, perhaps nothing really surpasses 'Blossomtime,' which has a tea fragrance, hybrid tea-type flowers, excellent disease-resistant foliage, and a habit of constant bloom. It continually pleases me that my predecessors on this present city lot had the grand wits to plant only first-rate climbing roses, including this one.

Among yellows, the obvious (to me, at least) choice is 'Golden Showers,' a constant-blooming thing of moderate growth, to ten or twelve feet, well suited to a wall. I am much interested in the climbing yellow 'Casino,' which I have no experience of. So celebrated a rose firm as Armstrong's considers 'High Noon' the best yellow climber. In this they err. It is too leggy, too thin.

What good can come of my saying 'Marechal Niel' is a glorious rose? Though it is. This great yellow climber has almost endless drawbacks for the normal gardener: it is a little too tender for the Washington climate, dislikes wet weather, has weak, short stems and skimpy, yellow-green foliage. Such a catalogue of vices should discourage anybody. It lacks almost everything but scent and color. Nevertheless, many gardeners (and I am one of them) are totally in awe of this rose. I would give almost anything if the Fates would allow me (or if my skill would, and thus far it has not) to grow the Marechal successfully before I die. Well. To come down to earth, the 'Climbing Sutter's Gold' suits me. Like other sports (in which a bush form takes off and becomes a climber) of hybrid tea roses, it does not bloom so much once spring is past. On the other hand, this one does bloom a little, off and on through the summer. Its flowers are intensely fragrant, and it is the best climbing yellow hybrid tea I know of, though if I had a plant of 'Climbing Golden Dawn' I would certainly not cut it down. The floribunda climber 'Climbing Goldilocks' is fine and free, with a little fragrance, but it is not for those who dislike sulfur-colored roses that fade to cream.

Climbing white roses leave something to be desired. Among hybrid teas, the old 'Climbing Auguste Viktoria' and 'Climbing Snowbird' are beautiful, and some speak well of 'Purity' and 'Mrs. Herbert Stevens.' The white 'City of York' often does not rebloom as well as it is supposed to, but I will say this for it, it is one of those roses that you can swag over an arch naturally (the climbing hybrid teas lack grace in growth and can be used on arches only by being dragged and hauled into place, and you always have the feeling that if the ropes are cut, they will leap to lose their chains, so to speak).

Among climbing red roses, you are on your own. I do not like them. I suppose 'Guinée' and 'Climbing Etoile de Hollande' are the best. 'Climbing Don Juan' repeats well. 'Parade' is a light red that repeats well and has a full old-fashioned look. 'Chevy Chase,' a Washington-bred rambler rose, should do for those who want a red rambler that does not get mildew. 'Climbing Crimson Glory' repeats better than most climbing hybrid teas. 'Climbing Christopher Stone' is peculiarly bright and rich. Oh, there is no shortage of red climbers, but I should remind you they can look dull and blah in a garden for all their redness—red is by no means a color that carries well, no matter what people think. My favorite red, insofar as I have one, is 'Dortmund,' a halfheartedly fragrant single bloom in clusters on a plant of dark fine foliage; everblooming, useful for a large shrub or climber to fifteen feet, and quite brilliant. Its color will kill almost any other color in the garden, but against a white wall it would look all right, I suppose, if you like red roses against white walls. Indeed I shall plant it myself, because I think it will brighten up the alley, yet I do not regard this as one of my more elegant selections.

Perhaps something should be said about those large-flowered ramblers that came out around 1900. You do not see, nowadays, the beautiful 'Gardenia,' an American white (it opens yellowish and fades) of about 1898. It does not repeat once spring is done. It is greatly fragrant. I am not sure it is still in commerce even. I would certainly give it space before I would find space for 'Climbing Peace' because it is, in a word, more beautiful. Similar, and probably somewhat better, is the French white, 'Alberic Barbier,' which repeats a bit until fall. These particular wichuraiana ramblers (the flowers are two to three and a half inches in diameter, however) are very graceful in growth and bloom, and quite vigorous, suitable for growing into trees. Speaking of trees, the old single white 'Silver Moon' will take care of anything up to forty feet. Its white saucers are fragrant, but it blooms only once during the year. It is good enough for them to grow it up trees at Kew in London. So there.

Not everybody likes the Pemberton Musks. These have good disease-free foliage, more or less constant fragrant bloom, and they are sort of half climbers and half big bushes. They were not all raised by the late Reverend Mr. Pemberton but most of them were. For a white climber that won't romp away over the roof and smother the house, 'Pax' is a fine choice. Smaller in bloom, and in various tints of pink, buff, coppery salmon, you are directed to those grossly neglected varieties 'Cornelia,' 'Bishop Darlington,' 'Felicia,' and (for a nice fading yellow) 'Thisbe.'

You must beware of "climbing musks," by the way, remembering it is the Pemberton Musk climbers that are lauded here. The wild musk roses are quite something else again. The lovely, single-flowered, wonderfully fragrant wild musks are too large for most town gardens. When last reported, the fine specimen of *R. filipes*, one of the wild musks, had extended to 150 feet in the garden at Kiftsgate where it is such a feature. Of course it is hard to keep a 150-foot plant from becoming rather a feature, but it makes life hard for any little forty-foot trees that happen to be in its triumphant path. Those with much space and taste, and with the energy and determination to track down sources of supply (I used to know a source for *R. helenae* but they don't list it now) will be interested in such grand wild climbers as *RR. longicuspis, filipes, helenae, gentiliana,* and the like. They grow them at various botanical gardens though not in Washington. *R. souleiana* has grayish leaves and is lovely, I should not have forgotten it, among the others. Mine died some years ago which was, on the whole, just as well. These are not roses for city lots, truly.

We have said nothing of noisette or tea climbers. They are tender to cold and hard to find, but among those still in commerce (but few modern gardeners care for them) are 'Gloire de Dijon,' the great 'Marechal Niel,' 'Devoniensis,' 'Reine Marie Henriette,' 'Lamarque,' 'Solfaterre,' and so on. Some day, for quite jaded gardeners, we should consider the old white microphylla, a difficult rose for difficult gardeners. A rose you may be weary of having me write about is 'Mermaid,' a single canary-yellow fading to creamy white. It is one of the greatest of all roses and quite flawless. Except, I suppose one should say, it can be hurt by unusually cold winters, and it is sheer hell to try to prune, and it resents pruning which makes it awkward since it is perfectly capable of covering the entire east wall of the White House (not that so great a rose is thought of for institutional buildings). But where there is room for it and shelter for it, this fragrant, disease-free (it does get thrips, sometimes) climber or heroic bush is desirable. If I ever have the money to cut down a vicious maple in the back I shall leave the stump fifteen feet tall and gain the sweetest revenge—for blessings are the best revenge—by growing 'Mermaid' up its otherwise revolting skeleton.

The trouble is, there are too many grand roses, and selections are odious, and yet one cannot grow them all. I see I have left out 'Mme. Gregoire Staechelin,' a fragrant vigorous ruffled pink that, alas, does not repeat. It blooms with irises. It makes a large plant not any more graceful than the average hybrid tea. It is also known as 'The Spanish Beauty,' though I have always felt if your name was Mme. Gregoire Staechelin and a rose was named for you, then people should go to the trouble of calling it by your name.

Anyway, despite the terrible defect of not repeating its bloom, it is a rose you need not be ashamed of. Sometimes writers say blandly and simply that it is "the best pink climber." Mme. Staechelin is not the catchiest name, and perhaps she needs a bit of a boost. When a rose with such a grave defect keeps being recommended, the reason may be sheer ignorance. On the other hand, it may be the rose has merits that atone for any shortcoming. As here.

If there were any decent roses at the National Arboretum you could go see many kinds and make your own selections. I do not mean any criticism of that eminent institution which has, I believe, more unlabeled crabapple trees than any other garden for three hundred miles. The conifers are extremely nice as well as the superbly grown camellias and a great many fine azaleas, and the cryptomeria glade is stunning. They have not got around to roses—roses are an obscure flower, after all. The nation is still young; give us another century to get going.

Old Roses

When Botticelli painted "The Birth of Venus" he sprinkled roses here and there—you recall the picture of Aphrodite sailing along in a seashell in a rain of pink roses—and the rose he painted is *Rosa alba*.

Let us not dwell on why pink roses are called *R. alba*, beyond the observation that this whole group of roses is now thought to be a hybrid group (the wild dog rose crossed with the damask rose) that came into vogue during the thirteenth century. Pliny says that England was called Albion either for its white cliffs or the white roses of that island ("ob albas rosas") but if so they cannot have been *R. alba*, which was not then in existence. This has never deterred anybody, however, from calling *R. alba* "the white rose of England" and it was, in fact, *R. alba* that was the white rose badge of the House of York. So the rose is storied enough, though not the white rose Pliny mentioned.

There is a barely semi-double white *R. alba*, and a full double white, and these are treated as if they were wild species and called *R. alba*. In addition, there are seedlings and varieties bred from those whites, and these are the ones called the alba roses of some old-fashioned gardens. The one most strongly endorsed by two preeminent connoisseurs (both dead, alas) is 'Celestial,' also called 'Celeste,' which is a medium light pink flower. It makes a large bush on the order of a lilac, say eight feet high, and has blue-gray-green foliage. Gertrude Jekyll's donkey, Jack, once ate the side off a large plant of this rose, and Vita Sackville-West once observed that if she had to settle for just one alba it would be 'Celestial.' These were both great authorities on roses. Others prefer 'Maiden's Blush' or (as the French call it) 'Cuisse de Nymphe Emue,' which is to say the thigh of a passionate nymph. It is quite similar to 'Celestial,' perhaps more a bluish color. Then we also have 'Queen of Denmark' ('Königen von Danemark'), which came out about 1800.

All these alba roses make impressive bushes and they have a powerful, sweet scent. They bloom in a great orgiastic spree in June and do not flower again until the next June. It is this spring-only habit that has done them in, as far as modern gardeners are concerned, because who wants a rose that does not bloom on and off all summer and fall?

So I do not urge anybody to plant 'Celestial' or 'Maiden's Blush' or 'Queen of Denmark.' I merely say that no roses surpass them in fragrance, no roses surpass them in delicacy of color and petal texture, and no roses surpass them in magnificent showiness when they are in bloom.

Now besides the albas, there are the damasks, the gallicas, the noisettes, the teas, the Bengals, the Scotch briars, and so on. These are all different types, strains or families of roses distinct from the hybrid teas and floribundas, which are all you will find in most gardens today. There is nothing wrong with our modern roses but there is no need to overvalue them or to ignore those other roses, now rarely seen, which are equally beautiful.

The damasks (there is one on Omar Khayyam's grave, and there is a variety called the autumn damask which blooms twice, in the spring and again in the fall, and this is the rose referred to in the verse of Virgil and Ovid) as a group bloom only in the spring. The flowers are as large as hybrid teas in some damask varieties, and powerfully fragrant with a (surprise) damask scent. The hybrid tea variety 'Etoile de Hollande' is somewhat of the damask shape and smell; but damasks lack strong color. There are no reds and yellows.

The gallicas, apart from being the "red rose of England," are also, of course, the red rose of France. The red rose that sometimes shows up in medieval church windows is a gallica. These bloom only in June and have a good scent, not as ravishing as the albas or damasks, perhaps. The red and white 'Rosa Mundi,' which either is or is not the rose of King Henry II, is a gallica. Some think it is a very old variety; other authorities think it relatively new. In any case, it is certainly a gallica and many roses of this group, mainly red, have spots, streaks, stripes, or a purplish cast and hence are called the "mad gallicas."

In extremely small gardens, one would have to love these old roses passionately to give them space that might be occupied by modern roses which bloom all summer. But where there is room for bushes that bloom only once a year (and of course lilacs, azaleas, mock oranges, and so forth bloom only once a year and nobody holds that against them), some of these roses might well be planted.

Now these old sorts of roses are sold sometimes by general nurseries—fine if you can locate them—otherwise from specialists. Also, gardeners who are not familiar with them will be at a loss over which varieties to try, hence a list of some of my own favorites, generally acknowledged to be among the finest of all roses. Not because they are my favorites, but the other way around. You might try: 'Celestial,' the alba already mentioned; 'Stanwell

Perpetual,' a constant-blooming Scotch briar that grows waist high, small grayish-green leaves, fragrant pink powder puffs; 'Tuscany,' a gallica with deep red flowers brushed black, it looks like dark red velvet and is fragrant; 'Celsiana,' a large soft medium-pink damask, very fragrant, a loose flower showing gold stamens, arching growth (in other words the flowers will drag in the mud if you don't do something), which has as good a claim as any other to be thought the most glorious rose of this world; 'Madame Hardy,' a white centifolia, very full of petals and fragrant, with a green eye; makes a sad ugly bush, but then who's perfect; 'Old Blush,' a pink Bengal or China, perpetual in bloom.

That should get anybody started, but I am appalled to see how cavalierly I describe 'Old Blush,' as if it did not deserve several pages of highly inflamed verbiage. It is, like the others, a very great rose which will, of course, still be around when nobody grows 'Peace' any more. 'Peace,' the great hybrid tea, will not last because it is not fragrant, so you may as well enjoy it in its century; your great-grandchildren will not know where to buy it at all. Thus, we see that justice triumphs.

Rugosas

Some gardeners, I know, will wonder why anybody would wish to grow any of the rugosas, those wrinkle-leaf and excessively thorny wild roses from Japan, plus a few of the hybrids between this wild rose and garden roses.

To begin with, no variety of rugosa will please the gardener who really wants a firm, fully packed rose five inches in diameter, with long cutting stems. Like 'Crimson Glory,' say. All the rugosas lack substance, the flowers are too thin of petal, and not one has good stems for cutting. Also, the foliage is usually dense, right up to the bloom. So anyone who is looking for the sort of rose you see in florist shops and whiskey ads may ignore the rugosas.

What is their charm, then, that so many ancient gardeners turn to them—limp and floppy—when the world is almost solid with roses of "better" shape and more spectacular color?

First and foremost, the beauty of the rugosa as a garden plant. Typically the rugosa makes a bush six or seven feet high and roughly globular or mound-shaped. Second, the fragrance with which the group is endowed, sometimes with a strong element of clove. Third, the repeat-blooming nature of the wild rugosas and many of their hybrids. Fourth, the fruit (like tomatoes an inch wide) which comes in late summer. Fifth, the general good health of this group (though the yellow 'Agnes' may be a martyr to blackspot) and their utter hardiness to cold. But none of these attractions would make much difference if the plant were not extremely beautiful.

I have never seen much point growing things merely because they perform well. And yet I know from experience that many gardeners do not, and would not, think the rugosas beautiful. There is no arguing with that, except to suggest that plenty of gardeners who have known all sorts of roses for nigh on to fifty years, etc., etc., would go to pieces if anything happened to their rugosas. Not that anything ever does.

The best-known white variety is 'Blanc Double de Coubert' which is semi-double and has a certain amount of fruit, or hips, and which is a very pure white, sweetly and strongly scented. It usually does not bloom much in the fall, but blooms heavily in spring and a bit all summer. I can think of at least two world-famous rose lovers who prefer the wild white rugosa alba to it, however. Doubling or tripling or quadrupling the number of petals in a rugosa is not quite the advantage you might think. In hot weather, the double flowers are usually pretty shapeless and ratty looking, while the singles are elegant. The wild white also makes a handsomer, more luxuriant bush than the other whites.

I used to grow 'Sir Thomas Lipton,' a white rugosa that bloomed before the garden bearded irises, and if the weather was right (not too hot) the flowers looked like white camellias and were superbly fragrant. It bloomed all summer, but I would have liked it better if it let it go with the spring display, since the summer flowers were never handsome. It bears no fruit, by the way.

I have mentioned the yellow 'Agnes,' which is very double and fragrant. Its non-rugosa parent was the Persian yellow rose. In some gardens it is a great carrier of blackspot, but others say it never gets blackspot with them. I would be very suspicious of it, since the yellow roses of the Middle East (*R. foetida*, or *R. lutea* as it used to be called, more charitably) are more susceptible to the blackspot defoliation than any other roses. Indeed, it was only with the influx of genes from those roses, in our present century, that blackspot became a real scourge to the gardener. To the Persian yellow and other roses of that group we owe the glorious brilliance of most garden roses such as 'Mme. Henri Guillot' and so forth—but the nearer the variety is to the wild yellows the more vigilant the gardener must be to spray against blackspot.

The main color of the rugosas, apart from white, is a sort of faded mallow pink, or else a sort of magenta, sometimes fairly strong. Lilac pink is about right for most of them. Pink fairly pale with a good bit of blue in it. If you do not like the color, you should not grow the pink rugosas, but I suspect many gardeners would succumb if they had a fine bush of, say, 'Belle Poitevine' in the garden. That one grows to perhaps eight feet, has four-inch flat blooms of light mallow and is well perfumed. Clearer pink, with less blue in it, is 'Frau Dagmar Hastrup,' with single (five-petaled) blooms, scented, in contrast to the double blooms of 'Belle.' The Frau may be kept to waist height without any trouble, and its fruit is crimson rather than yellow-red.

The semi-double white 'Schneezwerg' grows to perhaps five feet, not nearly so tall or fat as the wild white rugosa. The name means 'Snow Dwarf,' I am told, but the gardener should not imagine it is the sort of dwarf plant that can be used for edging rose beds.

'Hansa' is purplish red, and in the heat it can be quite lavender, very strongly scented of cloves, and double. Its flowers are floppy, even by rugosa standards. If the weather is just right, of course it can be very beautiful, but it is rarely considered a prize of the family. 'Rose à Parfum de l'Hay' is famous for its scent and for its relatively large (four inches or better) flowers of red touched with wine or purple. It sometimes grows poorly. The current darling of the family in this color range is 'Roseraie de l'Hay' which makes a bush to five feet or so and is intensely scented of clove and has flat double flowers, not too densely packed, of red flushed purple. (The "l'Hay" in both these varieties is in honor of the rose garden of l'Hay outside Paris, and has nothing to do with cows.)

'Sarah van Fleet' is a great favorite of mine, which blooms all summer and is scented, but has no fruit. As with all these rugosas, a big plant in bloom in May is quite a sight. They are very good along a country drive, and the tall ones make good summertime screens along an alley. The foliage turns yellow or yellow-orange and tawny in the fall, by the way.

Other rugosas in commerce (from rose specialists) include 'Will Alderman,' double mallow; 'Delicata,' a lighter and less double pale mallow, and the single wild reddish *R. rugosa*; the double and scented reddish magenta 'Magnifica'; the red 'Ruskin,' well scented and double with a good bit of substance, and less of the rugosa look than some; and the very tall (nine feet) 'Conrad Ferdinand Mayer,' pink, and 'Nova Zembla,' a lighter-colored sport from it (both the last two sometimes have disease problems, but that would not greatly discourage me). There are still others, of course, and I hope it is already clear that rugosas take a lot of space. In a border fourteen feet deep, they are fine toward the back, but you would not want to use them in the narrow borders or ordinary town gardens. Or maybe you would. Think of them as being as bulky as a lilac or forsythia bush.

They do not need any pruning to speak of, but will endure (the question is whether the gardener can endure) cutting or sawing back in late winter, without taking offense and sulking.

I suppose rugosas can die, but in comparison with most other roses in gardens they are virtually immortal. Some of them get blackspot here and there (Sir Thomas always did) but it never was very unsightly and never seemed to make any difference. They are all supposed to prefer a sandy soil to clay, and it is sometimes said they do not grow well on clay. Well, they will grow well enough on any dirt you may have.

Some gardeners are simply not going to get out there to spray roses for the various maladies to which roses in general are prone. It is too bad for such gardeners to plant roses that are almost certain to drop all their leaves in July from blackspot, and such gardeners may find in the rugosas an answer to their prayers. But—please—remember they are huge bushes.

Of Toads and Bronze Dogs

Ode to the Toad

Seventeen. ☐ Toads are conservative animals, I think, and not much given to expecting the best from fortune. Some weeks ago, well before the end of October, I accidentally dug one up while turning over some garden earth. I was surprised, naturally, when one of the clods heaved over on its side and there, in some annoyance, sat a toad.

These are more expressive animals than the average mammal thinks, and it is not just my imagination, surely, that makes me recognize emotions in them. Often in the spring I have seen them ecstatic—it must be something about the eyes—but more often I have seen them disgruntled and resigned to the absurdity of daily life. They look especially baleful when the gardener accidentally digs them up after they have begun their long cold-weather period of inactivity. They also register disapproval when a hound, or indeed any other dog, picks them up in his mouth. On several occasions I have seen dogs do this, and on all occasions the toad looked angry rather than afraid.

As most gardeners know, it is only young dogs that pick up toads, and they usually do it only once, though Luke, who as the vet correctly said was always going to be "a very slow dog," tried toads twice. I have never heard of even young dogs harming the toad nor, for that matter, carrying it in his mouth more than a few feet. Toads, I have been told, secrete a bitter or acrid substance which the dog does not like. Usually once is enough, and toads are left alone after that.

It seems to me odd that I have rarely seen a dead toad, although I know they are mortal. Do they die in ponds, or perhaps under a pile of brushwood?

There are many sorts of toads, and once years ago I went so far as to an order an assortment of several kinds from a dealer in Topeka, Kansas, whose name and address I have lost. The different kinds (except tree toads) strike me as rather much alike.

We have all read that each toad eats something like four trillion bugs a week, and that the toad is therefore good to have in the garden. I found that in my part of the city there was a shortage of toads; in fact I never saw any and my neighbors said there were none. Fortunately, I was able to find some tadpoles (toad tadpoles are easily recognized, since they alone are jet black) in a shallow rock pool along the canal at Great Falls last spring, and these grew nicely for a few weeks in the lily pool, then developed legs and hopped out. For some time I saw no young toads, but recently I have seen a dozen or so, about the size of ping pong balls. They have been very interested in going down some back steps into the basement. My Assistant often finds them hiding behind the washing machine, and I have pointed out the importance of checking that engine before starting it up. It does not seem, on the face of it, there is enough in the basement for a toad to eat, so I steadily remove them to the garden. I release them in a woodpile and trust they go on from there.

It is often said they eat slugs. I have kept my eye out to see this, without ever seeing it happen. It is true, however, that this year we had no five- or six-inch slugs (which we always had before) and for the first time I did not find slugs all over the walk leading to the alley.

The gardener should be more than cautious about spraying bugs, since poisoned bugs cannot be good for toads.

Ladybugs are also fine in the garden; they eat aphids. I never spray the aphids, knowing the ladybugs will soon come. If there are not enough aphids, there will not be any ladybugs, it's as simple as that.

Ladybugs have a terrible habit of getting into wet paint, in my observation, and I have no idea how to get it off them. A paper towel suffices for them to get their feet clean enough to get going, but I fear the chemicals of the paint on their shell cases may kill them.

Like many gardeners I am afraid of wasps and hornets and bumblebees, but honeybees do not alarm me. All these creatures commonly fall into fish pools. Some floats of wood are good for them to latch on to. Often a stick or a tuft from some plant can be extended to them to fish them out. It is astonishing how many bees, which seem dead in the water, will revive if fished out and set on the ground to dry. I do not say the gardener should keep watch night and day for waterlogged bugs, but if one is admiring the fish or the water lilies anyway, it is no extra effort to save a bee or a wasp.

I am not sure how we got going on garden animals, but since we're at it, the Carolina box turtle has not been seen for several weeks. He has lived in the neighborhood for several years, wandering from yard to yard. He thinks especially well of my neighbor's woodpile. Last year he hibernated in the ground (late October) in front of the house beneath a kerria bush. I did not think he was burrowing down far enough, but thought it presumptuous to do his digging for him, and apparently he knew what he was about since he emerged in April and has been healthy all summer. Box turtles are too often victims of cars going down alleys. I would never introduce a tortoise of any kind to a garden unless its security could be guaranteed. If one is already there, supplemental feedings of melon rinds are good in the summer. These of course have to be collected after the tortoise has scraped them clean.

Fauna Follies

Our herd of squirrels is coming along nicely, much better than I had desired, in fact, but since they probably cost no more than $6,000 a year to feed, perhaps they are worth it. There is a nest of them in a large oak in the front and another nest in another large oak next door. I believe Ken has a nest of them in his atrociously large maple, and darkly suspect Lillian and Dick and Murray all have vast squirrel-breeding stables of their own. In any case, there were nineteen of them eating birdseed at the back door last Wednesday.

It is only fair to say on behalf of the squirrels that, while they have of course rooted up a number of wild cyclamen, crocuses, and daffodils (they never eat daffodils, but when they bury nuts they are not averse to pitching daffodil bulbs they have dug up in the process on top of the ground), to say nothing of the pansies they have dug through in their storage policies, still they have never actually frightened the hounds. They bothered the hounds, but did not terrify them.

Once they saw we were not going to catch them for a Brunswick stew, and once they comprehended that the hounds were actually awake only on the rarest occasions, then the squirrels arrived like the guests at Andrew Jackson's cheese board. Needless to say, they are a mixed blessing. But in general, wild fauna can be a source of delight in gardens, even in the city. I myself am a city lad, but once spent a year in the country, and it converted me forever to the incredible merits of pavements.

Far more beautiful, though also less entertaining, than squirrels are the Carolina wrens who showed up abruptly (two of them), causing me to leap forth and construct a four-inch nest box for them under some garage eaves. They are obviously birds with an unusual desire to please, since they sat in the box for a week or so after it was put up. Perhaps they will nest.

A friend of mine had a broken pane in a small greenhouse through which some wrens entered. They were seen flying in and out, but nobody knew where they had settled until Dick tried to retrieve his hunting jacket which his wife had once borrowed, failed to return, and left hanging in the greenhouse. The wrens were nesting in one of its pockets. There was much talk at the time, of a domestic sort, which need not concern us, but the upshot was the wrens nested in the jacket for several years, and, perhaps I should add, it was also impossible to repair the broken pane in the greenhouse. The avalanche of morals here is such that you will need no help from me in deducing them.

An acquaintance in Georgetown has a small basin for fish and a water lily. It sits on the ground and is 29 inches in diameter. This was sufficient to attract a raccoon, whose paw marks are to be found on the fence nearby, which is painted black. My friend started putting an old fire screen over the basin each night to keep the coon out at night, but the coon soon learned to lift it off. Now it is also weighted down at night, and I am interested to follow this matter over the next few years to see who will give in first. The coon will win, most likely.

It cannot be too widely advertised, in short, that one does not need leopards and peacocks—or even mules—darting about to derive some amusement from the natural world. Even a slight exertion in the way of providing water, cover, and food (in that order, in my opinion) will surely attract our paw-bearing, tufted, or screeching friends in some measure.

The Art of Remaining Calm

"You're kidding," said an occupant of my house when I brought home the bronze dog.

Now just here let me say that the gardener who acquires a piece of sculpture for the garden must expect a great deal of yapping. It is rare, probably, that the flawless taste of the gardener will be shared by others. I set it near the pool during the time I constructed a masonry pedestal, and the household's three live dogs (live because the gardener is humble and takes no umbrage when they sit, dig, scratch, chase, and roll where they shouldn't) have checked out the statue of the bronze dog and found it wanting. One of them marked it, the way dogs do, but only because he thus marks everything living or dead. The gardener knows, if he has been around for any length of time, to stand silent when the family lights into him. In time they will see things his way. The day will come when the bronze dog will be remembered with affection by those of the family younger than I. But when I brought the sculpture home, the wit sprang from all sides along with the sarcasm.

I mention this only to reassure other gardeners who may have projects in mind (after long and prayerful thought) that the true gardener is not intimidated by wisecracks. And ought not be. The gardener must go his way serene, trusting in the talismanic virtue of righteousness, good judgment, etc., with faith that others will in time see the light.

Since it was so traumatic for me, I might add that sculpture should only be acquired if the gardener knows—*knows*—he will love it forever. Nothing less than the gardener's certainty about the sculpture will ease the taunts he is likely to receive. It is not important for gardeners to agree on what garden sculpture should be. It is very important for the gardener to be sure in his mind what the sculpture (if any) in his own garden should be.

Often I have warned against ornaments in gardens, on the firm ground that ornament usually detracts rather than adds to the ornamental effect. The true ornament of the garden is proportion, balance, luxuriance, repose, and so on, and it is usually a mistake to put sculpture in it. I know one garden that has a huge Henry Moore sculpture at the end of a walk and it looks fine. But usually sculpture does not look fine at all. Better effects are usually had from a great bulky holly or an arbor or a lily pool than from sculpture. And possibly I err in making the bronze dog an exception in my own case.

I paid a lot more than the blasted thing is worth, I am sure. But a lot less than it is worth to me. And maybe that is one test whether the sculpture is right for the gardener, if not for the garden.

He is not exactly a dog. He is equally a lion, a chimera, a dragon. He came from Bangkok and, I suspect, is one of seven hundred cast a year ago to lure dollars away from tourists. There is no reason to think he is not brand new. So he has no attraction of the rare antique. His front legs come straight down like a piano's or (as they used to say, though it is not true nowadays when they are so elegant and beautiful) the ladies of Charlottesville. His paws are indicated by three rows of knobs. A raised formal band runs up the middle of his chest, and raised lines from his chest to his back. The Chinese lions or monsters often had wings, and I figure these sweeping lines are an illiterate adaptation of the winged lions of ancient dynasties. His hindquarters (a middle-aged model, no doubt) swell out extravagantly and his tail, which rises in and curves up over his back, looks rather like a flame. There is a gilded bronze flame at one of the buildings of American University, the flame of knowledge, presumably, that always struck me as singularly dumb. A pity they did not model it on my dog's tail which is, as I have hinted, beautiful.

Anyhow, I like the mutt in the garden. I like to sit in the summer house I built and look through the white arch across the bricks to the raised pool faced with weathered tiles and then through the screen of black wood arches (now hung nicely with fleece vines) to the circular horse trough. This elegant basin (from Sears) is faced with stucco colored with yellow oxide of iron and a few rather chipped tiles from Spain, and back of it (raised up on cinder blocks stuccoed over with buff mortar) sits the Great Dog I have been telling you of. His tufted paws rest on some polished dark brown hexagonal quarry tiles in a frame of oak.

He is sort of green (probably an instant patina of copper nitrate, and I turn him just a bit sideways, because if you see him head-on you don't see the splendid tail. Paw to paw is twenty-odd inches, and he's forty-one inches high, up to the crest over his head. His mouth is wide open, the tongue curving up and down like a roller coaster, and he has a little beard and some rather neat fangs. Very fierce. I am counting on the slugs' being terrified next spring.

It's a Jungle Out There!

Eighteen. ☐ Some gardeners like tropical luxuriance and some do not, and I am in no position to argue my passion for jungles. We do not live in the tropics, and a sound argument can be made that it's esthetically silly to desire tropical touches in a temperate-zone garden. All the same, if somebody showed me a plant with leaves twenty-five feet in diameter, I'd probably tear down the garage to accommodate it.

There are prim gardens and they are very nice, but I would not want one. I remember at Versailles, the garden of Louis XIV, wondering how anybody could spend so much money and construct canals on so large a scale and have so many trees and still achieve a sparse and stingy look.

Probably if you grow up in the Arctic Circle or Bangor, you learn to admire a hunk of granite and some nice lichens. If your country is the Mississippi Valley, on the other hand, you think there should be vines in the trees, alligators in the pond, and night jasmines around the horse trough (or "stock watering tank" as they call horse troughs up here).

Well. I have given up thinking of coral vines, fat gardenia bushes, and much else, but I have not given up the notion that a garden should have a lot of leaves in it, preferably hanging from the air and preferably large or astonishing in texture. I have always had trouble with docks, among the weeds, because I can never quite pull them up all the way. They are handsome, and one can easily imagine them on the Equator—and first thing you know, you have a lot of them to dig out.

My summer house, if that is not too grand a name for four small wood posts and some one-inch trellis, is fairly embowered from the hot western sun by a grape vine and two clematis plants. The floor is brick, and around the perimeter are dracaenas and so on, sitting out in their pots for the summer. The pool beyond is raised 24 inches above the ground level. It is silly (though gardeners will understand it) to think how many years I spent deciding what kind of tiles to face the outside concrete with. And, of course, there was the grave matter what to plant around it. The creeping fig is not properly hardy here, so of course that was the first choice. Nothing else has such small neat leaves or hangs so close to masonry. It has survived three winters, and every summer I persuade myself it is gaining a little strength. But there is also a yellow-leaf ivy called 'Buttercup' that is utterly hardy, so that one of these outrageous winters won't completely break my heart.

From my fortress, under the tangle of common almond-scented clematis, I can see not only the pool (the creeping fig is not yet big enough to show up, to my annoyance) but some of my favorite plants.

There is the great Japanese butterburr, *Petasites japonicus*, which at the moment is sulking in an oak whiskey barrel, for it really is not safe to let loose. Its leaves, with me (and in its somewhat cramped confinement), are no more than eighteen inches in diameter. On hot days they wilt and you have to flood it, and by twilight it revives. Not a plant for everybody, of course, which is why it is rare.

There is also the ligularia called 'Desdemona,' with waxy circular leaves of dark green, purplish beneath, and acrylic-yellow daisy flowers. The leaves reach about eight or ten inches across. They too wilt if it's dry. The great reed or ditch grass, *Arundo donax*, looks much like field corn, except it is more graceful and reaches twelve feet in height. Daylilies would pay for their space even if they never bloomed, because of the beauty of their bright green leaves in April. They shade out weeds, to a considerable extent, and are handy to stick in between large-leaf plants, since daylilies are almost endlessly accommodating. I like that old herb, the lovage, which grows to the height of a man once it settles in, and its sheaf of celery-type foliage is agreeable. It may be too wet for fennel. It never self-sows and the bronze-leaf form (like shoulder-high feathery clumps of mist) has always sulked.

The wild American rudbeckia, *R. maxima*, is a plant I would never willingly be without. Possibly because it is wild, it is ignored. Its flower stems reach nine feet, but the great thing is the leaf, which is as blue and glaucous as a cabbage, and fleshy like one, too, and the leaves grow to eighteen inches long when well fed in a very sunny moisture-holding soil. They make big fat clumps, not quite rosettes, a yard wide. I know of no source for this wonderful plant except to roam about the South and to dig it up somewhere. All other rudbeckias including 'Goldsturm' are, of course, merely weeds, as far as I can see, though they probably do very well for those who like them. So, for that matter, does goldenrod.

My crinums have been a terrible disappointment. That is because the crinums I bought at a local garden center, as dormant bulbs, were not crinums at all. Sometimes I marvel at the gall of those who not only mislabel daffodil bulbs left and right but who sell ismenes for crinums. Some day, God willing, I will make an enormous effort (which is what it takes these days to acquire almost any plant except marigolds) to acquire some of the crinums I used to grow. Their long amaryllis-like leaves make clumps often four feet in diameter, and nothing so firmly announces the coming of settled warm weather as those big stalks of lilies, some of which have a foul smell and some of which are intensely sweet.

I have little hope for the gunnera, now sitting in a pot. It should be hardy in Washington if given a little mulch in winter. It likes full sun, endless water, and plenty of rotted manure, in response to which it can produce leaves ten feet in diameter, though I would settle for leaves four or five feet across.

The ordinary cooking rhubarbs are handsome enough, but far handsomer is *Rheum palmatum* from Asia, a wild fellow that reaches seven feet. The individual leaves are no larger than washtubs. Again, it is rare because nobody wants it and because nurserymen do not like to give it space, I suppose, and also because the general level of interest in magnificent wild plants is slight.

You go through hell to import a plant from abroad (my rheum came from England)—and if it ever grows, I'll try to spread it around.

Other things with tropical leaves that please me are cannas (of which more anon), my grape vines, the white-striped Chinese miscanthus, a grass that grows ten feet high, the blue-leaf hostas, the plume poppy with leaves ten inches or a foot wide, like giant aces of clubs, and yuccas. All these are of course totally hardy and need no protection whatever. But I know they are a bit of a shock to those who run more to columbines and pinks (neither of which does well with me). You can't have everything, but I never begrudged the space some of my big babies take up.

A Few Kind Words for the Canna

The canna got such a bad reputation from its mistaken and trite use in Victorian gardens that it has never quite recovered the favor that its majesty entitles it to. The asinine custom of treating plants as mere blobs of color in a design spread out like a rather ugly rug may still be seen in some of the parks in Paris, at the Alhambra in Spain (though one may expect the Court of the Lions to be purified any year now since a moderate and enraged series of protests was promptly lodged when they started massing marigolds and salvias in that beautiful cloister), and indeed wherever such gardening is preserved as an example of the vulgarity of the past or where the designer does not himself have any taste at all. Ribbons of white mugwort or dusty miller, backed up by bands of blue lobelia, red saliva, and the like, were often centered by a "dot plant" which indeed provided a dot and was supposed to "give height and emphasis" to the general mess, though a good bulldozer would have been a far more precious ornament to such plantings.

Anyway, the canna commonly grew in such places and when revulsion set in among gardeners at the banality and cheapness of the effect, the canna was commonly blamed and banished from many gardens. Elephant ears, geraniums, wax begonias, crotons, and several other innocent victims also suffered for years because people remembered well how ridiculous they had looked in the wormy little dribbles of Victorian gardens.

And yet, as anyone who has eyes can see, the canna surpasses all other common plants in the tropical luxuriance of its broadened, swordlike leaves. The one most often grown is called 'The President' and it is usually called cherry red, but it is a knock-you-down red closer to the shade of a stoplight. It grows superbly, carries over the winter in storage much better than many other cannas, blooms earlier than many, and continues nonstop until chilly weather in the fall. Its leaves are rich medium green, and like all cannas I am familiar with, it is worth growing for the leaves alone. I have never, myself, had any use for this particular variety, but it would look handsome enough in clumps and drifts with wormwood (*Artemisia absinthium*) and ligularias and rhubarbs and so on.

Nowadays there are many softer colors of canna, and many are only knee-high or a bit more. They come in buff and salmon and begonia-rose and yellow, and there is no reason they should not look good in big tubs or boxes on a terrace. Or, needless to say, in clumps in a flower border.

The old wild 'Indian Shot,' which grows perhaps five feet high, is a canna with good green foliage and small flowers of bright red. You see it, or used to, around the most modest dwellings in the rural South, and some day it will return to favor, since the small spikes of brilliant red look less bloated than the usual canna blossom.

Some people do not like plants with reddish-purple or bronze leaves, and they should avoid such dandy cannas as 'Wyoming' and the bronze-leaf form 'King Humbert.' I am sorry to say I have now quite forgotten which is which—I preferred one to the other—but the foliage of both is admirable, and one has orange flowers verging to red while the other has red flowers with much less orange. The one with more orange struck me as the handsomer, but I usually grow both since, as I say, I never can remember which one I like better. They grow five or six feet high and are splendid with gray and bronze. They also look good with straw-yellow or buffy flowers like daylilies, and as far as I am concerned they look fine with sharp lemon, too. I admire them with figs and pomegranates, or near brick and quarry tile pavements, but best of all with chest-high mounds of gray wormwood and black-green yews. The foliage of the bronze cannas is so handsome it is perfectly possible to cut off the flowers, if the colors are too flashy for you, and just think of them for their leaves.

All cannas are best dug up (they have fleshy roots about half-way between a peony and a potato) in late October, cut back, dried off and stored in the basement, which (according to myth) is cool but not freezing. Perhaps storing them in an unheated garage in a bucket of sand is safer—I know they will not endure being too warm and dry in the winter. In sheltered spots, many cannas will live outdoors through the winter, but for me they don't, not in my heavy water-holding clay. You sometimes see them doing well in courtyards or against south or southwest walls. The roots are acquired in April and planted outdoors about lilac time, and they are at their best in really hot weather, reaching the ultimate lather of excitement about Labor Day.

Some cannas have leaves striped with white, and some have flowers of yellow spotted red. I can think of much worse things than a patch of cannas grown together for one's general amazement, mixing many kinds together. The trouble with that is that they vary a good bit in foliage, habit, vigor, and freedom of bloom. If there is a spare strip near the alley, however, cannas of various sorts planted with four o'clocks will make you smile when you come home from work.

The Shady Life of the Caladium

Now fancy-leaf caladiums, to turn to them, are important for a jungly effect in those dank shady holes that many townfolk fondly call a garden. Tiny places where the brick is mossy and where the main gardening task is to clean up the dog messes. Yet such a garden, with a couple of chairs and a basin or pool for goldfish, and a few clematis vines (if there is enough light for them to struggle up into the sun), can be very pleasant—or better than nothing. And if it's all you've got, you may as well call it paradise and get on with it.

Caladiums are worth their weight in gold in such shady gardens. You can acquire a large tub, or a half-barrel that once held whiskey, perhaps, and fill it with good *light* soil: lots of leaf mold and peat moss and sand nicely mixed. You do not want heavy loam or plastic clay. The caladium bulbs should be 1½ inches in diameter, to produce the finest leaves, and they should be started in barely damp peat moss or sphagnum. Just a three-inch-deep wood box (or clay pots will do) filled with peat moss. Set the bulbs an inch below the surface. If convenient (and it never is), give some bottom heat. I have tried setting the box on top of the furnace and also on top of the hot-water heater with excellent results, but it all depends—you don't want to cook the things. Once the bulbs are sprouted well, plant them individually in smallish pots of the light soil. Then in mid-May plant them in the great tub (or in a shady border along the terrace, etc.). These fancy-leaf creatures do not require direct sun, and will in fact burn if given very much sunlight. Some more than others.

The leaves are one to two feet long, each growing on its stem direct from the bulb. The most popular, and maybe the most dramatic, is called *Caladium candidum*, which has a white leaf with green veins. There are a number of other white-and-green sorts ('Aaron' and 'White Christmas' among them), while others are deep rose with green borders, or deep bronzy red blades with green edges, or white with red veins. Once I planted a batch of mixed colors, not labeled as to variety, and was well pleased with the results, though gaudy and startling. You may find (but then you may not, either) the white with green veins is the best.

Caladiums must never be allowed to dry out once they start growing. They are good by a shady terrace or by the pool because you will not forget them and their thirst. In October, you dig them up and store them dry over winter. The bottom of a bedroom closet (preferably someone else's) will do quite well.

If this peat moss and pot business seems too much, you can plant the caladium bulbs in the earth outdoors in mid-May, but in that case the leaves will not be large by June, like the ones started indoors.

Dahlias—A Lot at Stake

Nineteen. ☐ Sometime in late August there suddenly comes a hint —maybe you feel something in the air—that summer is passing. It is then that dahlias are in their glory, and while none have yet been bred that are quite as large as TV sets or as bright as atom bombs, they will bloom magnificently and conspicuously enough through September and October, when few other things do.

Dahlia fanciers, who, like all other horticultural fanatics, tend to be somewhat lopsided in their enthusiasms, profess to see great delicacy of shape among dahlia flowers, and to hear them talk you'd think these great, flamboyant daisies had every elegance, every grace. Let us admit it once and be done with it: the dahlia somewhat lacks the charm of the lily of the valley, the dramatic tension of the iris, the fragrance of the nasturtium, and so on. What it does offer is a brazen contentment with its flaunting color, so to speak; and when all is said and done it looks best in a sunny field among the corn and pumpkins. I cannot think of a more vigorous, spectacular, up-and-at-'em flower for late summer. Regular tigers they are.

Nothing is more comforting to a gardener on bad days than to examine the dahlias as they grow from tubers (planted in April or May) to maturity during the summer. There is so much material in dahlias—the roots are huge, the leaves are lush—that you feel you have quite a property there; and this is all very different from the anxious uncertainty of many aspects of gardening. The dahlia has lawful and orderly habits, too, there is nothing effete or sinister about it; and it looks great planted in neat rows with neat green stakes. Few labors are more pleasant than buying five-foot stakes (once one recovers from the criminal price charged for them) and painting them dark green in the basement on damp, cold spring nights. I can never resist setting the stakes out immediately to mark the places of the forthcoming dahlias. One also, of course, spends a good bit of time on catalogues and charts and tentative ground plans; and much innocent amusement may be had by putting 'Lavender Perfection' next to 'Empire State'—no, it would be better, surely, next to 'Croydon Masterpiece.' Or would that be too blatant? Ah, 'Fairest' should do it. Reckless, of course.

There are two ways of handling dahlia tubers. The commonest way, which I do not like much, though I have tried it and it works, is simply to dig a hole, set the roots in more or less flat, at five or six inches—that is, the top surface of the root is five or six inches beneath the ordinary ground level. These roots should be covered with two inches of soil. They are planted in lilac time. Once the shoots are growing vigorously, fill in the hole with another two inches of soil, and a few weeks later, add the rest of the soil. A stake rising three or four feet above ground will have been set when the roots were planted—twenty to thirty inches apart for the chest-high sorts, or fifteen inches for the lower kinds that only grow a foot or two in height. These very low kinds do not need stakes. Depending on weather, growth will be rapid or slow, and gardeners will worry in cold spells in May. If dahlias are planted outdoors, dormant, as the lilacs fade, however, the cold rainy spells that come along will not be disastrous though the gardener (especially the first time he tries dahlias) is sure to complain that everything must be rotting.

Really heavy growth does not occur until late May and June at the earliest. It is only in late July that you see the stakes are none too tall, and only in late August (when incredible winds are likely) that you are finally convinced that the stakes were a great idea. (Possibly it should be said here that the dahlia stalk is tied with strips of old shirts or sheets to the stake. Once I heard of a gardener whose dahlias were laid low by September storms, though staked. Nobody had told him the dahlias had to be tied—he assumed they sort of leaned, like a drunk with a lamp post.) The great foot-wide or ten-inch-wide dahlias that are not so popular nowadays grow to shoulder height if they are carefully pinched and groomed, or six or more feet high if left alone and merely disbudded. They will need stakes a minimum of five feet high, and one-by-two lumber will be found a lot safer than light stuff. Until you have seen it (and seen a vast dahlia plant snap off) you may have trouble imagining the stress a stake must bear when a fifty-mile wind tangles with a freshly luxuriant mass of leaves six feet high and three feet wide. So resign yourself, if you grow the tall sorts, to providing adequate stakes at planting time. Do not imagine you can safely drive stakes in on July 19.

Now the other way of starting dahlias is to set the roots flat in a three-inch cardboard box—the kind garden centers usually set small plants in will hold about six dahlia roots—and pack damp peat moss around them. Peat moss should not be dry, or wet either, but about like a washcloth wrung out and set on the side of a bathtub. Shoots will pop up in a day or week. At this point, you can do one of two things—you may keep the roots damp in the moss (once the fine hair roots start growing from the big tubers, more water is necessary) and set the whole root mass out in May, say May 10, just as you set out the dormant roots in April. The only difference is that the plant has started growing, and you avoid the slight risk of a prolonged spell of damp cold weather which greatly delays growth of the dormant roots. (Thus by early June, the dahlias started in peat moss and planted out in May are likely to be more vigorous than dormant roots planted outdoors in April.)

But now back to the box of peat with dahlia shoots three or four inches high. If you like, you can also make cuttings of these shoots. Plant them firmly in a sand-peat mix or potting soil mix and keep slightly damp. They root in a couple of weeks, as I remember, and when nicely rooted they are grown in pots—first three-inch, then five-inch, until they look sturdy enough to plant in the open garden. Dahlias rooted this way in April will make full-sized plants with full-sized blooms by Labor Day. Until I tried a dahlia cutting (three inches) I did not believe so tiny a creature in late April could make a plant as good as one supported by six fat tubers. But it did. But if you do not want to fool with cuttings, just set the whole root mass in the six-inch hole.

Three or four shoots only should be allowed to grow—the dahlia root may send up more, but these should either be used as cuttings or else pinched off. Nothing is gained and a lot is lost by letting an old dahlia clump send up a forest of stems like a peony.

In buying dahlia roots, it is best if the eyes or growth buds are just barely visible, but often they will be already sprouted. If sprouted, remember they are brittle and snap off easily. Do not be too upset if they are pale greenish white—with care and a bit of sun they will soon straighten up and look wholesome. But do not cover a root with long pale shoots with five inches of dirt—the shoot may very well rot.

If you have a root with six or eight tubers dangling from a central point (the stub of last year's stalk) like sweet potatoes, you should let it sprout in the peat moss, then divide it into sections. Each section must contain at least one sprout. Often some of these sweet potato-type tubers will break off. If they contain part of the old stalk, they will send up a shoot, but if they do not have part of that old crown, they will not do anything. Throw them out. Do not divide the root system until you see where the new shoots are. If you just pull the tubers off, none will produce plants, but if part of the old crown is attached to each tuber or small cluster of tubers, you may get three or four plants from one cluster. It is not always easy, by the way, to "divide" the tubers, even when you can see the new shoots, since the old crown is both woody and spongy, and the dickens to cut through, sometimes.

The commonest error with dahlias, if I may speak from my own experience, is failure to give them the water they require in summer. A profound soaking every week or so is useful, from July onward. And they need sun, as much as possible. In woodsy, shady places, forget dahlias.

Dahlias are of best quality in September and October, so there is some sense in not letting them bloom in July, which is when many of them will try to bloom. Of course, you can leave the dahlia to bloom when it jolly well pleases, even if the July blooms are not so grand as September, but you need not expect a dahlia (or anything else) will produce an unending succession of fine flowers for three and one-half months straight. You may decide not to let them bloom (simply pinch the flower buds off when they are like peas) until after mid-August.

Now for varieties. The large decoratives (a class of dahlia) have blooms eight to ten inches wide, when disbudded; the smaller medium decoratives have flowers six to eight inches, and the small decoratives are four to five inches. The same size divisions are found among cactus dahlias, so called because they are supposed to suggest cactus flowers. The petals are quilled—somewhat rolled, that is—rather than flat. Often they curve up and inward like football chrysanthemums. The smaller cactus varieties are thought grand as cut flowers—indeed, all dahlias are. No dahlia gets too large for me and if they were available with flowers twenty inches in diameter I should certainly acquire them. But I am aware that many people prefer smaller varieties for their vases. The pompons are two or three inches in diameter, shaped like balls (the Dutch have produced some a bit flatter than globes, like the rosy orange 'Magnificat' which is usually considered a fine pompon) and they bloom their heads off and need not be pinched or otherwise fussed at, but can be allowed to flourish in the most total abandon. The same is true of the collarette dahlias (single flowers with a sort of sunburst of different-colored petals in the center) and the mignons (low-growing single flowers) and others used for mass bedding displays.

It seems almost pointless to name varieties, since there are thousands, and many that are highly praised in one nation are no better than many bred elsewhere but not so widely grown or exhibited for awards. American, Belgian, Dutch, English, Australian breeders have all been busy with dahlias, and there is no need to be chauvinistic about flowers.

Not to make any secret of it, but with the reminder that my own selections are merely standard sorts and others are doubtless as good or better, my own dahlias this year (not counting those whose labels are lost or the few my wife persists in buying without names) include these: 'Bacchus,' 'Cleopatra,' 'Gina Lombaert,' 'Golden Autumn,' 'Nocturne,' 'Orfeo,' 'Peters' Yellow,' 'Poros,' 'Royal Sceptre,' 'Gerrie Hoek, 'Holland's Festival,' 'House of Orange,' 'Lavengro,' 'Prairie Fire,' 'Red and White,' 'Tartan,' and 'Terpo.'

An Edible Complex

Twenty. ☐ The peach tree is, I suppose, as beautiful as any subject of the vegetable kingdom, and of pear trees what is there to say beyond open gratitude for their most excellent beauty. Apples I do not care for, partly because I find the taste of the fruit unattractive—nobody will ever persuade me it was an apple that tempted our first mother in Eden—and partly because apples do not grow in the South, which was my country. The bloom of the apple is all very well, in its modest lust toward something approaching pink, and in open pastures out past Gaithersburg there is much to be said for the cherry tree as well.

All these things are very good in Michigan, Indiana, Oregon, and places of that sort where space is ample for buffalo, Ford factories, and large gardens; but in this capital, or any place else where the cost of land is a factor, we should give some thought to what we plant.

I know that humans are irrational and that ideas are fixed as well as foolish, so it cannot be expected that what we say here will be recognized as truth, but fruit trees are generally a disappointment and frequently a menace. Let us except the fig tree and, for the venturesome, the pomegranate. Those are sensible trees, worthy of space. The peach also is not too large for roomy town gardens, and if there is space for one large tree, the pear might be considered for its beauty (*not* for its fruit).

For some reason, people who eat a total of fourteen apples a year often decide it would be "an economy" to grow their own tree. This involves an expensive spraying machine and a nice assortment of chemicals that should be kept securely locked in a stout wooden cabinet lest children and dogs be poisoned. It also involves repeated spraying throughout the growing season, and even so there is nothing to show for it but a lot of apples greatly inferior to those of Mr. Magruder's grocery. Pears are even more futile than apples, since edible sorts (often called dessert pears) do not, as far as I have ever observed, grow in this climate. Except for those grown in the Far West, American pears are inedible unless cooked, and nobody has ever figured out what to do with pears grown in this part of the world except feed them to hogs or else make preserves to give as Christmas presents, in which case they may sit on a shelf in a jar for some months before being discarded.

The grubby-peasant approach to life, which one often remarks in growers of fruit trees, is so overwhelmed and seized by the thought of saving a dime a year by eating wormy produce instead of buying it from good farmers, that the main point is overlooked: the production of high-quality (that is, edible) orchard fruit requires much time and labor and some expense. People who cannot collect their wits sufficiently to plant an azalea (now there is something worth having in a town garden) are perfectly capable of racing out to buy enough fruit trees to plant Albemarle County.

Now the folly of mankind is hardly our concern, and anyone who wishes to grow apples and pears and cherries is quite free to do so. But it is my opinion that he who plants fruit trees is engaged in fools' work. Apart from fouling the air with poisonous sprays and attracting wasps to the carpet of rotting fruit which invariably comes along in a few years, no great harm is done, except that cherry tree roots make it difficult to grow anything agreeable within many feet of them.

I do like birds and hope they will forgive my removal of three quite hideous cherry trees. Occasionally I give the mockingbirds an orange, and I have planted various viburnums, cotoneasters, and so on which have fruit for them. Furthermore, the bill for birdseed here is not to be believed, to say nothing of corn for the crows, which is quite an item even when you buy it in fifty-pound bags. Feeding birds is possibly a foolish thing, but it amuses us and we are quite faithful about not starting to feed them and then stopping. God, I was once instructed, feedeth the ravens who continually do cry, and the sweetness of the language is worth remembering. Starlings and sparrows are as handsome as other birds, once you get used to them. In any case, there they are, and I for one rejoice to see them.

But let us not stray from our topic of fruit trees, for the point is not that the birds should starve or that people should never eat pears again, no. Rather, the point is that the gardener of this capital who has a very small garden should buy fruit at the grocer's and should feed the birds (if that is his bent) some more sensible way than by growing fruit trees.

Daffodils and lilies, tulips, peonies, roses, poppies, tuberoses, nasturtiums, grapes, roses, figs, camellias, viburnums, lilacs, rue, basil, box, yew, magnolias and oaks (if there is room); and above all, I suppose, irises—these are the great and worthwhile things to grow. Violets and pansies, larkspurs and hollyhocks, pinks and sedums and daylilies, a few dahlias, even—where are the great flowers to go if the garden is full of wretched trees?

Trees belong in forests. Fruit trees belong on farms. There may be exceptions, after much thought, but the promiscuous and willy-nilly planting of trees is an offense and should be considered one.

The Blueberry: Give It a Gold Star

For years I have thought it would be good to grow blueberries, without, of course, going so far as to devote any space in the garden to them. It is extremely ornamental, as berries go, making rather twiggy bushes six or eight feet high with reasonably handsome leaves (there is a strong azalea look to it) which often color a nice red in the fall, with green stems in winter tipped with red buds. The flowers in spring are white, or flushed with pink, and the general effect is somewhat like a fat shadblow. In fact, there is no season in which the blueberry is actively ugly—and you must give a plant a gold star if it has no season in which it looks wretched.

Its fruit does not have a great deal of flavor to begin with, so its lack of intensity can hardly be considered a fault, any more than it is a fault in grits. And the fruit, too, is ornamental, or would be if the birds did not eat it instantly. It strikes me funny that people are often in a fit to plant things for birds to eat, searching out obscure plants from Asia or somewhere. Actually, a planting of ordinary blueberries, strawberries, grapes, and raspberries will be found to attract more birds than all the other things in this world.

The gardener frequently wishes, in his greed, to eat the berries himself. In that case, he would do well to cover them with nets or (in the case of grapes) white paper bags. Once, years ago when we netted a fig tree, the squirrels got under the net and raised terrible commotions until they were let out, so I am not as sold on nets as most people. I do know that some gardeners build permanent cages of pipe covered with one-inch mesh to keep out birds, and still other gardeners say (and one hesitates to call them liars to their face) they never have any trouble with birds anyway. Where do they live? One can but wonder.

Blueberries like soil even more acid than most azaleas and camellias, but around Washington this is no great problem. If the planting stations are half ordinary soil and half peat moss, the results are good, though people who like to play with soil-testing devices may also enjoy playing with sulfur or aluminum sulphate to increase the acidity of the soil to a perfect point. I have always disliked aluminum sulphate myself.

Blueberries begin to bear when young—say three years old— and by the time they are eight or ten years of age they can produce between eight and fourteen quarts per plant. At least two varieties should be planted—somewhere around April Fool's Day —men of blueberry-land say, to improve pollination or fruit set. Blueberries ripen over a period of six weeks or more. If I were planting them, I probably would rely on some or all of these varieties, starting with the earliest and proceeding through to the latest ripener: 'Earliblue,' 'Blueray,' 'Bluecrop,' 'Berkeley,' 'Herbert,' and 'Coville.' There may be others even better, but the ones I mention are fairly well known—anyhow, they are the ones I would plant. If I were planting just two sorts, possibly 'Earliblue' and 'Blueray' would do. Do not plant just one variety. I suppose it is clear that two or three blueberry bushes (six bushes are often recommended for a family of five) will produce more blueberries than none.

Often in the summer even a handful or two of blueberries goes well with peaches, apples, grapes, pineapples, and so on in a compote, over which you can dribble some honey if everything happens to be a bit poor in quality.

The Raspberry: A Question of Good Taste

The raspberry is one of those rare plants that nobody has ever called ornamental. It has nothing to commend it to the gardener who broods over beautiful leaves and flowers and bulks and outlines. But there is a place in this world for selected uglies. The fruit of the raspberry makes all objections irrelevant, since it is incomparable in intensity and richness of flavor.

Mankind, indeed, is best thought of as the raspberry-eating animal. Biologists classify mankind as "sapiens" or brainy, and philosophers sometimes say we are the only animal that laughs, and the only animal that blushes. But my own view is that we are best identified by that single activity of total and unalloyed ecstasy (not followed by any sadness at all) which is the ingestion of red raspberries.

Enough readers have been kind enough to write me that their raspberries bear heavily without any trouble on their part and without any interference from birds. But the gardener must not count on that, and must be prepared to net or cage his bushes or else learn to admire the lively sight of birds rejoicing.

Raspberries should have full sun, or perhaps a bit of late-afternoon shade from the west. They like sandy loam, deeply dug and lavishly enriched with compost. Back to reality, they grow well enough in ordinary gardens if there is sun, and if the clay is given a few inches of compost or peat moss dug in. Needless to say, the gardener should have done this last year, before he decided to plant raspberries this March. In the event this preparation has not been attended to, the gardener must manage as well as he can.

Plants are ordered from nurseries, as a rule, and planted three or four weeks before the last killing frost (let us say we plant them in mid-March here, though there is nothing especially magical about March 15) covering the roots with two to four inches of earth.

Usually there is a stub of an old stem which is handy in setting the plants. Once new growth starts, or before, this old stub is cut off at ground level. This is supposed to reduce the chance of anthracnose.

The diseases of raspberries are impressive, and I feel that the less said about them the better. Raspberries should not be planted where tomatoes grew, lest they pick up verticillium in the ground from those previous occupants. Also the raspberry plants should be virus-free. Nurseries nowadays can supply virus-free bramble fruits, and if nothing is said about "virus-free," then you get your plants elsewhere.

In small town gardens (I am assuming the passion for raspberries has overthrown the gardener's mind, and that the gardener is determined to grow raspberries despite their lack of good looks, and despite the space they take that could otherwise be given to irises, peonies, roses, lilies, and so on) the dormant raspberry plants may be set as close to eighteen inches, though thirty or forty inches is "proper." The extension division of Virginia Polytechnic Institute and State University says no closer than thirty-six inches.

Varieties they mention as doing well include these: 'Sunrise'— good quality early red, firm, fine-textured, tolerant to cold, anthracnose, leaf spot, can blight. 'Latham'—vigorous, productive, somewhat tolerant of virus, and the standard red raspberry of the East. 'Pocahontas'—large, firm, tart, hardy, productive. 'Cherokee' —ditto, good for the Piedmont, and an "everbearer." 'Heritage'— everbearer, and if all tops are cut down in late winter it gives one crop starting in August.

There are several other raspberries with various claims to attention, but since I have not grown any raspberry myself, I relay the VPI sorts, with the observation that I keep hearing good reports about the amber-colored raspberries such as 'Fall Gold' and 'Amber,' and I know that many have had good harvests from 'September' and 'Hilton' (both red) and some say 'Milton' is the very best. It is dumb to name two varieties Hilton and Milton, but there it is. 'Heritage' has the reputation of being self-supporting, and not flinging itself about in all directions. I notice that correspondents sometimes tell me it is "reasonably" upright. But in general there should be stakes reaching about five feet above the ground, to which the bushes are tied. Or posts with wires at three and five feet. Red raspberries, if pruned back to three feet, will be reasonably self-supporting. The variety 'Heritage' is simply cut to the ground and left to grow as it will through the summer, then cut to the ground the following winter.

The idea with raspberries is to cut out the canes that have fruited, relying on new canes from the ground to provide the next crop of fruit. Once a cane has fruited, cut it to the ground, either in the fall or the winter (some gardeners like to get rid of it immediately, others say no, wait till full dormancy). In a row, you allow four young canes per running foot to produce that year's crop. The width of a row of raspberries (at ground level) should be kept to eighteen inches or even twelve inches. It is wrong to be delighted at the number of new canes appearing, and it is wrong to let new canes spring up outside the foot-wide row. If one is not ruthless, the raspberry row will soon become a dense thicket, into which the gardener gazes while wondering how to pick the berries.

Rotted manure, chemical fertilizer 10–10–10, and cottonseed meal have all been used successfully as fertilizer, and since raspberries are shallow-rooted, they greatly appreciate a mulch (two inches of sawdust, or five to six inches of bulkier stuff) especially since it is tiresome to try to pull weeds out from a forest of thorny stems.

Fortunately the raspberry usually does quite well without any spraying, but sanitation in the removal of canes is important.

Both blueberries and raspberries are susceptible to one or more annoying diseases and to various pests, but the gardener can often ignore these (except birds) and get by all right. Cats, by the way, are no answer to anybody's bird problem, since then you would have cats.

Vegetables—Interim Report

By October, most likely, my tomatoes will be coming along just fine, but I need not expect them on the Fourth of July. Seven seeds were planted, to produce six plants, but it was June before these seedlings were large enough to set out. Other gardeners, needless to say, had plants in bloom by then.

Pole beans, planted toward the end of April, all rotted in the ground, thanks to the outrageous cold this capital always endures in May. Beans were replanted but the first one only emerged after June had begun. Beans have always seemed to me the most desirable vegetable to grow, partly because you should not touch the plants when there is moisture on the leaves (it is supposed to encourage fungus, to touch them when they're wet). And since everything is always wet here, you can thus save yourself a lot of work.

There are bush cucumbers nowadays that theoretically can be grown in pots. I do not for one minute believe it, but I do have several pots of them sitting about. The directions say you can grow one cucumber plant per six-inch pot. Ha! That will be the day. They do not tell you how many cucumbers you get from a plant in so small a pot. Two?

A lattice summer house is a fine place for cucumbers, letting the vines grow up the slats. Last year, although my summer house is completely canopied by a large Norway maple, I grew a cucumber plant in utter shade and actually got one cucumber.

Needless to say, most vegetables require sun—and certainly cucumbers, beans, and tomatoes do.

The obvious place to grow such things, at my place, is along a waist-high picket fence thirty feet from the far end of the garden. The fence is maybe twenty feet long. Unfortunately it is not available for food crops, being occupied by a satisfyingly vigorous blue clematis, 'Perle d'Azur,' and other goodies. There are some daffodils at the foot of the fence, and a couple of dahlias, and the akebia vine and the tub with the gigantic Asian rhubarb, and a fat clump of 'Lady Bountiful,' a tall daylily that blooms in early June before most others, and a clump of tradescantias, the old blue Virginia spiderwort. There also is an upright juniper and a young plant of white Japanese wisteria that is supposed to take off into a tree about fifteen feet away. The fence is also slightly overhung by a dwarf plum and a dwarf peach. There is, therefore, not all that much space left on the fence for my field crops. Along the fence also are a few plume poppies (these are whacked back or rooted out from time to time, since they are as invasive as they are handsome) and a clump of *Rudbeckia maxima*.

It's astonishing, when you think of it, how quickly a sunny spot in any garden fills up. You have to have the clematis and all those other things. Still, no wonder we starve to death.

Daffodil-irious

How Many? What Kind?

Twenty-one. ☐ Once a friend offered me several dozen bulbs of the cluster-flowered daffodil 'Cheerfulness,' but I said no thanks, since I did not like to plant fewer than a hundred bulbs of a variety. It was only later, when I became less greedy, that I came to see that one bulb is often enough, and that flowers have other merits than mass display.

Now, when I replace 'Cheerfulness' (for I do not have it in my new place), I will probably buy three bulbs of it, well knowing this will give the effect of a small clump even the first year, and a fine, fat flowery clump the second and third. Moreover, when I divide it some five or six years hence (gardeners have a way of looking well to the future, you will notice, and counting all chickens before they hatch) the Lord only knows how many bulbs I will have.

Another thing I have learned—or that I feel, since it is not technically correct to say I have learned anything much—is that the difference between great daffodils and common ones is not so vast as one thinks in the first flush of excitement when one starts being serious about daffodils.

Some years ago I remember seeing a fine daffodil collection of the newest Irish varieties, some of them selling then at a good many dollars per bulb. At a distance of a few feet, I was rattled to notice they looked much the same, and gave the same general effect, as the cheapest varieties available.

The point of all this is to encourage all gardeners who have not yet gone berserk for daffodils to make a beginning this fall. Increasingly it is possible to buy splendid daffodils in garden stores locally, and the days are long past when you could only find six or eight varieties. Now there are dozens. Most of these are pretty standard kinds, but let us not be snobbish, recalling that some of the most standard varieties, like 'February Gold,' are among the finest of all.

My suggestion, to those who are not going to send off for catalogues from specialists, is to go to several garden stores and visit the daffodil bins. Over each bin is a colored picture of the variety offered in that bin, with the price clearly marked. A gardener new to daffodils could do much worse than simply look at the pictures, choose ten or so that appeal to him, and buy one bulb of each.

It is generally said daffodils should not be planted in warm earth and should not go in before mid-October here. My own experience has been that the earlier they are planted the better. In a former garden near the Mississippi-Tennessee line (which is in the South to be sure) I had slightly finer blooms when I planted them early in September, though most gardeners there hold out for late October.

Also, I have planted them in November, December, January, February, and March, though anybody should be too ashamed to admit he was too slothful to get his daffodils in by the end of October. I say this only to encourage beginners with daffodils with the truth that they are endlessly obliging flowers, enduring a great deal of abuse.

Nothing is worse than for connoisseurs of any flower to frighten off gardeners new to that flower. It may be said, if a generalization must be made, that almost anybody will be pleased with almost any daffodil now in commerce.

It may also be said that Washington is far more favorable to the culture of daffodils than most other parts of America. If the gardener (who perhaps does not know beans about daffodils) simply buys sound bulbs (almost all of which are raised in Holland, though the varieties may have been bred in other countries) in September and October, and plants them with three or four or five inches of earth over the top of the bulb, in any ordinary garden soil that will grow roses or lilacs or apple trees or tomatoes or beans or good dandelions, he will have good daffodils in the spring.

The height of the daffodil season here is about mid-April, though the early varieties are in good bloom by late March and the late ones go into May.

Begin modestly, I say that easily, though I used to be greedy about daffodils. Do not be too impressed by novelties, do not rule out the cheapest varieties you find at garden stores. Plant them with confidence, knowing that once you plant them there is nothing further to do.

Among the First

Daffodils, as you know, come before the swallow dares, and they seize the winds of March, as a wit once observed, with beauty.

The question arises, *which* daffodils do this?

The easy, careless answer is that they all do. Some go as far as to say they never met a daffodil they didn't like. But without intruding any of my own prejudices—there are a number of daffodils I not only dislike but positively will not grow if you give them to me—I might mention a few especially early daffodils that no sane man can possibly dislike; indeed, they all happen to be favorites of mine, as good luck would have it.

First there is the wild *Narcissus asturiensis*, which used to be called *N. minimus*. It is perhaps two inches high, a regular miniature yellow trumpet. Many gardeners find this daffodil is not very permanent. My dark suspicion is that none of the wild daffodils goes on forever. They should seed about and in due time there will be good colonies of the wildlings (the scenario goes) and if not, then you had best resign yourself to planting a few every year.

There are some miniature garden hybrids in the yellow-trumpet division, among them such sorts as 'Wee Bee,' which used to last about four years with me, and 'Little Gem' and 'Little Beauty,' small versions of trumpet daffodils, a trifle rough and coarse, but fairly irresistible. The last two are excellent for ordinary gardeners, since they are freely available in September from the bulb importers at a dime each or thereabouts, and they are relatively permanent in the garden, and they also seed themselves and the

seeds sprout freely. With me they usually start blooming about February 20 and continue for three weeks, though as the weather warms up they have a disconcerting way of lengthening their stem to eight inches. As they start out, however, they are only two inches high. They are irresistible if planted in clumps of six or a dozen bulbs, with (a foot or two away from them) fat clumps of snowdrops and other early flowers.

In Washington, bulb flowers providing color before the end of February include most forms of *Crocus chrysanthus*, *C. tomasinianus* and its dark red-purple hybrid called 'Ruby Giant'; the early big fat Dutch crocus called 'Dutch Yellow Mammoth'; the big Dutch crocuses 'Purpurea Grandiflora' and 'Pickwick' (solid rich wine purple and mauve with violet stripes, respectively), and the wild *Scilla tubergeniana*, which starts out pale chalky blue, not so deep as sky blue, and which winds up some weeks later as white.

Also blooming with these earliest trumpet daffodils are occasional flowers of certain anemones of the *A. blanda* type. The first one out with me this year was the somewhat startling raw rich red 'Radar,' like a dandelion that fought at Shiloh, so to speak. For some reason I do not have any early *Hyacinthus azureus*, though that is one of the grandest of all early bulbs, like heavy sky-blue grape hyacinths only earlier. These things depend on the season, of course. This year the truly beautiful soft *C. sieberi* 'Violet Queen' was through blooming before the earliest daffodils began, but in other years they bloom together. All I am trying to do is to remind you of some of these bulbs so that next fall you will say "Yes, that fellow keeps yapping about them, so this year we will try a handful or two."

I digress into these accompanying whites, reds, blues, and purples because the early daffodils are all lacking in those hues. Two other companions you must not forget are *Iris reticulata* (the plain purple form, plus the incredibly rich blue forms called 'Joyce' and 'Harmony') and *Iris danfordiae*, which is one of the sharpest lemon yellows of the entire gardening year, a color quite unknown in daffodils, by the way. The little iris flowers are not much bigger than ping pong balls, and the style arms are marked with beautiful grass green, an extraordinary and lovely thing that fortunately is more often seen in gardens nowadays. Remember, these irises grow from little bulbs planted in the fall; they do not cost much, and you cannot live a reasonable and proper life without them. I always find the first green aphids of the year outdoors in February on these little yellow irises. They do no harm.

Now then, having opened the daffodil season with *N. asturiensis* and its garden forms, and got a few things going for other colors, what other daffodils do we find? Usually no other daffodils open quite so early as these, but again it all depends. Certainly by the first week in March you may expect a number of other daffodils, especially the ample tribe of hybrids from *N. cyclamineus*. Now *N. cyclamineus* makes a bulb the size of an English pea, and it likes a medium-sunny dampish spot, such as you would find in short grass (not a dense lawn in the open, but sad-looking grass such as you find a few feet away from big old oaks) with a bit of peat. It likes to be spongy and wet in February and March, then it likes to bake nice and dry all summer. Do not let this alarm you—it is one of the easier wild daffodils to grow, it's just that you may have to plant it a few times before it settles in.

Anyhow, its numerous hybrids have something of its beauty, with the petals swept back as if suddenly surprised by a small tornado, or like a mule who has suddenly seen a Great Dane in a tree. You know how mules throw their ears back when something frightens or baffles them or if they suddenly decide to kick for no particular reason. Well, the petals of the cyclamineus daffodils flare back like mules' ears. Very easy to grow are such kinds as 'Tête-à-Tête' and (somewhat larger) 'Peeping Tom,' 'February Gold,' 'March Sunshine,' 'Bartley,' and 'Little Witch.' These can all bloom in February in mild winters here, but usually in the first half of March.

That should hold us for the moment—enough little daffodils to get us started. I like to grow this first wave in a place apart, with the blues and violets and lemons and whites of the other bulb flowers mentioned.

Then I like a second wave of daffodils—varieties like 'LeBeau' and 'Beryl' and *N. obvallaris* and so on, with such early shrubs as the fragrant viburnums and some patches of the blue star-flower, *Ipheion uniflora*.

This second wave may well include the wild *N. bulbocodium conspicuus*, the yellow hoop-petticoat daffodil, which, if it is happy, will seed itself in nice ratty lawns that are not overly manicured or too-soon mowed. With the second wave, we add such bulb flowers as the gentian-blue chionodoxas, the main flush of wild anemones, early grape hyacinths, blue Roman hyacinths, maybe even an early trout lily or two and the demure, elegant (for the name, I confess, does not promise such beauty) toad lilies.

Then after all that, the main flush of garden daffodils in endless variety, but let us stop here with these earliest of all. Remember the past few early springs, and tell me truthfully if some of these early sorts would not be a great addition to the garden. Then why are you not growing them? I told you last fall. And the fall before.

But peace. I know you are trying. As I always said of Luke, my personal hound of excellent and dear memory, it took him quite a while to get going on anything, but he was just fine once he started.

A Matter of Breeding

Today's garden-variety daffodils were bred over a number of generations from modest wild daffodils that are still to be found in the mountains of Portugal and Spain, in alpine meadows, and in lowlands of Europe. Virtually all progress has been made within the twentieth century, and at the moment the Irish and English breeders lead the field. G. W. Wilson and Lionel Richardson, both Irish, have accounted for most of the daffodils that win shows, though since their deaths other breeders have come to the fore, among them Americans, such as Grant Mitsch of Oregon, whose pale 'Daydream' was, and still is, a glorious flower.

The blooms are crossed like those of any other flower: pollen is collected and dusted on the sticky pistil; pods form and ripen and are sown, with flowers appearing in about five years. They are observed for several years to make sure there are no further surprises (the first blooms of a new variety can be rather deceptive, and it is impossible to predict the bulb's hardiness or general constitution) and then they are grown on, to increase into a salable stock.

Prices can be very high when a new daffodil is first introduced. If the gardener sees a daffodil at a show, badly wants it, and finds it sells for $7.50 per bulb in a specialist's catalogue, he might do well to go ahead and buy it. It might be many years before supplies permit what the gardener would call a "reasonable" price. Usually I have bought just one bulb, and within three or four years have had a sizable clump. Often one can swap with friends. Needless to say, you want to be sure your circle hasn't all bought the same variety.

There is no inherent reason why the best daffodils have been bred in Britain, although admittedly daffodils reach their greatest size, clarity, and perfection of texture when they grow slowly in cool weather. They are never so good in our continental gardens where tropical heat can force them from green shoots to full-open flowers within a few days.

On the other hand, we can usually enjoy our daffodils in balmy spring sunshine quite unknown at daffodil season in Britain, so things even out.

A long-lasting daffodil that has almost vanished from commerce, and which I miss nowadays, is 'Brunswick,' a large-cup sort that flowers a few days after the early ones mentioned above, and which sometimes lasted in bloom outdoors for a month. It has white petals and a yellow cup that bleaches out a good bit, retaining a sort of lemon flush at the brim of the crinkled cup. It had a grand disposition, and refused to rot, and it never seemed to be bothered by narcissus fly or nematodes or virus ailments, though that was probably mere lucky accident. Anyway, I regret the relative rarity of daffodils like this, the ones that have beauty, distinctiveness, and vigor, all in one plant.

A fairly old white trumpet sort, 'Cantatrice,' has a way of getting basal rot so that you never know whether you are going to have it next spring. There have been many white trumpet varieties since this one was introduced, but none more beautiful, perhaps. The year the white 'Empress of Ireland' was introduced (it was then selling for $100 a bulb, though now it is as reasonable as any), its breeder sent a bulb to a friend of mine, and we all went over to admire it. It had everything, I thought, except that radiance and tension that excite one in the most beautiful flowers. I thought at the time it would probably turn into a fine workhorse of a daffodil. It can grow large, and often it displays much finer health than 'Cantatrice,' and I find myself thinking of it along with 'Mrs. E. H. Krelage,' 'Roxane,' 'Mount Hood'—all of them just a bit gritty where they should be silky.

'Ceylon' is a yellow with red cup that we all regarded as sensational twenty-five years ago, and a clump often provides color for a full month. There are newer and better ones like 'Falstaff' in this color pattern, but they are not all that much better. Most gardeners who do not make the effort to deal with daffodil specialists wind up with 'Red Rascal' or 'Scarlett O'Hara' for their red-and-yellows, since these are Dutch varieties sold at garden centers. They are not very good daffodils, compared with 'Ceylon,' since they burn in the sun, fade, lack fine stems, and have not substance of petal to take bad weather. The Dutch growers attach no particular importance to superlative beauty, I believe, and are quite content if a flower makes a great show at fifty feet and never mind the rest. On the other hand, the Dutch taste is a useful corrective to over-refinement. The trend in Irish and English breeding of daffodils has always led to utter utterness, if you follow me—a kind of preciousness in which a mystical beauty of the flower was everything, and its garden uses forgotten. A good dose of barbarism from outside is a corrective to this, and I think it unjust to say (as an English critic did) that Dutch daffodils tend to resemble pats of cow dung in a pasture. Some of my best friends would be Dutch if I knew any, and I count it wrong to forget how the Dutch have developed the tulip and how they have mastered, more than anybody else, the problems of bulb storage, propagation, and other techniques so that prices are brought down.

At the same time, it is worth reminding the gardener that daffodils can have a beauty more complex and profound than the simple healthy, hearty, windblown good looks of daffodils in an old orchard. They can also have elegance and polish, and that high refinement that is always, of course, a bit threatening to us plain gardeners. I have noticed, strangely, that the grubbiest gardeners are usually the ones who first go wild for the most delicate daffodils, and who first notice the gulf between a superb daffodil and a good old boy of a flower.

Fragrant Flowers—A Potpourri

Moonflowers

Twenty-two. ☐ How glorious the hot weeks of the year are for our tropical visitors—the petunias, zinnias, marigolds, lantanas, verbenas, and so on. But I think the progress of the moonflower has pleased me most. Roger Pineau gave me some seeds which I started in pots but did not get planted in the open ground until early July. Really the seeds should be started in pots indoors in late April and planted out the end of May.

The moonflower since 1773 has been a summer treasure of Western gardens. Its name, *Calonyction aculeatum*, refers to its beauty at night and the little bumps on its stem. It is like a very large morning glory—six inches across—only it is less trumpet-shaped than most morning glories. The moonflower blooms are flat like a tray, dazzling white, and they open about 9:30 at night, closing the next morning, sometimes as late as noon. It is found in the tropics of both old and new worlds, and I do not know its original home. The flowers are strongly scented, a trifle sickly in character. They are like thin strong silk, so white they appear to be illuminated, even on a fairly dark night. They do not care much for moderate balmy weather, but if it gets really hot, the sort of weather corn grows in, these vines spurt into growth, sometimes far exceeding the ten feet that is given as their ultimate height.

They love full sun, or as much as they can get, and plenty of water and fertilizer. I try to keep a circle a couple of feet in diameter clean around the stem of the vine. If this dirt is lightly scratched with a trowel (an inch or so deep) after it begins to dry (say the day following a watering) and if the vine is given maybe five gallons of water two or three times a week, and if a scant handful of fertilizer is dug in once every ten days or so, the vine will soon come into its own. It has to reach a good size, eight feet or so, before it begins to bloom well. It twines and is very happy on tall chain-link fences around factories. If grown on a sunny wall, it needs wires or netting to twine on. Once it gets going, side shoots emerge and a dense fountain-canopy effect is produced.

You can tell in the afternoon which buds will open that night. In the South, where I used to live, it was the custom to keep an eye on the moon vine and, when sixty or so buds showed they would open that night, to ask people over to watch them. Unfortunately, people in that country talk so much that I cannot recall seeing the buds open very often. They tremble and vibrate when they open. Usually someone would say, "the flowers are out," and everyone would run over to admire them, then back to jabbering. Equally festive is the night-blooming cereus. In our neighborhood there lived an old cereus in a tub. It was ninety-seven years old, the last time I saw it, and produced 120 flowers open at once. When it bloomed (and you can tell by late afternoon which buds will open) its proud owner would phone round the neighbors and there would be punch or champagne (rather dangerous in hot weather) and cucumber sandwiches for refined persons, and ham and potato salad for mere mortals.

These parties, once such a feature of the American summer, were always spontaneous, since you had only a few hours to plan them and invite people. It was always astonishing to see how many people could come at the last minute.

Phlox

The garden phlox blooms madly in late July and August as the daylilies begin fading away. In tiny gardens in town I doubt you would want phlox, since they take as much space as peonies and have a somewhat weedy air to them even when well grown. But in wide borders or, for that matter, in a solid bed, nothing is more festive in late summer, provided there is full sun, deep soil, and plenty of water available. Phloxes usually fail in half-shady places, but where tomatoes flourish, the phlox does very well.

In May, you will see phlox plants in cans on sale at garden centers, and if these are planted promptly and watered well they will bloom freely the same summer.

Pink, white, crimson, scarlet, and purple are the main colors. I do not, myself, despise the magenta phlox (which is what you often get if you let the garden hybrids go to seed and grow up) but most gardeners sneer at it. In case you wondered, the lavender and purple varieties like 'Amethyst' and 'Russian Violet' are distinct shades of violet and are not magenta. White phloxes are especially admired at night when they show up well. 'Miss Lingard' is an early sort that blooms off and on, about knee height, and vastly admired. It is not so big and bouncy as the later kinds, like 'Mount Fujiyama' or 'White Admiral.' Pinks tend toward salmon—yellow in the pink—like 'Sir John Falstaff' or toward rose—blue in the pink—like 'Charles Durant' and 'B. Symons-Jeune.' One of the handsomest of all phloxes is 'Dodo Hanbury Forbes,' which is a pink with a trifle of blue in it and passes for clear pink. It consorts better with the rose pinks than the salmons, however. The standard red phlox nowadays is 'Starfire,' which is scarlet, but there are also rose-reds like 'Windsor.'

Two common nuisances with phlox are red spider mites and mildew. I prefer to ignore both (as who does not) and often they are no problem, especially if the phlox are given good sunny open positions and rich soil to begin with. More distressing are the eelworms which make the plants so stunted they are not worth growing. They are avoided by growing new plants from cuttings, instead of dividing the roots.

Greedy gardeners have trouble thinning their phloxes, but the best results—the flowers are larger and showier—come from pinching out all but five of the stems. Every third year the clumps should be divided, either after the bloom season ends or in spring when the new shoots are not more than three inches high. (Otherwise it is a nuisance to keep them watered enough to prevent wilting.)

The Giant August Lily

The hostas or plantain lilies are, to begin with, distinct and beautiful in foliage and will many of them grow in deep shade.

The one most likely to be noticed in late summer is the broad-leaved *Hosta plantaginea*, sometimes called the August lily, though I never heard anybody call it that. All hostas lose their leaves in winter, but if slugs don't eat them they are beautiful all the rest of the year, and their great merit is their beautiful foliage.

Before getting into the confusion over names, which I do not expect to be ever sorted out as long as the world is full of botanists, all of whom have variable sets for Hosta, I should say that the plant we are discussing now has conspicuously broad leaves growing in luxuriant clumpy rosettes that may reach knee height, with thick-stalked tufts of flowers borne only slightly above the leaves.

The flowers, like smallish white lilies, are highly scented, moderately agreeably in my opinion, and they are bunched instead of being neatly spaced along the stalk. Thus in full bloom, the flower stalk looks, and is, top-heavy and usually leans sidewise. The flowers are white, not whitish, and the scent is sufficiently strong that you don't have to keep sniffing or say, "Now I wonder if this is what he means by scented."

Various other hostas are "scented," but the August lily is the only one I know that is heavily scented, blooms in August and September (depending a bit on location) and has leaves fatter than a canna's.

This plant is often called *Hosta subcordata* or *H. subcordata grandiflora* in catalogues, and it has also at various times been grown as *H. grandiflora* and *H. japonica*, as well as *Funkia grandiflora*. And I say nothing of the times it has probably been acquired by gardeners as *H. fortunei* or *H. fortunei grandiflora* or *H. fortunei subcordata*. It is never, so far as I know, called *H. lancifolia* or *H. tarda* or *H. sieboldiana* or *H. ventricosa*, if that is any help.

From time to time we run into thundering articles that roar against the confusion of names among hostas, and usually the writer of them is prepared to set everybody straight. A certain number of gardeners think, "Ha, at last I can get at least the fifteen commonest kinds straight in my mind," but the genus Hosta has always reminded me of the novelist Kafka and of various disorders of international politics. Everyone is sure something serious is going on, but few have any idea what it may be. The gardener, like a character in a Kafka story, knows his fate is being decided somehow or somewhere, but has not a clue beyond that. Well, the hostas are being taken in hand by authorities, but I, at least, have no idea at all about whom to rely on. For my part I think the best thing is to acquire any hosta one admires and not make a large claim for its name, since it is probably the wrong name anyway.

Part of the difficulty is that these perennials from Eastern Asia, and perhaps there are thirty-nine (and perhaps not), readily hybridize. In the past century, and in this, many hostas have risen to meet the sun as beautiful bastards, if it is not rude to say so, and many of these are given species names as if they were a true wild species. Some garden hybrids (crosses either intentional or accidental between distinct wild species) have been listed by species names, and some true wild species have been listed by vernacular garden-hybrid names. And even in garden hybrid names (such as 'Thomas Hogg,' for example) there is no assurance that if you buy a plant called that from six different nurseries, you will not get several quite distinct plants. All of which is to warn the gardener not to be surprised at anything that may come his way in Hosta-land. And yet the August lily, *H. plantaginea*—white, fragrant, and wide-leaved—is a particularly grand plant for the garden.

Like most hostas it prefers light shade, and will endure heavy shade (though I do not swear it will grow in a basement) and is splendid in woodland, provided tree roots do not use up all the moisture (for it requires moderate moisture) and provided its striking huge leaves do not seem to you too great a contrast to the usual modest occupant of an American woods. They are fine plants for dampish borders north of a house. They are beautiful in ordinary garden borders where, however, they must not be allowed to bake dry. I think them marvelous with yuccas, though the contrast between sharp spikes and opulent arching leaves may seem too gross or violent to the refined gardener.

There are some hybrids commonly met with, such as 'Honeybells' and 'Royal Standard.' I am not so reckless to say what these hybrids are, or where they come from, but 'Royal Standard' looks much like the plant we have been considering. It takes sun better, with fewer moults and mutterings if it gets a bit dry. It also has taller bloom spikes with somewhat showier flowers, and I think it blooms more freely. That is, a bushel basket-sized clump of *H. plantaginea* might have four spikes of bloom, while 'Royal Standard' might have nine. That is simply my impression of the two plants, not a scientific study, but I will say I have been more pleased than I thought I would be with 'Royal Standard.' Let me add that when the plant was quite young, it showed no sign of turning into anything much. Its leaves were far too narrow to suggest *H. plantaginea*. But after a year or two, it came on strong with great vigor and gives the impression, ultimately, of *H. plantaginea* with taller and more abundant blooms.

One great comfort, amid the confused names, is that there does not appear to be such a thing as an ugly hosta. So feel free.

Nasturtiums

The nasturtium has been on my mind lately, though it has been years since I grew any. When you think of it, the nasturtium is vastly more complex, colorful, fragrant than the zinnia, marigold, petunia, lantana, verbena, geranium, and so on. But somewhere along the line it developed an image—call a dog mad and hang him—as a common flower unworthy of attention in gardens.

Now gardening may well be one of the world's important fantasies, but within that fantasy there can be some clear sight and relatively sane judgment, which leads us to my point: the nasturtium is eminently worth growing.

The seeds alone justify planting it. That is, even if they did not sprout (and they sprout infallibly) it would be worth the effort, merely to sow them in neat little rows, one by one (for the seeds are relatively enormous). Few seeds are so agreeable to handle. Even the clumsiest child can sow them without mishap. And when they sprout, they grow quickly, the peltate leaves like small circular trays of soft blue green. Very like the leaves of a lotus, only smaller.

Now aphids are supposed to be a great problem in growing

nasturtiums. Once or twice I have had infestations of aphids, dense on the growing tips and youngest leaves, but without resorting to any special poisons except water, I have got rid of them with no real trouble.

They like full sun, and require at least half-sun; no point planting them under great shade trees.

The scent is often compared with such fragrances as those of marigold or tansy—"nose-twisting" smells. I find them, on the contrary, very sweet with little or none of that nose-twisting marigold or chrysanthemum quality. They are much more like the smell of sweet peas, carnations, roses. But such is the force of words that many gardeners can smell only what they have read; and if nasturtiums are supposed to be nose-twisters, then many gardeners will find themselves unable to notice the fine perfume.

Too much is made—another instance of the force of tradition —of the nasturtium's preference for poor soil. In poor soil, they simply do not grow very well, at least for me. I find they always do best in fairly rich soil in a well-run border, the sort of place inhabited by peonies, roses, Oriental poppies, irises, and the like.

If the plant were tricky to grow, and if the seed could be acquired only by getting special import licenses and ordering from Vladivostok, we would be making great efforts. But, because nasturtium seed is to be found on every seed rack, we ignore it; and because we ignore it, we soon come to think it worthless.

The world is so full of remarkable plants that nobody can grow more than a ten-thousandth of the dandy things that could be grown. I understand that all right. Still, I have the strong feeling that the nasturtium is neglected not because gardens are too crammed with meconopsis, gentians, and so on, but merely because nobody ever says anything nice about the nasturtium.

Lilies

It is interesting that although November 1 is the correct time to plant lilies, they give better results, as a rule, for most gardeners, if planted in very early spring.

As a group, they all like good drainage, and dislike having their roots agitated—what they like is full sun in porous gritty soil loaded with leaf mold with plenty of water that filters right on through. A cool root-run, a light dapple of delicate branches over them to prevent undue baking, but plenty of headroom without overhanging branches.

To be very blunt, lilies are not likely to be permanent in gardens with heavy soils, and as you get older you sometimes acknowledge you are not really going to give the lilies a slope and two bushels of leaf mold and all that. If this is the case, you can often plant them in the spring, have them flower a year or two, and when they dwindle away (as they certainly will with anything less than first-rate drainage) you can pretend you got inferior bulbs.

Lilies as a group are very difficult. Those who have just started with them usually swell up in the head like a pumpkin and boast of their marvelous clump of *Lilium langkongense* or some such thing. But we who have been through much and endured much will merely congratulate them. It would be too brutal, I guess, to call on such gardeners five years later and ask to see all the marvelous lilies. What is especially difficult and infuriating about lilies is that they grow like virtual weeds and bring on a great flush of triumph and, alas, hubris. Then they totally disappear or steadily decline, despite much activity and bustle with the leaf mold, aphid sprays, and urgent prayers. We would be lost indeed, most of us, except for the tireless (and doubtless profitable) energy of commercial bulb growers, especially de Graaff in Oregon whom I have always supposed to be possessed of unearthly powers.

To take only one sort of lily—the hybrids between *L. auratum* and *L. speciosum*—it may be said that these have been brought to undreamed-of vigor and health, sufficient to make them last a year or two or three in the average garden. Theoretically they should be permanent, and for some gardeners no doubt they are. The lilies of this group are known as 'Imperial Crimson,' 'Imperial Gold,' and 'Imperial Silver' hybrids, but even Communists would love them. In color they range from white with gold pimples (if you will excuse so vulgar a word for so delicate a beauty) to white with gold stripes and rosy red bumps, to white with rosy crimson flushes to rosy crimson with dark bumps. They are superlatively worth growing even if transitory. They bloom in August on stems four to six feet high as a rule. The individual flowers are perhaps eight inches wide, of incomparable waxy texture and unrivaled elegance of form. Though large (and they may be even ten inches wide) they are anything but coarse.

Lilies of this height (and they may exceed the heights mentioned) are best staked, unobtrusively. It is almost true that "they do not need to be staked." Suit yourself. But you will gain nothing by throwing a large fit next July 23 after a summer storm. Remember that.

But not to wander, these lilies should have the sort of position an azalea is given; that is, good drainage and plenty of leaf mold. Peat does not come amiss, but it should be thoroughly mixed with the earth, not dumped on in a thatch at the surface. The bulbs should be planted with the base of the bulb about eight inches deep. I know the books suggest greater depths. Ha.

Do not trim off the roots when you plant them. Do *not* let these (or any other) lilies sit around in sacks a day longer than necessary. Order them for late March delivery—by then it should be mild enough for the gardener not to find excuses for not planting them promptly. If it should snow (one learns all too soon the vagaries of weather) in late March, keep the bulbs cool—if necessary pack them in peat and keep them in the garage a few days. Don't let them heat.

The cucumber mosaic virus, basal rot, and a number of other terrors await the innocent when it comes to lilies. In spite of which, when these great and noble flowers bloom, even if just for a little while, you will say "Mine eyes have seen" and be thankful.

To Shrub It Up

Viburnums and a Kerria

Twenty-three. ☐ The viburnums are one of those plant families that everyone should grow. Depending on the particular viburnum species, some are outstanding in flower, some in fruit, and some in fall coloration. Almost all have an air of security about them, you might say—they are not forever apologizing for their shabby leaves or gawky branches or cruddy blooms.

My tiny lot, as I have complained on numerous occasions, is encumbered by a house and several outrageous forest trees which I have neither the heart nor the energy to take down. So I have little enough space. And yet I have plants of the following viburnums, which I cite not as the best, necessarily, but to show I think so highly of them I give them space even in a smallish garden:

V. 'Dawn,' a garden form that blooms in the winter, if the winter is bloomable. It is a hybrid of what we used to call *V. fragrans,* now given some ridiculous new name. The hybrid originated at the Aberconway garden in Wales.

V. × *Juddii,* with small tennis balls of white heavily flushed pink, rather waxy, very sweet of smell, neat in habit (to perhaps seven feet) with good foliage till November, sometimes coloring well. It is very similar to *V. carlesii,* which is as beautiful but which is sometimes tricky to grow (though you may see superb healthy plants of it here).

V. dilatatum, notable mainly for masses of red fruit in fall, neat handsome foliage, big shrub to ten feet or so.

V. opulus sterile, the common old snowball bush, with white tennis balls of flowers, which children have pulled off and thrown at each other for some centuries, or millennia perhaps. It has no scent but is very handsome. Because you see it everywhere, there is a snobbish aversion to it, which is silly. Often its leaves color bronze and orange and so forth in fall. It has no fruit. It is dandy hanging over a fence or wall with bearded irises below. They bloom together.

V. tomentosum plicatum 'Mariesii,' which blooms with the dogwoods or a few days after dogwoods start. It has horizontal branches strung with white flowers and the effect is flat horizontal layers of white. It sometimes fruits well; usually the leaves color well. It grows to perhaps ten feet.

V. tomentosum plicatum sterile, the Japanese counterpart of the snowball bush, with deeply veined, almost pleated leaves and neat white tennis balls of flower, unscented and without fruit. The leaves usually do not color much in the fall. It too blooms with irises. It has a neat, well-fed look to it.

V. setigerum, from which the Chinese make tea when they go to one of those sacred mountains, with flowers in April, not very showy but quite pleasant, and magnificent red fruit, extremely showy, coloring in August and holding on till hard frost. It likes to shoot up narrow stems to ten or twelve feet, arching over a bit and thickening up greatly with a few seasons' growth. Like virtually all viburnums, the leaf buds are beautiful as they open.

V. wrightii, a rounded bush to seven feet, with clusters of rich crimson berries and wine-red leaves in fall.

Another April-blooming shrub I like is *Kerria japonica*, which has arching green stems up to six or eight feet, with canary-yellow single (five-petaled, not double) flowers the size of quarters or half-dollars all along their length. It abides shade far better than most flowering shrubs. I planted it where it will follow the somewhat clotted flamboyance of Kurume, Gable, and Glenn Dale azaleas. Unfortunately, where I have it, it blooms right with the azaleas, adding a strong yellow which is fairly outrageous (to be plain) with the pinks and scarlets and whites. In the open garden, without the shelter of a wall, it will bloom with the early tall bearded irises, and looks better than with azaleas. There is a double form, like pompons, the old Jew's mallow, and some prefer it. I think the single is better.

The Pussy Willow: A Fuzzy Interlude

Early March is a time of year which can usually stand a good bit of improvement. Flowers are few, unless the gardener has been foresighted enough to plant some of the little early bulbs that garden writers are forever recommending, or has a pussy willow in the garden or along the alley. The usual one makes a bush the size of a lilac, say twelve feet.

It is easy, as early as January, to cut branches and set them in pails of water for the house. The catkins or pussies are sheathed by only one scale which readily parts, allowing the silky catkin to emerge. After a few days the stamens (the male sexual parts) ripen and shed their yellow pollen, and I think many people are allergic to it, but if so they probably know it. As you doubtless know, the cut branches root freely in vases of water and can be planted outdoors, though most of them fail to survive the shock of transplanting.

It is better, if the idea is to raise pussy willows, to stick cuttings directly into the ground in November or, for that matter, in March, without bothering to root them in water first. The gardener would only want one plant, I should think, and it is inconceivable that one way or another there should be any problem rooting a plant. Pussy willows can, of course, be bought at nurseries and this saves the anxiety (but also misses the pleasure) of seeing the shrub develop from a cutting.

Willows in general have a variety of names, and I am never sure which ones are correct. The usual pussy willow is often called *Salix discolor*. I used to grow one that made a tufty bush only four or five feet high called *S. gracilistyla*, which looked nice with its pinkish catkins over a colony of the pretty blue flowers of *Chionodoxa sardensis*. Nearby were an extremely deep pink form of star magnolia and also one of the very early tamarisks that bloom before the leaves. I had to whack the pussy willow back regularly to encourage plenty of new growth for a good show of catkins the following year, and also to keep it from lounging into the tamarisk, which it inclined to do. No plant can stand indefinitely to have severe pruning year after year; this pussy willow succumbed after about five years. The truth is, the gardener has a short attention

span and after five or ten years may prefer to let a plant go rather
than not.

But then there are those days in late winter when the sky is
bright blue and the temperature is in the 50s, and one trots about
the garden to see if anything is going on. It will be weeks before
the dogwoods—or even the forsythias—bloom, weeks before the
trees leaf out, and we are then grateful for things like the snowdrops, the Asian witch hazels, and the pussy willows, which would
hardly be noticed in spring or summer.

Bordering on the Sublime

Sometimes people complain that a border of evergreens along
the side or front of their lot is oppressively dense, and others complain that their shrub border of flowering bushes looks like a mere
collection of brushwood or odd sticks.

I do think we too often ignore the fact that from November
to April such a planting is going to be without interest unless we
take steps to make it cheerful in, say, January, and I do not think
the solution is a solid wall of yew or holly. And, apart from mid-
winter, there is that awkward period from October 20 to Thanksgiving to be thought of.

The prostrate junipers, creeping about on a slope and occasionally lifting their heads a bit to see what's up there, are to my mind
priceless plants for sunny and rather dry slopes such as you often
find along city sidewalks. I would resist the gardener's normal
temptation to plant a dozen different kinds of these junipers along
a thirty-by-fifty-foot strip, but would choose one or two, with other
things besides junipers. I like the Andorra juniper, which turns
rosy violet in cool weather, and young plants from pots or cans
could be set two or three feet apart, then leaving a space of some
feet and having another clump. In between there could be small
patches of crocuses to brighten the days of late February and early
March.

One of our native wild andromedas, *Leucothoe axillaris*, has
evergreen glossy lance-shaped leaves that turn wine and purplish
in winter, making a sort of small weeping fountain, and grow
taller than the junipers and consort well with them.

Some of the prostrate contoneasters—*C. horizontalis* or *C. salici-*

folia—would bring a touch of bright berries and woody twigs. If you thought the violet and wine-colored evergreens were getting a bit much, you could use any number of barberries with bare winter stems or some of the evergreen kinds.

The dwarfest types of yew (*Taxus baccata repandens* and *T. cuspidata densa* among them) could give intense dark green.

The somewhat despised form of the Oriental arborvitae called 'Berkman's' with its gold spring foliage and somewhat insistent shape (like an egg, or a seriously squeezed pudding) is easily overdone, no doubt, but I have always liked its dense luxuriance and its green-black-bronze-gold look in winter. It gives great solidity and weight to a mixed planting, and so does the slower growing Hinoki cypress in its dwarf forms like *Chamaecyparis obtusa nana*, which is black-green with whorled tufts of foliage.

Above these plants of the slope, up on the brow of the rise (maybe eight feet from the sidewalk) I would consider a few shrubs that lose all their leaves. Because we do not want something that looks like the planting around a dog cemetery.

Among shrubs I would like in such a position are the Maries variety of the Japanese snowball, with horizontal branches and flat—not snowball-shaped—patches of white flowers in May. Also there are Japanese maples sometimes to be found in nurseries that would do. The green-leaf kinds please me best, especially the seven-leaflet kinds of *Acer palmatum*. They grow slowly and can be discreetly whacked to keep them from their usual aim of making a dense round canopy. Their handsome small leaves lighten the mass of other things, and in December the foliage turns burnt-orange and crimson and so on (if freezes are early, sometimes they do not color at all).

The Chinese witch hazel and its hybrids are handsome, and while they eventually turn into small trees, they too can be pruned smaller, and in any case the gardener's problem is how to get them big, not how to keep them small. Their fall leaves are orange and purple red and tawny, and their flowers in late winter are a substantial comfort to the early bees and, of course, to the gardener.

Judd's viburnum, *V.* × *juddii*, has fall leaves of various oranges and reds, and small tennis balls of intensely sweet pinkish flowers in late April. Other viburnums—but remember these become six to twelve feet high, depending on variety—are equally splendid.

Both the tea viburnum (*V. setigerum*) and Wright's viburnum (*V. wrightii*) have handsome berries in that awkward period around Labor Day, well before the fall-coloring leaves have started. The tea viburnum has brighter showier scarlet berries but Wright's is a more compact plant and has better crimson foliage in late October and clusters of dark crimson berries.

Another suitable plant is the euonymus with fall leaves (in November) of dusky pink-red, as beautiful as any plant known to gardening—*E. alatus*. This is usually grown in its dwarf (up to seven feet or so) form called compactus.

The beauty of box (*Buxus sempervirens*) hardly needs to be pointed out. It deserves and requires good treatment, plenty of air and light, and occasional mulches of manure. It could figure near the walk up to the house, say, but you would not want to lose its distinctive billowy shape by crowding it in with other things.

Other evergreens for the brow might be such hollies as 'Foster No. 2' and 'Nellie R. Stevens,' both hybrids and a bit different. If you dislike hollies (and I admit their fallen leaves make weeding something like hell, over the years) you could use one of the evergreen photinias (*P. serrulata* becomes a globular mound 15 feet high in time) or such a cherry laurel as 'Otto Luyken' or the fine-foliaged berry-laden nandina.

Mahonias, especially *M. bealei*, the commonest one in nurseries, provide quite different texture with large dull hollylike leaves that look fine throughout the year, and yellow racemes of bloom in February followed by dense clusters of blue berries.

An occasional azalea, allowed to become a 6-foot bush, could be used, such as the white 'Treasure,' and there are several kinds of purple-leaf barberries (*Berberis thunbergii atropurpurea*) that can shoot up and fan out where the gardener is interested in that effect, and their bare stems in winter have a lightening effect on the evergreens.

It is apparent, probably, that not all these plants could be used in a shrub screen along a thirty-foot lot. It is also clear, I hope, that the gardener could make his shrub border more dense and green, or more light and open, by varying the mixture of such plants to suit his own tastes.

Also, there are people made extremely anxious if more than two kinds of plants are used per acre. They should, of course, continue on their monotonous way, clucking at hodepodges to their heart's content, and these suggestions are not for them.

It is not possible, by the way, to achieve a richly textured effect that will last indefinitely. Plants grow. If your young hollies are twenty feet apart and you fill in with other things, the time will come when something has to yield. You may have to move a large azalea, or saw down an old mahonia, or chop out the viburnum. This is obvious but always comes as an outrageous surprise to the gardener, as I well know. On the other hand, I do not see much sense in planting stuff at the proper distance for a fine effect fifty years from now. Such plantings will come to perfect maturity just in time for some jerk to bulldoze the place to sell french fries on.

Earthman's Earthly Paradise

Twenty-four. ☐ Sometimes the gardener (if he is incredibly lucky) has the problem of a long narrow strip of land along a walk or beside a garage. I will tell you what I am doing with such a strip. I do this to inspire you to think of even better ways to manage it yourself, not because I think my way is particularly fine.

The walk runs north and south, and the land (forty inches wide) parallels its east side. The west side of the walk is a border about thirteen feet wide, backed by a wood fence, but all that concerns us here is the forty-inch-wide strip along the walk's east side. The stretch of walk being discussed is forty feet long and it receives almost full sun. When I look at it, I quite envy myself for having forty feet of land in full sun, because for many years I have been much afflicted with trees. While trees are excellent for apes, owls, and arboreal fauna in general, they are annoying in a small garden where one hopes to grow something besides a compost pile and a continental championship collection of slugs and sowbugs.

This strip does not exist in a vacuum, of course, but runs down the center of my garden, and whatever I did with it had to take into account the following realities:

• The plants in the strip could not sprawl all over the walk, which is only four feet wide.

• It could not be planted solid with irises (an obvious and charming solution) because other persons associated with my gardening feel there should be "some sense of proportion" and there are "enough irises already, God knows" elsewhere.

• There cannot be dense shade cast by plants in the strip, because of the irises that grow in a moderate-sized bed just to the east of the strip.

• There needs to be some illusion of height, however, to lend drama to the otherwise uniform height of the iris foliage to the east. I should say, perhaps, that while the irises occupy only the most modest amount of land, still, they do receive the lion's share of the best land of the garden, naturally. And their leaves, as I have so often and so honestly been the first to admit, are extremely dull to look at for most of the year. But then so is grass.

• The strip should somehow be related to a garage at its north end. The walk continues along the west side of the garage.

• Since the garden is small, the space should be fairly intensively used. Just here let me say all land in town should be intensively used. If there is a patch of simple bluegrass, then it should exist only because the gardener thinks nothing else would do so well for the general beauty of his schemes. In other words, intense use does not necessarily mean jamming the largest number of plants possible in a given space, but it does mean there are no dull spots in which nothing at all is going on.

• The strip, because it is only forty inches wide, should have a somewhat uniform look. As you might say, it should vibrate evenly, without one part striking the eye much more than another.

The first thing I did was dig it about twenty inches deep, working in two or three inches of sawdust. In theory the sawdust should be rotted (this was not rotted at all) and in theory it should have been dug thirty inches deep instead of twenty, and theoretically it should have had at least four barrow loads of humus worked in, but we do not live in a perfect world or even a theoretical one, and our backs, our time, and our wallets are not all they might be. I did this digging in early winter.

As for plants. I decided on hybrid tea roses, grapes, rue, dusty miller, tuberoses, and forget-me-nots, not all dumped into the blender together, as it were, but sorted out thus:

Three poles were set up. They were 4-by-4 sawed lumber painted with wood preservative, set in concrete, given two coats of primer and two coats of surface black paint. They rise to eight feet above the ground and are twenty feet apart. They are set right up against the east edge of the walk. They are connected by chains.

I am a little embarrassed to say these were a half-price sale on dog chains from West Germany at my friendly neighborhood hardware store, which lost its lease. Each chain therefore snaps on to the next chain, instead of being one unbroken length, and of course there are days I go out and worry about that. The chains are also painted black and hang in broad curves.

Two grape vines have been planted (not at the posts but in between the posts, at roughly the lowest point of the descending arc of the chains) with the idea they will grow along the chains and form a garland, as you might say, of grapes along the walk between the house and the garage. It is unnecessary, I am sure, to remind you that grapes require annual pruning, that they attract Japanese beetles, that they get two kinds of mildew, each worse than the other, and that they have no colorful blooms nor fragrance nor fall coloration of leaves, nor winter beauty. Furthermore, the grapes they produce are inferior to California or South African grapes at the store. Nevertheless, if you are of my mind, nothing is more beautiful than grape vines employed as I am doing them.

At the south end of this narrow strip there will be a moderate mound of common yuccas, with a smallish saxifrage or two and a hosta chosen for its flowers ('Royal Standard') as well as or more than for its foliage, and perhaps a few palmettos, not that people believe these are hardy, but I am sturdily raising a few from seed.

At the extreme north end is a shrub or semi-climbing rose, 'Nymphenburg,' which is what I call shell pink and which has good foliage, vigor, and fragrance and which blooms off and on all summer. It will lean against (that is, will be frantically tied to) the last pole.

I am proud to say I am not growing anything up the other two poles. When you think of the clematises, jasmines, akebias, etc., etc., that would relish such a site, you will say anyone who resists those temptations is a hero. Nothing is being grown up those poles for two reasons. There is no point having the strong vertical accents if they are to be obscured by shrubs or thick vines, and since the poles actually touch the walk there is not really space for plants, too. Also, the grape is a great one for going its own way, and from its vantage point on the chains between the poles it would certainly be forever tangling with any plant trying to grow up the poles. I know, indeed, that a happy activity for me for years to come will be pruning out the grape's attempts to infiltrate 'Nymphenburg.'

Now beneath this long garland of grapes (provided by two plants of 'Steuben,' an American grape that ripens soon after 'Concord' in late summer—I do not say 'Steuben' is the best grape for this purpose, but obviously if I had been able to think of a better one I would have used it) is a row of roses. These are ten plants of 'Sutter's Gold,' 'Helen Traubel,' and 'Mojave.' They are spaced forty inches apart, for no better reason than I like them that way. It is always said the varieties of roses should not be mixed up, but that 'Helen' should be all together, then 'Suzie' or what not, but I like them mixed up. Mine alternate and repeat. Rose people as a class do not approve of that, but then I do not approve of rose growers so much (at least on the subject of roses) that I feel obliged to consult them. It will be noted that the three varieties of rose, however, are all in the apricot-pink color range, and they all have a common parent (they are all 'Charlotte Armstrong' seedlings) so mixing them up is not so daring as to mix up varieties of widely different colors and types. The roses will grow (and did, of course) to four or five or six feet the first year if given sun, water, space, and reasonable attention. The first winter after planting I like to prune them only very slightly. It greatly disturbs me to see eight-year-old rose bushes with one scrawny stem or two, and it suits me better to leave almost all the first year's growth on the bushes, then to prune a bit more severely the second and third years, but always with the idea that the rose is to be a shrub, not merely a rootstock with an orange blob the size of a cabbage on it (which is what many roses remind me of strongly).

Beneath and between the roses, so generously spaced out, I find room for forget-me-nots, and a dozen clumps of rue (*Ruta graveolens*) and dusty miller (*Senecio cineraria* 'Silver Dust' or 'White Diamond' or something of that sort) and, at the extreme eastern edge, a row of single Mexican tuberoses. These are lifted every winter, and of course you want to watch out for the rose branches and thorns as you dig tuberoses in November and plant them in late April. I also have a number of strawberries running about here and there, and a columbine or two and a batch of blue bugle and two or three clumps of lamb's ears, and a rose campion or two, and some portulaca and coral bells, all of which are frowned on by cultivators who think the rose should be grown in regal isolation.

You will ask, "But won't the roses object to that garland of grape vines growing above them?" and yes, I think they will not like it much. They are big roses now and must learn that life is not just a bed of roses. You can hardly have too much rue.

Garden Account Book

Responsible people who are also gardeners take great care not to spend too much on the garden. I have myself kept accurate records for years and years, though of course most of the past accounts were somehow lost. The best way to do it is to make plans on graph paper first, showing the entire garden, then divide it into sections and make lists of plants that go into each part of the garden, the list showing both the name of the proposed plant and its price. This is time-consuming, but gardeners somehow manage to find the time. Only this past week I was browsing through the Dictionary of Gardening and behold, out fell my rose list for 1957 which I distinctly remember looking for in 1957. I was so interested to see that prices have advanced only 50 percent in the interim, and I was also fascinated to notice that my great choices of 1957 are virtually identical with my choices this year.

Well, the advantage of such lists, as I do indeed intend to make a point here, is that if you make them at various times you will soon have a tremendous list of plants you cannot possibly afford. That is important. Otherwise, you will not be able to explain to your wife, "It is true that $46.75 sounds like a lot, but when you consider the original list was $618.10, you will see how much has been cut down."

The gardening account book must show, of course, the $46 you actually spent, complete with date, etc.

There are several legal ways to keep your garden account book from being embarrassing. When ordering bulbs in the fall, for example, I list the sum I mail off to various firms, but it would be picky and petty to bother with, for example, ten Dutch irises picked up at the garden center for 70 cents. During the fall, I am obliged to drop in at many places where they sell bulbs in Washington (how else could I get the "feel" of what is available to readers?) and while I'm about it, I sometimes get 60 cents' worth of this or 85 cents' worth of that and of course Bolgiano's had that half-price sale. These incidentals are not reckoned in the garden account book, because they are really incidental rather than "garden purchases." I think of them as a beer, and surely nobody would expect me to charge the garden if I dropped in for a beer while checking out garden centers.

The cost of removing trees can be considerable. This is not, however, a garden expense. It is essentially a safety measure. If there should be a tornado from the northeast—and nothing is less reliable than tornadoes, though usually they are from the southwest—there is no doubt the tree could damage the roof tiles of the house. Normal prudent safety measures need not, and should not, be charged to the garden budget.

Fungicides are a problem. I noticed the package of benomyl for blackspot on roses costs more than $25, but of course it would last for years and besides I will get a smaller package anyway. Let's say we get the $5.95 size packet. If this were something I wanted for the garden, I would write it down as a garden expense. But in fact I dislike having to get it in the first place, and it is only because another member of the family is wild about roses—in short, the rose spray is virtually the same as taking your wife to a cafeteria for supper.

A garden hose, or two garden hoses, is a garden expense. It is also a general maintenance item. If your wife buys it, not needing any special gardening knowledge or interest, then clearly it is not a gardening expense in the way that two very particular philadelphus bushes are. As it happened, another member of the family recently bought two fifty-foot hoses. Even she saw the necessity of it. Hence, she will enter that in her book under household costs instead of my entering it as a garden item.

Blades for bow-saws can add up. These are medical items. I certainly would not want my son to break a blade and injure himself while cutting up tree branches—one replaced blade in good time can save a trip to the emergency room, and preventive medicine is the best kind.

Vessels used in the garden, originally from the kitchen, such as various pans, cannot be considered garden expenses if they were bought to roast chickens in (etc.) and are only temporarily used for some outdoor purpose.

Lawn mowers come under civic betterment, but if you sell yours, the money goes into the garden fund, naturally.

Seeds are a garden expense. I deduct 60 percent, in my books, as the share the birds eat, but the 40 percent that does not fall under entertainment goes as it must under garden costs.

As I review my accounts, I am gratified to say that sound planning, careful buying, and fastidious attention to cost have resulted in surprisingly moderate expenditures. It is not necessary, we all would agree, surely, to spend a fortune in order to have an agreeable garden of repose.

Masterful Plants Undo Master Plans

Someone has given me two nice young seedlings of the Arabian thistle, *Onopordon arabicum*, and I gave one to my elegant friend who has great success with everything.

The other I planted, after some weeks of thought (or some weeks of avoiding thought), on the west wall of a shed. This thistle is precisely the sort of plant I admire—easy to grow, monumental and architectural in scale and stature, with superb foliage like gray acanthus leaves with fierce spines.

And virtually impossible to site in a jam-packed garden.

It is a biennial, having a two-year life cycle. Surely I do not need to warn gardeners against ordinary thistles of our pastures, which are immortal and cannot be got rid of in less than two centuries. Our wild thistles are relatively beautiful, but they spread underground and are a great terror. The Arabian thistle is also a terror, but since its root is not perennial, and since it relies on seed to maintain itself, it is quite easily controlled. It makes rosettes the size of a bushel basket the second year and sends up a flower stalk maybe ten or twelve feet high. But the main thing is the silvery gray foliage. If you happen to have a wall of clipped yew fourteen feet high, as I do not, this thistle is very beautiful, planted about four feet in front of it. The trouble is that its large basal rosettes, sitting on the ground, effectively smother any little plant in the way. Another trouble is that when the flowering stem reaches ten feet, it is vulnerable to wind and can come crashing down like a small redwood in a summer storm, its spiny leaves doing moderate damage to any fleshy plant or animal in the way. Of course, all you need is a good stake, somewhat like a telephone pole, and very firm ties, like insulated wire, to keep it upright. One small problem, needless to say, is where to find space for such a plant. Fortunately, in digging foundations for the shed, several clumps of daylilies were smothered (my chart at the time showed I had moved them, but some error transpired) so that is where the thistle went. Not boldly, in a fine well-prepared site. But niggardly, sort of under the eaves. Maybe it will not exceed five feet in height. I do not want it to flourish too much, or it will mean trouble for the 'Red Bengal' on one side.

How much better a garden would be if it were planned in all details at the start, and the plan adhered to. But when we start gardening we do not, as a rule, know any more about gardening than an architect. We learn as we go and we accumulate as we learn. I have several times planted seed of this very thistle with no luck. So years ago I gave up the idea of growing it. But when you get two nice young plants in pots, nobody can just say "Thanks, take them back, I have no space." At least I cannot, at least in the case of the Arabian thistle that I so admire.

Another case: when I moved to this new small garden I ordered the lily 'Black Beauty,' a rather foolproof dark red hybrid of *Lilium speciosum*. The lily specialist was unable to provide it, so I settled for something else. No sooner did I have all the space filled up than someone presented me with several small bulbs of 'Black Beauty.' Naturally, in they went, somewhat jammed up against *Clematis tangutica* and a clump of the lily 'George C. Creelman,' or what is said to be Creelman, not that I believe it.

I had temporarily forgot, needless to say, that *Astrantia major* was on the other side. And I had not quite counted on the red valerian expanding northward quite as far as it did, and at that time I had no way of knowing I would add a lavender bee-balm. It was in the way of some bulldozers. I only got a tiny root. Of course it grows superbly from a tiny root, and is heading north like Lee on a bender.

Another thing that seemed all right at the time was the propagation of a dozen bulbils of one of those yellow de Graaff lilies (by now I have forgotten exactly which) and it took some thought to

figure out what they were when they came up, somewhat indig-
nantly no doubt, through the skirts of the yellow clematis that has
of course grown a bit since the time the bulbils were put in.

The original plan, which I look at as one might look at the city
plan for Ur, shows the cypress post with the clematis and the rose
'Helen Traubel' beside it, and nothing else. The three clumps
of lilies (the rose died, mercifully), the astrantia, centranthus,
alstroemeria, the daffodil 'Liberty Bells,' and possibly a few other
oddments that I seen no point in mentioning have somehow all
moved in.

I shall give another example. Along one length of a lily pool
I dug a shallow ditch to carry off any surface rainfall. Of course
I did not want it to look like a trench. It is between some brick
paving and the raised walls of the pool, faced with tiles from
Spain. So I did not want a raw ditch. It is only eight inches deep,
and the master plan calls for one clump of *Iris tectorum* at the pool
corner, and a gentle rug-like cover of the Corsican mint (*Mentha
requienii*) and yellow creeping Jenny on the surface of the shallow
ditch. Very well. The iris up and died (it flourishes in another spot
not nearly so well suited to its needs) and so did the mint. The
creeping Jenny wants more sun and has headed west, coveting a
spot occupied by a blue geranium. Well away from the pool. But
in the meantime a friend wearied of planting primroses and gave
me three white and yellow ones. These were stashed out. These
soon got in the way of the Corsican hellebore, and they increased
mightily. So I dug them up, divided them, and planted them at the
base of the pool wall along the ditch.

In the ditch itself I planted the wonderful waxy skunk cabbage (*Lysichitum americanum*) that I had a chance to acquire,
and two Italian arums somebody found in New York. Also, some
seedling foxgloves were temporarily set there (two years ago) and
it turns out that a lady's mantle (*alchemilla*) managed to seed
itself all over before departing this life. Now I do not know any
gardener who can pull up alchemillas when they are babies. Those
tiny star-shaped leaves are as beautiful as anything I can think of.
In the space of two years, however, the original plan has been
slightly altered to the extent that the wild iris, mint, and so on
have gone utterly, and a whole batch of unplanned things have
arrived.

The trouble with master plans in gardens, then, is simply that they do not take into account masterful plants. Nor addled masters.

I Never Promised Me a Rose Garden

Gardening, it sometimes seems to me, takes more time than seems reasonable or probable, so it comes as no real surprise that digging and planting operations for three (3) tomato plants requires a full day.

By 10:00 A.M. the gardener is at work, if I may speak of myself in the third person which is now such a trendy thing to do. The gardener has had his second cup of coffee and in the genial warmth of a glorious spring day is examining tadpoles in the lily tank. Tadpoles in great shape.

Also the shrub or climbing rose (it will serve as either, depending on how you wish to prune it) called 'Joseph's Coat' is in fine color, a red and yellow bicolor, though that gives no idea of the flower. It is a soft orange blend, opening fiery hot yellow with red flushes, somewhat like the old 'Talisman.' This changes within a day to a curious mixture of carmine and rose bengal at the edge of the petals, while the inside is ivory. The next day the carmine softens and the ivory intensifies to yellowish buff. Then the whole thing changes to a kind of lifeless carmine which is attractive nevertheless. Meanwhile, other buds are opening and going through their color changes, so the effect is, at the very least, lively; and if you like such goings on, as I do, you will think the plant beautiful. Allow me to say that, in spite of all this color-changing, the effect is also civilized.

But on to the tomatoes. Proceeding toward the back of the garden to the Tomato Site, the gardener marvels that the rose 'Mojave' is backward in leafing out. Plants of 'Sutter's Gold,' 'Medallion,' and 'Helen Traubel' planted at the same time are four or five days farther along in growth. The great rose 'Charlotte Armstrong,' which is rose red, never appealed to me for some reason and I never grew it. It's very like Beethoven, a towering composer, no doubt of that, and yet you may dislike most of his music, though the late quartets sound much like Mozart. In any case, 'Charlotte Armstrong' for me has always been rather like 'Peace,' a great rose but it will be the day when I give it space. But the interesting thing is that 'Sutter's Gold,' 'Helen Traubel,' and 'Mojave,' which are possibly my favorites of all hybrid teas, are every one a seedling of 'Charlotte Armstrong.' If you meet someone you dislike (gardening is full of morals) you may remember 'Charlotte Armstrong' and reflect you might like the children.

Roses are not the gardener's favorite flowers, but if you grow them, you may as well grow them well. So the gardener, before getting to the tomatoes, gets out the sprayer and applies Benlate and Phaltan.

The gardener also discovers that an old tie pin shaped like a safety pin is an excellent device for poking loose bits of debris that stick in the spray nozzle. This takes no more than twenty minutes, once he discovers the nozzle is clogged and once he discovers the tie pin.

As in most gardens, all operations such as spraying have to stop while the aged hound is shut up in the garage. She has no sense at all, but then she has the best voice imaginable so things even out.

The gardener can but marvel that the catmint seems to have died (*Nepeta* × *fassenii*, usually called *Nepeta mussinii*) because while it can stand great cold, it cannot stand waterlogging in the winter, and this one was planted at the foot of a small slope, with the idea of moving it to a better drained site, which was never done. Still, one is always annoyed that plants behave as one knew they would.

Scratching about 'Wyoming,' one of those mahogany-leaf forms of the garden canna, the gardener sees the roots have not rotted, though the plant has not yet sprouted. It is well known that cannas like a warm sunny site, in light friable soil, and in such places they sprout promptly in April and make good growth by June. If, on the other hand, one grows them in damp, tenacious clay in a good bit of shade, of course progress is slow in the spring.

The first requirement of the tomato, the gardener has always presumed, is sunlight. It is better to grow three or six plants, properly cared for, than half an acre just stuck in any which way. The first hole is made twenty-four inches or so in diameter and dug eighteen inches deep, with perhaps a peck of weathered sawdust and other humusy litter dug in at the bottom. Then dry friable soil is added. The tomato, from a smallish peat pot about the size of a tennis ball, is planted at the top. The hole, I should add, is not filled all the way up with earth, but a three or four inch depression is left, to be filled in later as the tomato plant grows, so that by July the bottom of the plant will be several inches beneath the soil level.

There are hormone solutions that reduce the shock of transplanting, and while expensive, when you buy a jar of the crystals, still a quarter-teaspoon is all you use with two gallons of water and you only need about a cup or two per tomato plant. Of course, it takes time to read the directions, find the plastic bucket you use for mixing, chase the hound (whom you forgot you had shut up in the garage and who bolts out if the door is opened to find the Transplantone, of course), go to the far end of the garden to turn the hose on, find the two-gallon measure, fill it up, and return to turn the hose off.

On the way the gardener notes a blue-eyed grass in flower (*Sisyrinchium*) among some irises raised from seed. The blue-eyed grass looks exactly like an iris when it sprouts from seed—it is a relative of the iris, in fact—and is often carefully nursed along with the infant irises. Within a few months, however, its tufty manner of growth (and perhaps I should add its extreme vigor) assure the gardener it is no iris, but it remains because who wishes to cast out blue-eyed anything in this world? Well, there it is. The first iris seedling, it turns out, appears to be lemon yellow. This can be ascertained before the bloom opens by squatting down and looking at the sun through the iris bud, taking care not to step on the Shasta daisies or the other dog (who has somehow got out of the house) and keeping in mind the danger of looking at the sun. The second dog is skillful at getting through the thicket of stakes that "protect" the irises, one notes. He is very excited to see the gardener, whom he has not seen for an hour.

Meanwhile, the hose, not yet turned off, has flooded the platycodon, one of the best of the blue flowers, surely. Also, it is noticed, the old hound has got out of the garage again and is loping down the row of strawberries at twenty-four miles an hour.

But eventually the tomatoes get planted, all three of them. I have said nothing thus far about the hazards of "digging a hole for the tomato." I should say, in truth, that tree roots may be encountered. Happy is the gardener who, after swearing through two holes' worth, can call on his peerless son to dig up the roots from the third hole. The gardener is thankful when the son worries it out, after ax, hatchet, and saw fail. Iron wedges, driven by a sledge hammer, are useful in dealing with such roots. Your neighbor will have the hammer. You already have the wedges. While borrowing the hammer, one admires the grape blossoms the neighbor is rightly proud of. The phone rings and one is summoned home. The small dog, not the hound, is dozing in what used to be the hyacinths and is chased indoors.

As the sun westers, the gardener heads bathward. He collects the wedges, hammer, ax, hatchet, bow saw, sharpshooter spade, trowel, Transplantone, Benlate, Phaltan, four buckets, two tin coffee cups, one glass, a hundred feet of hose, suntan lotion (stuck and refusing to squirt when you squeeze), T-shirt, jacket, and other incidentals of labor. The hound is free, free at last, and yowps sweetly. The gardener is well content with a very full day, for he has much to show: three tomato plants with wire cylinders around them.

He eats his tuna salad with joy and happiness. He will bathe as soon as the hot water tank fills up again (the peerless son, prime axman, has beat him to the showers) and the gardener even goes so far as to eat a doughnut, ordinarily forbidden for weighty reasons. The laborer is worthy, however, of his hire.

Index

Index